THE
PANIC-PROOF
PARENT

Creating a Safe
Lifestyle for Your Family

DEBRA SMILEY HOLTZMAN, J.D., M.A.

CB

CONTEMPORARY BOOKS

Library of Congress Cataloging-in-Publication Data

Holtzman, Debra Smiley.
    The panic-proof parent : creating a safe lifestyle for your family
/ Debra Smiley Holtzman.
       p.   cm.
    Includes bibliographical references and index.
    ISBN 0-8092-2392-9
    1. Safety education.   2. Children's accidents—Prevention.
3. Home accidents—Prevention.   I. Title.
HQ770.7.H65 2000
613.6--dc21   99-38647
                                    CIP

Disclaimer: In a time of rapid change, it is difficult to ensure that all of the information contained in this book is entirely up to date. Therefore, the author and publisher accept no responsibility for any errors or omissions and specifically disclaim any liability, loss, or risk, which is incurred as a consequence, directly or indirectly, of the use and/or application of any of the contents of this book. Readers are encouraged to confirm the information contained herein with other sources. The ultimate responsibility for child safety resides with you, the caregiver. The mention of specific products or services in this book does not constitute or imply a recommendation or endorsement by the author, unless it is explicitly stated.

Note: The first aid procedures described in this book are designed to assist you in the event of an emergency until medical treatment can be obtained. They are for reference purposes. The author advises all readers to complete a certified first aid course and CPR course. This book is not intended as a substitute for proper first aid training. In the event of a medical emergency, readers are advised to promptly consult with a physician or other health professional. Accordingly, the author and publisher expressly disclaim any liability, loss or damage, or injury caused by the contents of this book.

Cover design by Monica Baziuk
Interior design by Precision Graphics

Published by Contemporary Books
A division of NTC/Contemporary Publishing Group, Inc.
4255 West Touhy Avenue, Lincolnwood (Chicago), Illinois 60712-1975 U.S.A.
Copyright © 2000 by Debra Smiley Holtzman
All rights reserved. No part of this book may be reproduced, stored in a retrieval
system, or transmitted in any form or by any means, electronic, mechanical,
photocopying, recording, or otherwise, without the prior written permission of
NTC/Contemporary Publishing Group, Inc.
Printed in the United States of America
International Standard Book Number: 0-8092-2392-9
00 01 02 03 04 MV 19 18 17 16 15 14 13 12 11 10 9 8 7 6 5 4 3 2 1

To my husband, Robert, and my beautiful children, Adam and Laura. Thank you for sharing this journey with me. You are my inspiration and I love you so much.

To Mom, Dad, and my sisters, Madeleine and Karen, thank you for always loving me, believing in me, and motivating me to higher achievements.

To Grandma Lily, Julian, Monte, Neil, Elena, and Bruce and my other nieces and nephews, David, Marisa, Deanna, Elyssa, Chelsea, and Steven for your understanding, appreciation, and support.

To Janet, Debbie, Cindy, Howard, Cecilia, Ira, Daphne, Lenny, Michele, Steve, and Martha, thank you for your longtime support and friendship.

To Nana, Grampsie, and Joan, your values helped shape my life; you are always in my thoughts.

"One hundred years from now, it will not matter what kind of car I drove . . . what kind of house I lived in . . . how much money I had in my bank account . . . nor what my clothes looked like. But the world may be a little better because I was important in the life of a child."

—Anonymous

Contents

Preface

With nearly two decades of experience in the safety and health field, it is hard for me to remember a time when I wasn't in the safety business. In my early twenties, after receiving a master's degree in occupational health and safety, I worked as a safety consultant, surveying work premises and analyzing work practices. My job was to provide technical advice to insurance policyholders so that they could create a safer and healthier workplace.

Later, as an attorney, I worked on environmental and tort cases, witnessing first-hand the devastation a family suffers when a loved one is seriously injured due to unsafe working conditions or practices or becomes ill because of environmental exposure.

When I started my own family, such problems came even closer to home. I worried about the safety of my own children. With that concern came a deepening regard for the safety of others' children.

For the past few years, I actively volunteered to teach child safety, gave TV news interviews, appeared on talk shows, sat for interviews with newspapers and magazines, and wrote monthly safety and health columns for *Today's Parent*, a parenting newspaper. Through my volunteer work for the Broward SAFE KIDS Coalition, the Florida Poison Information Center, and the Broward County Chapter of the Sierra Club, I have met thousands of parents and grandparents and have listened as they gave voice to their anxieties.

Listening to the fears and concerns for children's safety and health, I realized that parents are panicking more. They feel they have little control over the environment in which their children move, and they doubt their ability to safeguard their children. Parents want to know how to protect their kids.

That's why I wrote *The Panic-Proof Parent*: to give parents and grandparents solutions—simple, effective ways that would enable them from the first day they picked up the book to begin to protect their children. I used government pamphlets and brochures, fact sheets, and books, medical journals, and periodicals. I gleaned facts from the Internet and popular media and interviewed leading experts across the nation. The very wealth of material can be so daunting, no wonder parents panic!

It's all here, all in one place, in an easy-to-access format. My prayer is this: that it will be used to save a child!

Acknowledgments

I especially thank my editor, Drollene P. Brown, whose wisdom, extreme talent, and patience were enabling factors in my completing this three-year journey in pursuit of my dreams.

Thanks to my husband, Robert Holtzman, M.D., for his invaluable medical expertise provided throughout the entire book—and for the hugs, too!

Also, a warm thank you to Madeleine Levy, my sister, who not only encouraged me, but also was the person who got me started on this project.

Thanks to the many organizations and governmental agencies—and the people who spoke for them—that promptly and graciously answered my inquires, supplied me with information, or reviewed sections of the book: National SAFE KIDS Campaign, especially Dr. Angela Mickalide, Camilla Taft, Beth-Ellen Kane, and Jennifer Carr; Centers for Disease Control and Prevention, especially Dr. Lawrence B. Schonberger, Dr. Enzo R. Campagnolo, Dr. Joseph Piesman, Dr. Kathy Orloski, Dr. Oona Powell, and Dr. Paula Yoon; Consumer Product Safety Commission; Environmental Protection Agency, especially Kevin Rosseel, Mary Smith, and the Office of Asbestos Ombudsman; Food and Drug Administration; National Highway Traffic Safety Administration; U.S. Department of Agriculture, USDA Meat and Poultry Hotline; Florida Department of Health, especially Dr. Lisa Conti and Mr. Walter Klein; David Karmol, National Spa and Pool Institute; Dr. Louis Slesin, *Microwave News*; American Academy of Pediatrics; Art and Creative Materials Institute, Inc.; NSF International; American Lyme Disease Foundation; Pupil Transportation Safety Institute; SIDS Alliance, especially Phipps Cohe; National Center for Missing and Exploited Children; Child Watch of North America; March of Dimes, especially Richard Leavitt; National Reye's Syndrome Foundation; Washington Toxics Coalition; Center to Prevent Handgun

Violence; National Fire Protection Association; International In-Line Skating Association; Alliance to End Childhood Lead Poisoning; Environmental Working Group; LaLeche League International; National Program for Playground Safety; Kids in Danger; Burn Prevention Council, especially Joanne Mclaughlin; Child Abuse Prevention Center, especially Amy Wicks; Dr. Keith Florig of Carnegie Mellon University, Department of Engineering and Public Policy; National Youth Sports Safety Foundation, Inc., especially Rita Glassman; Dr. Richard Mass of Environmental Quality Institute; League of American Bicyclists; s.t.o.p. (Safe Tables Our Priority); Shriners Hospital; AAA Foundation for Traffic Safety; Farm*A*Syst/Home*A*Syst and Door and Access Systems Manufacturers Association.

Thanks also: Dr. Carolyn Dunn, Dr. Wilma Hammett, Ron Sheffield, Dr. Katherine Shea, and Pat Fossella.

A special thanks to my colleagues and friends in Florida: Jerry Goodman, Mike Petrozzino, Mark Horowitz, Carol Young, Monnie McCauley Mazorra, Broward SAFE KIDS Coalition, the Florida Poison Control Center, Broward County Cooperative Extension Service, Pamela Santucci and Tom Mueller of Broward County Health Department, Yoli Buss, Judy Kaplan Wener, Page Ashley, Joy Riddell, Dan DeCoursey, Kevin O'Brien, Bonnie O'Brien, Dyanna Jamiel, Andrew Cuddihy, Bonnie Wolansky, and Dr. Paul Goldberg. I thank them for answering my endless questions and supplying me with information.

And I give thanks to my mom, my grandmother (Nana), and my mother-in-law, whose love, wit, and wisdom permeate this book and my life.

Introduction:
A Word to Parents

E ach chapter in this book provides step-by-step guidelines or simple and practical ways to protect your child. This is a child safety and health reference guide for the new millennium, providing quick reading for busy parents and one-stop answers for every question. No longer will you need to consult a stack of books when you have an urgent need for an answer. Everything is here, in a user-friendly format that, I hope, will help you stay calm in every emergency. In fact, my goal is to prevent as many emergencies as possible.

Having the most up-to-date information should be liberating, not frightening. In alerting you to potential hazards, I am enabling you to take charge. For those who want even more information, I provide avenues for parents on every path of the information age: websites, fax numbers, telephone numbers, and postal addresses.

Chapters are designed to give you facts at a glance. You may want to read the book from front to back to help familiarize yourself with the format as well as to introduce areas that you may never have considered before. You may also skip around from chapter to chapter, based on your own concerns and curiosity. In whatever way you become familiar with *The Panic-Proof Parent*, you will want to keep it in a readily accessible place, for quick reference. Also note that you will see numbers inside parentheses throughout the book, such as (1.1). These refer to endnotes that start on page 230.

When I set out to pull all this information together, I wanted to present the facts so one could easily understand them, without needing a Ph.D. As I wrestled with the mountain of material, I was determined to make it user-friendly and warm. To do that, I wove in my own experiences as a child and as a parent, and I inserted the "Mother used to say" lines to set the tone.

I believe children are life's most precious gift, and in this book I celebrate my life with my family. The time I used to spend worrying and panicking I now use to relax and enjoy the time I have with my loved ones. I'd like to give that gift of time to you. Please don't feel overwhelmed as you read about things that can go wrong. You already know we live in a dangerous world. It is my heartfelt hope that you will use this information to develop the tools you need to keep your children safe and healthy and to acquire the skills that will assist you in instilling safety awareness in your children.

The three years it took to write this book have taken me on a wonderful journey, a time for reflecting on the love and wisdom handed down from my mom, grandmother, and mother-in-law—three very special women in my life. I hope their warmth and abiding calm will inform this work as much as anything else, resulting in a book that will make you a panic-proof parent.

1

Starting at the Beginning
Guarding the Fetus

Mother used to say to an expectant mom:
"You're eating for two."

Although the adage "eating for two" was sometimes interpreted as advice to eat twice as much, the fact is that what the pregnant woman puts in her body can go into the body of the unborn child as well. Some illnesses she gets can affect the baby, whose immune system is too immature to fight back.

As a mother-to-be, you should know that every time you sip an alcoholic drink, take a drug (prescription or otherwise), consume a caffeinated beverage, or smoke a cigarette, your baby does, too. If you are currently pregnant or thinking about getting pregnant, offer your baby the best opportunity for a healthy start by following these guidelines.

Foods to Avoid

Reduce your risk of contracting a food-borne illness.

- Never eat raw meats.
  - Steak tartare
  - Undercooked poultry
  - Undercooked pork
  - Rare hamburgers
  - Raw or undercooked seafood, such as oysters, clams, sushi, or sashimi
- Don't eat raw eggs or products made with raw eggs.
  - Caesar salad
  - Homemade ice cream (unless the base is cooked)
  - Cookie dough batter

- Avoid raw sprouts, such as alfalfa, clover, or radish.
- Don't eat food that contains raw (unpasteurized) milk.
- Don't drink unpasteurized milk or unpasteurized juice.
- Don't eat foods that may be contaminated with the bacterium *listeria monocytogenes*.
  - ❖ What does this bacterium do?
    - —It can cause a serious infection called *listeriosis*.
    - —It can cause miscarriages and also illness in newborns.
  - ❖ To reduce your risk, avoid soft cheeses such as feta, brie, camembert, blue-veined cheeses, and Mexican-style cheeses.
  - ❖ Some cheeses are OK: hard cheeses, processed cheeses, cream cheese, and cottage cheese.
  - ❖ Yogurt is OK.
  - ❖ Cook leftovers to 165°F or ready-to-eat foods such as hot dogs until they are steaming hot.
  - ❖ The risk of listeriosis from eating deli foods is relatively low, but pregnant women and adults with weakened immune systems may choose to
    - —avoid cold cuts (to be on the safe side) or
    - —heat cold cuts thoroughly before eating.
  - ❖ Control listeria.
    - —Refrigerate any food marked "refrigerate."
    - —Don't buy or use foods past their "use by" date.
    - —Use or discard open packages within three to four days.
- Limit your consumption of shark and swordfish.
  - ❖ The Food and Drug Administration (FDA) recommends that pregnant women and women of childbearing age who may become pregnant limit their consumption of shark and swordfish to no more than once a month.
  - ❖ Why?
    - —These fish have much higher levels of *methyl mercury* than other commonly consumed fish.
    - —Exposure to high doses of this substance during pregnancy, especially the first trimester, may seriously harm a child's developing nervous system. Note: Examples of other fish that may be contaminated with mercury, or industrial pollutants such as *polychlorinated biphenyls* (PCBs) are large tuna (typically sold as fresh steak or sushi), bluefish, striped bass, and freshwater fish.
    - —Contact your local health department or Environmental Protection Agency for advisories about water bodies or fish species where mercury or other industrial pollutants are of concern.

Watch Consumption of Other Substances

- Check on medicines and food supplements.
  - Discuss with your doctor any medication you might take:
    — Prescriptions
    — Over-the-counter remedies like aspirin or cold medicine
    — Food supplements—mineral, herbal, or vitamin
- Limit caffeine.
  - In moderation, caffeine may not be harmful. I have to admit that I really look forward to my morning coffee, but when I was pregnant, for my baby's sake, I allowed myself only one cup. I slowly savored the five-ounce serving! You may wish to call the product manufacturer of coffee or chocolate-flavored products to find out how much caffeine they contain. Meanwhile, watch your consumption of
    — coffee;
    — tea;
    — soft drinks that contain caffeine;
    — hot chocolate, cocoa, or chocolate; or
    — chocolate or coffee yogurt or ice cream.
  - One or two cups of coffee daily are not considered dangerous for developing fetuses (1.1).

Habits That Endanger the Unborn

- Don't take street drugs.
  - Stop now if you are planning to get pregnant or are currently pregnant.
  - Drug use during pregnancy has been associated with a variety of birth defects and miscarriage.
  - The newborn may be exposed to the painful agony of drug withdrawal.
  - If an expectant mother is taking street drugs, it is imperative that she ask her physician for assistance in stopping. (See the phone numbers listed under "For More Information" at the end of this chapter.)
- Don't drink alcoholic beverages.
  - Stop now if you are planning to get pregnant or are currently pregnant.
  - Consumption of alcohol leads to low birth weight and can cause abnormalities.
  - This is the leading preventable cause of birth defects and mental retardation.

❖ Fetal Alcohol Syndrome (FAS)
 —What is it? A serious, lifelong condition that is characterized by facial deformities, growth retardation, and central nervous system deficiencies, including mental or developmental disorders.
 —Are all symptoms always present? No. Some children with FAS have only some or one of the abnormalities.
 —What causes it? Pregnant women who are heavy drinkers put their babies at risk for FAS.
 —How much is too much? No one knows. It's best to avoid alcohol completely during pregnancy. (If you had a glass or two of an alcoholic beverage before you knew you were pregnant, please don't panic! You probably haven't harmed your baby.)
❖ If an expectant mother drinks alcohol, it is imperative that she ask her physician for assistance in stopping. (See "For More Information" at the end of this chapter.)

■ Don't smoke.
 ❖ Stop now if you are planning to get pregnant or are currently pregnant.
 ❖ If an expectant mother smokes cigarettes, it is important that she ask her physician for assistance in stopping. (See "For More Information" at the end of this chapter.)
 ❖ (See "Secondhand Tobacco Smoke" in Chapter 11 for the dangers of smoking while pregnant.)

Good Habits That Protect the Unborn

■ Take folic acid to help neural tube defects (NTD) such as spina bifida (open spine) and anencephaly (incomplete or entirely absent brain). Each year, approximately 4,000 pregnancies in the United States are affected by such abnormalities.
 ❖ How soon should you take folic acid?
 —All women of childbearing age should consume 0.4 mg. (400 micrograms) of folic acid per day.
 —It is important that women begin taking folic acid at least a month before becoming pregnant, because these defects develop in the first month after conception (1.2).
 ❖ Why should you take it? Studies show that if all women received that amount daily, taken one month before conception and throughout the first

trimester, the incidence of neural tube defects might be reduced by 50 to 70 percent each year.

❖ What are the sources of folic acid?
— The best source is a multivitamin supplement, one taken every day.
— Other sources:
  • Orange juice
  • Green leafy vegetables
  • Peas and beans
  • Fortified breakfast cereal (Beginning Jan. 1, 1998, enriched grains such as bread, buns, flour, pasta, and rice were required by the FDA to be fortified with folic acid.)

Preconception and Prenatal Health Care

❖ A prepregnancy medical checkup to evaluate your health and to identify any potential health risks for yourself and your baby is an important part of prenatal care.
— Discuss with your doctor all chronic diseases, such as diabetes, seizures, lupus, heart problems, thyroid disease, and hypertension.
— Be screened for sexually transmitted diseases.
— Other risk factors include repeated spontaneous abortions and previous delivery of a low birth-weight infant.
— A woman who is overweight, underweight, younger, or older than the ordinary childbearing range may face special risks. She should consult her doctor.
❖ The Centers for Disease Control and Prevention (CDC) recommends testing for Hepatitis B and HIV (AIDS).
❖ If already pregnant, continued doctor visits are essential, as recommended by your physician.
▪ Get screened for these diseases:
❖ Rubella
— A woman who develops rubella (German measles) during early pregnancy can have a baby born with birth defects such as hearing loss, eye problems, heart defects, and mental retardation.
— If you are planning to conceive, you should be tested for rubella immunity and vaccinated if necessary.
— Note: Because the vaccination may pose a small "theoretical" risk to a developing fetus, the CDC recommends that women wait three months after vaccination before becoming pregnant (1.3).

- ❖ Chicken pox
  - —Contracting chicken pox (varicella) while pregnant can also pose risks to the fetus. Contact your physician immediately if you have been exposed to the virus. An injection of VZIG (varicella zoster immune globulin) may be necessary; if promptly administered (within ninety-six hours of exposure), it can lessen the severity of the disease.
  - —If you are planning to conceive, you should be tested for chicken pox immunity and vaccinated if necessary. (A chicken pox vaccine was approved by the FDA in 1995.)
  - —Note: The possible effects of the vaccine on the fetus are unknown at this time. The CDC recommends that women should avoid pregnancy for one month following each dose of the vaccine (1.4). However, the manufacturer recommends that conception should be postponed for three months following vaccination.
- ■ A number of birth defects are inherited, triggered when a child inherits a matching pair of disease-causing genes, one from each parent (1.5). Blood tests can identify if you are a carrier of the following:
  - ❖ Tay-Sachs disease
    - —It causes fatal brain damage.
    - —It primarily affects people of Eastern European Jewish descent.
  - ❖ Sickle cell anemia
    - —This is a blood disorder.
    - —It primarily affects African-Americans.
  - ❖ Thalassemia
    - —This is a blood disorder.
    - —It primarily affects people of Mediterranean or Asian descent.
- ■ Couples who are at greater risk for genetic disorders are those who know of genetic disorders in their family; those who already had one child with a disorder; or couples who are closely related (such as first cousins).

Maintain a Healthy Lifestyle

- ■ Take care of yourself.
  - ❖ Eat a well-balanced diet. Your doctor or health-care provider can give advice on dietary requirements and may be able to offer sample meal plans.
    - —Drink at least six to eight glasses of water, fruit juice, or milk every day.
    - —If a prenatal vitamin has been recommended for you, be sure to take it!

- ❖ Exercise regularly.
    - —Consult your physician before beginning any kind of exercise program. A pregnant woman should check with her physician for specific guidelines.
    - —Some good choices are walking and swimming.
    - —If you become tired, feel pain, or bleed after exercising, stop your routine and contact your health-care provider.
- ■ Avoid non-essential or elective x-rays until after the baby is born.
    - ❖ Let all health-care professionals, including your dentist, know if you are pregnant or trying to become pregnant.
    - ❖ Make sure your reproductive organs are shielded with a lead apron when you are undergoing x-rays. This is important for every woman, all the time.
- ■ Avoid contact with toxic substances.
    - ❖ Substances to avoid include:
        - —Pesticides (See Chapter 5.)
        - —Dry-cleaning fluids
        - —Paint thinner
        - —Lead (See Chapter 9.)
        - —Mercury
    - ❖ Take care when using household cleaners.
        - —Carefully read and follow safe handling procedures. (See Chapter 8.)
        - —Use in a well-ventilated area.
        - —Wear gloves.
    - ❖ If your job requires that you lift heavy objects or work around fumes, chemicals, or radiation, consult your health-care provider. Always
        - —practice proper lifting techniques;
        - —wear appropriate personal protective equipment, such as gloves and masks; and
        - —have adequate ventilation.
- ■ Don't get too hot.
    - ❖ Places and activities to avoid:
        - —Hot tubs
        - —Saunas
        - —Steam rooms
        - —Exercising in hot, humid weather
    - ❖ Why? Studies show that prolonged elevated body temperature in early pregnancy may increase the risk of neural tube defects.

❖ (For more information on hot tubs, please see Chapter 16. For more information on heat-related illness, please see Chapter 15.)

■ Take precautions against *toxoplasmosis.*
  ❖ What is it?
    —A flu-like illness
    —Caused by a parasite named *Toxoplasma gondii*
    —Adults who don't have immune disorders may have such mild symptoms that they do not know they have it.
  ❖ How is it transmitted?
    —Through cat feces
    —Through raw meat, especially pork
  ❖ Its impact on a fetus is extremely harmful.
    —If you are pregnant and become infected with Toxoplasma for the first time, you can pass the infection on to your baby.
    —It can cause birth defects such as mental retardation, liver and spleen damage, and visual impairment or blindness (especially if the fetus becomes infected in the first trimester).
  ❖ Get tested.
    —If you are planning to get pregnant, you may wish to be tested for Toxoplasma.
    —If the test is negative, you need to take steps to avoid infection.
    —Individuals with a weakened immune system need to follow these steps as well because they can develop severe toxoplasmosis.
  ❖ Take steps to avoid toxoplasmosis.
    —Cleaning the litter box
      • If you already have a cat and you can't part with it, have your spouse clean the litter box.
      • If you must change the litter box yourself, make sure you wear gloves and change the box on a daily basis. The parasite found in cat feces needs only one day after being passed to become infectious (1.6).
      • Immediately wash your hands thoroughly with soap and water after cleaning the litter box.
    —Protecting your cat
      • Consult with the veterinarian to learn more about your cat's risk for toxoplasmosis.
      • Feed him commercial cat food products instead of raw or uncooked meat.

❖ Take other precautions.
  — Avoid working in the garden or handling soil or sand—all of which may contain cat feces.
  — If you do engage in these activities, wear gloves and wash your hands thoroughly with soap and warm water afterwards.
  — Make sure the meat you eat is cooked thoroughly. Do not eat steak tartare, rare hamburgers, or undercooked pork.
  — Follow all food safety guidelines outlined in Chapter 3.

For More Information

For assistance in stopping habits that harm you and your baby, use the following hot lines or websites.

Drug addiction. Contact Drug Help (staffed twenty-four hours, seven days) by calling (800) COCAINE [262-2463], (800) 662-HELP [662-4357], or (800) 378-4435, or by visiting their website: www.drughelp.org.

Alcohol dependence. Contact the local AA (listed in the white pages of the phone book), or call (800) ALCOHOL [252-6465] (staffed twenty-four hours, seven days), which is a national referral and help line.

Tobacco addiction. To reach The Cancer Information Service (a program of the National Cancer Institute), which is staffed M–F, 9 A.M.–4:30 P.M. EST, call (800) 4CANCER [422-6237], or visit their website: www.nci.nih.gov.

To reach help from the American Cancer Society, twenty-four hours, seven days, call (800) ACS-2345 [227-2345], or visit their website: www.cancer.org.

To ask questions about prepregnancy, pregnancy, birth defects, genetics, drug use, and environmental hazards during pregnancy and other related topics, contact the March of Dimes by writing to Birth Defects Foundation, National Office, 1275 Mamaroneck Avenue, White Plains, NY 10605, or call the March of Dimes Resource Center: (888) MODIMES [663-4637]. Specialists are available: M–F, 9 A.M.–6 P.M. EST, or by faxing (914) 997-4763, or by E-mailing resourcecenter@modimes.org, or by visiting their website: www.modimes.org.

To be advised about high concentrations of chemical contaminants in local fish and wildlife, access the Environmental Protection Agency's fish and wildlife consumption advisories by visiting their website: www.epa./ost/fish.

2

Aspirin
A Good Medicine That Should
Sometimes Be Avoided

Aspirin is a good, effective drug when it is directed by your pediatrician. However, the National Reye's Syndrome Foundation, the U.S. Surgeon General, the Food and Drug Administration (FDA), and the Centers for Disease Control and Prevention (CDC) recommend that aspirin and combination products containing aspirin not be given to children and teenagers during episodes of flu-like illnesses or chicken pox before a doctor is consulted about Reye's syndrome.

Why Avoid Aspirin During Illnesses?

The primary reason for avoiding giving aspirin to children is the risk of Reye's syndrome. It is a rare, life-threatening condition that affects many organs of the body, but characteristically, it is most harmful to the brain and liver. The syndrome is characterized by abnormal accumulation of fat in the liver and other organs in addition to a severe increase of pressure in the brain. When Reye's syndrome occurs, it almost always affects people in the age range from infancy through young adulthood.

Most patients have a viral illness during the three weeks before the onset of Reye's syndrome. The mechanism by which aspirin may trigger Reye's syndrome is still unknown. Aspirin's causative role in this potentially fatal childhood illness, however, has been strongly supported by both case-control and national Reye's syndrome surveillance data in the United States and United Kingdom.

Aspirin Aliases and Similar Medications

Read the label, but don't be content simply because you don't see the word *aspirin*. Look for its aliases or the presence of chemically related medications:

— Acetylsalicylate   — Salicylic acid
— Acetylsalicylic acid   — Salicylates

Always consult your pediatrician before giving your child any medication. The doctor may recommend that you give your child nonaspirin products such as acetaminophen or ibuprofen.

Reye's Syndrome

Symptoms (2.1)

■ Early
  ❖ Persistent or continuous vomiting
  ❖ Listlessness (loss of pep and energy)
■ Later
  ❖ Personality changes
    — Irritability   — Aggressive behavior
  ❖ Disorientation
    — Confusion   — Delirium
    — Irrational behavior   — Convulsions
  ❖ Loss of consciousness
■ Difference for infants
  ❖ Symptoms do not always follow the typical pattern.
  ❖ For example, vomiting does not always occur. Sometimes diarrhea is present.

Appropriate Response

■ Persistent vomiting or signs of brain dysfunction in children and teenagers soon after the onset of a viral illness, particularly if they have received aspirin or aspirin-containing medications, may be an indication of the development of Reye's syndrome. Medical attention should be sought immediately because serious complications, including death, may occur.

■ Even medicines that do no harm can mask symptoms. Do not administer *any* drug to treat the flu, chicken pox, or any viral illness, without first consulting with your doctor.

■ Good news: statistics show that 80 percent of patients recover if diagnosed and treated at an early stage of illness.

For More Information

Contact National Reye's Syndrome Foundation by writing to P.O. Box 829, Bryan, OH 43506-0829, or by calling (800) 233-7393 or (419) 636-2679, or by faxing (419) 636-9897, or by E-mailing reyessyn@mail.bright.net, or by visiting their website: www.bright.net/~reyessyn/. A staff specialist is available M–F, 8 A.M.–5 P.M., EST.

Contact Reye's Syndrome Surveillance Officer, Office of the Director, by writing to Division of Viral and Rickettsial Diseases, Mailstop A39, Centers for Disease Control and Prevention, 1600 Clifton Road NE, Atlanta, GA 30333, or by calling (404) 634-3091, or by faxing (404) 639-3838.

3

Making Sure Our Food Is Safe

Mother used to say:
"Eat a little something. It will make you feel better."
When you felt ill, she would ask:
"What did you eat?"

Mother and food, for many of us, will be forever linked in our minds—a hot breakfast, a carefully packed lunch, an after-school snack, a favorite meal, or a special tray when we were sick.

Now that you're a parent, your child depends on you to prepare food that will make him or her feel better—not make him or her sick. Food-borne illness is not just a problem found in other parts of the world. In fact, millions of Americans suffer every year because of it, and, according to the Centers for Disease Control and Prevention (CDC), it causes 9,000 deaths each year in the United States (3.1). Infants and children are more at risk from food-borne illnesses because they have less developed immune systems. Common symptoms include diarrhea, abdominal cramping, fever, blood or pus in the stool, headache, vomiting, and severe exhaustion. In a child, these symptoms must be treated immediately because such illness can be life threatening. Be aware that symptoms may appear as early as half an hour after the contaminated food is consumed or they may not develop for several days or weeks (3.2).

The Bad Guys: Bacteria and Where They Hide

To stop food-borne illness before it begins, you must know the enemy. The bad guys in this case are bacteria. They cannot be seen, smelled, or tasted, and they don't wear identifying black hats. You have to know where they hide (3.3). Be on the lookout for these bad guys and their common food hideouts.

Campylobacter jejuni: raw or undercooked poultry, meat, unpasteurized milk, and untreated drinking water.

Salmonella: raw or undercooked eggs, poultry, meat, and seafood; unpasteurized milk and dairy products; uncooked fruits and vegetables.

Escherichia coli (E. Coli) 0157:H7: raw or rare ground beef, unpasteurized milk, unpasteurized apple juice and cider, untreated drinking water, and uncooked fruits and vegetables. Important note: Hemolytic Uremic Syndrome (HUS) may develop as a result of E. Coli 0157:H7 consumption, particularly in the very young. HUS can cause permanent kidney damage or failure, possibly resulting in death (3.4).

(Note: Fruits and vegetables can become contaminated by these bacteria at several points along the route from field to table: fertilization with raw manure, irrigation with contaminated water, rinsing with contaminated water, or contamination by food handlers.)

Listeria monocytogenes: soft cheeses, unpasteurized milk, raw leafy vegetables, meat, and poultry. These bacteria can grow slowly at refrigerated temperatures. Watch out if you are pregnant! (See Chapter 1.)

Vibrio species: raw and undercooked seafood, such as molluscan and crustacean shellfish, and untreated water.

Clostridium botulinum: improperly canned food, garlic in oil, vacuum-packaged and tightly wrapped food. Important note: The symptoms of botulism are neurological. If not treated, this illness is fatal in three to ten days; everyone, regardless of age, must seek immediate medical attention. The symptoms are double vision, blurred vision, drooping eyelids, trouble speaking and swallowing, difficulty breathing, dry mouth, and muscle weakness. Infants with botulism appear lethargic, feed poorly, are constipated, have a weak cry, and have poor muscle tone (3.5).

Clostridium perfringens: any food left out for long periods, either on inadequately maintained steam tables or at room temperature. This is called the "cafeteria germ." Keep hot food hot at or above 140°F. Keep cold foods at or below 40°F.

Staphylococcus aureus: "staph" bacteria can be found on our skin, in infected cuts and pimples, and in our noses and throats. It is spread by improper food handling, such as not thoroughly washing hands and utensils or letting foods sit at room temperature too long, particularly cooked and cured meats, cheese, and meat salads (3.6). This bacterium produces a toxin (which cannot be destroyed by reheating) that can cause vomiting shortly after ingesting.

Shigella: outbreaks can occur in any food, but especially in salads, when a human carrier does not wash his or her hands properly after using the toilet and then handles liquid or moist food that is not cooked thoroughly afterward. *It's extremely important to wash your hands!*

In other words, they're everywhere! We can't stop eating, but we can be careful in the way we choose, store, and handle the food for our family. Now that we have identified bacteria as the bad guys, the next step is to find the good guys. The first one is our own vigilance—our own knowledge about the bad guys. Two others are at your fingertips at home: soap and hot water. You may also have an antibacterial or disinfectant product at home, such as bleach. We can think of it as a good guy sidekick (or the hero's best friend). How can you use the good guys to keep your child safe from food-borne illnesses? Here's how.

Good Guy #1: Vigilance with Groceries

Examining Products as You Shop

- Make sure to shop at clean and well-maintained markets, which have meat and poultry supplied by USDA or state-inspected plants.
- Look for the "sell by" or expiration date. You should buy the product before that date.
- Look for the "use by" date. Use the product by that date.
- Do not buy an animal product that is slimy, has a foul odor, or appears discolored.
- Buy only pasteurized milk, cheese, juice, and cider.
- Select fruits and vegetables that are free of mold and decay. Avoid products that have brown spots, soft areas, or discoloration.
- Make sure *any* food you buy is in good condition: canned goods free of dents, cracks, or bulging lids; grade A or AA eggs with clean, uncracked shells. (Make sure eggs have been refrigerated in the store.)
- Examine every bag or box to make sure there are no rips or tears.
- Buy only meat, poultry, or seafood that has been tightly packaged—no leaking juices! Buy from a refrigerator or freezer case.
- In addition to shopping at a clean and well-maintained market from which supplies are bought from state-approved sources, become a seafood savvy shopper by following Food and Drug Administration (FDA) seafood safety tips (3.7).
  - Fish should be displayed on a thick bed of fresh, not melting, ice, preferably in a case or under some type of cover.
  - Fish should be arranged belly down so melting ice drains away from the fish.
  - The fish's eyes should be clear and bulge a little. (Only a few fish, such as walleye, have naturally cloudy eyes.)

❖ Whole fish and fillets should have firm and shiny flesh. Fresh whole fish should have bright gills free from slime.

❖ Fresh fish springs back when pressed.

❖ There should be no darkening around the edges of the fish or brown or yellowish discoloration.

❖ Fish should smell fresh and mild, not fishy or ammonialike.

❖ Do not buy cooked seafood if displayed in the same case as raw fish because cross contamination can occur.

Handling Perishables

▪ Put raw meat, poultry, and fish into a plastic bag, even though you are careful to choose a package that looks intact. The package can tear during handling at the store. In addition, you don't know whether other bags have leaked onto the package you chose.

▪ Put fruits and vegetables in the plastic bags provided in the store; do not place uncovered raw items on the checkout conveyor belt.

▪ Purchase perishable foods last; keep them in the coolest part of the car or a cooler with a cold source in the car until you get home.

▪ Go straight home. If you have other errands, do them before shopping for perishable food.

Keeping Vigilant

▪ Store perishable items immediately.

❖ Immediately freeze ground beef, poultry, and fish that won't be used within one to two days.

❖ Put any packages of raw meat, poultry, or fish on a plate before refrigerating so their juices won't come in contact with cooked foods or foods that will be eaten raw, such as fruits or salad ingredients.

❖ To keep eggs fresh and prevent breakage, store them in their carton. However, do not store them in the refrigerator door, where the temperature varies due to opening and closing.

▪ Set your refrigerator temperature at 40°F or below and the freezer at 0°F. Keep an appliance thermometer in both sections and check them periodically.

▪ Check labels on cans and jars to see if foods must be refrigerated after they are opened.

Keeping It Cold

Do not thaw meat, poultry, or seafood on the counter. Bacteria can multiply at room temperature. There are three safe ways to defrost food:

1. In the refrigerator. This requires planning ahead because a number of hours are required. Only food defrosted in the refrigerator can be refrozen without cooking, but there may be loss of quality.
2. In cold water. Put frozen food in a watertight plastic bag and submerge in cold water. Change water every thirty minutes.
3. In the microwave. This method is the quickest way to safely defrost. Follow the manufacturer's directions for your microwave model. Foods defrosted by this method should be cooked right away.

The Good Guys at Home: Soap, Hot Water, and Bleach

Keeping It Clean! Let Soap, Water, and Bleach Chase Away the Bad Guys.

- Tie your long hair back.
- Make sure any open sores or cuts are completely covered. If you have an infected sore or cut or a diarrheal illness, let your spouse cook!
- Wash hands with soap and warm water for at least twenty seconds—and use a nail brush—before and after handling food or food utensils.
- Clean the cutting board.
    - Wash your cutting board, knife, and countertops with hot, soapy water after raw meats, poultry, fish, or eggs have touched them.
    - To sanitize cutting boards, counters, and sinks, first wash with hot, soapy water.
    - Make a solution of one teaspoon chlorine bleach to a quart of water and let the solution set on surfaces for a few minutes.
    - Rinse with clear water and pat dry. To sanitize products effectively, one must follow directions carefully.
- I recommend that you have two cutting boards: one for cutting produce and other ready-to-eat foods and one for raw meat, poultry, and fish. Do not put cooked food on an unwashed plate or platter that has held raw meat, fish, or eggs. If the boards can be cleaned in the dishwasher, so much the better.
- Wash lids of canned foods and drinks before opening to keep dirt from getting into the food. Clean the blade of the can opener frequently.

- Wash kitchen cloth items often in the hot cycle of your washing machine. Harmful bacteria multiply quickly on kitchen towels, sponges, and clothes. Consider using paper towels to clean up meat and poultry juices.
- When serving, too, make sure your hands—and the hands of everyone at the table—are clean.
- Use clean dishes and utensils at the table. If you used them in preparation, wash them thoroughly with soap and hot water before using them at the table.

Hand Washing 101

Mother used to say:
"Did you remember to wash your hands?"

It's extremely important to get your children into the habit of washing their hands. Frequent hand washing, when performed correctly, can help remove harmful bacteria and other germs that you or your child may have picked up from other people, contaminated surfaces, or from animals or animal waste. It's really just that simple.

When children (and parents) need to wash their hands:

- Before eating and after eating
- After using the bathroom or having their diapers changed
- After blowing their nose
- After handling pets, pet cages, or other pet objects
- After playing outdoors
- When their hands are visibly dirty
- More frequently when someone in his or her home is sick

Other times when parents, caregivers, or older children need to wash:

- Before, during, and after preparing food
- Immediately before preparing bottles or feeding children
- Before giving or applying medication to child or self
- After handling animal waste
- After wiping child's runny nose, or cleaning up spit or vomit, or similar substances
- After assisting child in using the toilet or changing diapers
- After cleaning the house
- After working or gardening outdoors

- After handling trash
- After removing gloves used for any purpose

How to correctly wash your hands (3.8)

- Use warm running water and a mild liquid or clean bar soap.
- Wet your hands and apply soap. Put the bar soap on a rack and allow it to drain.
- Rub your hands together vigorously until a soapy lather appears. Continue for at least twenty seconds. (Suggestion: It takes about that amount of time to recite the alphabet. So sing the alphabet, then add words that you and your child make up to finish the tune while you are drying hands. That way, they learn how much time to spend washing and also have a fun and positive experience!)
- Make sure to scrub under fingernails, between fingers, and around the tops and palms of the hands.
- Rinse thoroughly under running water.
- Dry hands with a clean towel.

Cooking with Vigilance

Waiting till It's Safe

- Don't taste any food of animal origin—meat, poultry, eggs, fish, or shellfish—when it is raw or during cooking.
- Yes, this means homemade cookie dough, too! It contains raw eggs.

Cooking till It's Safe

- Cook meat, poultry, and fish thoroughly.
  - ❖ Cook ground meat to at least 160°F.
    - —It's best to *always* use a food thermometer.
    - —Digital instant read thermometers, for use toward the end of cooking time for beef patties, should be inserted at least one-half inch into patties. (If patties are thin, insert into side).
    - —USDA researchers prepared and cooked patties of ground beef purchased from various locations across the country. More than a quarter of the "fresh ground beef" patties turned prematurely brown before reaching the safe temperature of 160°F. The lesson to be learned from this experiment: it is best not to depend on visual inspection. Use a food thermometer.

❖ Poultry: cook a whole chicken or turkey to at least 180°F, measured in the thigh; cook breasts and roasts to at least 170°F.
— It's best to always use a food thermometer.
— Visual check: cook till juices run clear.

❖ Fish is done when it is opaque and flakes easily with a fork and reaches 160°F on a food thermometer.

■ Cook egg dishes to 160°F.

❖ Visual check: cook until the yolk and white are firm, not runny.

❖ Hard-cooked eggs should be safe for everyone in the family to eat. Avoid giving your children soft-cooked or "runny" eggs.

❖ Don't use recipes in which eggs remain raw or only partially cooked, such as in ice cream, mayonnaise, or Caesar salad.

■ Never interrupt cooking. When partially cooking meat, poultry, or fish for the grill, do it while the grill is heating up and then bring the food to the grill immediately. Remember: Don't put cooked foods from the grill back on the plate that contains raw juices. Don't overlook the tongs that were used to put the raw meat on the grill! Thoroughly wash them before using to remove the cooked food.

■ Allow extra cooking time if your microwave is low wattage. Rotate foods manually in the microwave if there is no automatic rotation device.

Grilling Concerns

Some studies have suggested there may be a cancer risk related to eating foods cooked at high cooking temperatures. Based on recent research, eating moderate amounts of grilled meats—such as fish, beef, and poultry—cooked without charring to a safe medium temperature, does not pose a problem (3.9). Tips to reduce charring:

■ Choose lean cuts and remove visible fat before cooking.

■ Precook meat for two to five minutes in the microwave and discard the juice; finish cooking on the grill immediately.

■ Raise the cooking level of the grill so food is farther from the heat.

■ Clean the grill well after each use.

■ Avoid eating charred or burned portions of food.

The Right Stuff(ing)

■ Slow cookers are not advised for frozen or stuffed products.

■ For optimal safety and uniform doneness, cook stuffing separately.

■ If you do decide to stuff the foods, stuff them immediately before cooking. Take stuffing out immediately after cooking.

■ Cook a turkey until the temperature reaches at least 180°F in the innermost part of the thigh and the center of the stuffing inside the turkey (or in a casserole) reaches 165°F. Using a thermometer is essential when a turkey is stuffed. Bacteria can survive in stuffing that has not reached the safe temperature of 165°F.

What's Hot; What's Not

■ Avoid the danger zone of 40° to 140°F, the zone in which most bacterial agents of food-borne illness thrive.

■ Oven cooking at temperatures below 325°F is not recommended.

■ Handle leftovers with care.

   ❖ Thoroughly reheat leftover foods or ready-to-eat foods such as hot dogs until they are steaming hot.
     — Leftovers should be reheated to 165°F.
     — Wet foods such as gravy should reach a rolling boil.

   ❖ Refrigerate leftovers within two hours after cooking—within one hour if it's a hot day, 90°F or higher.

   ❖ Divide leftovers into shallow, covered containers before refrigerating, so that they chill rapidly and evenly.

   ❖ Never reuse marinade.

Taking Care with Fruits and Vegetables

Raw fruits and vegetables can also harbor disease-causing bacteria. Before eating any raw produce, it should be washed. This is true even for organic fruits and vegetables.

■ Wash the produce thoroughly under running water. If appropriate, use a small scrub brush.

■ Wash and scrub produce that has a rind, too, such as cantaloupe and pineapple. Why? Pathogens on the outside of the rind can contaminate the inside when you cut it and it won't necessarily be cooked to destroy the bacteria.

■ Toss out produce if the skin is broken. Organisms may have crawled into the pulp, and you won't be able to wash them out (3.10).

■ Wash lettuce and other leafy vegetables.

   ❖ Discard the outer leaves.

   ❖ Separate the inner leaves and thoroughly wash.

■ Decide where to buy.

   ❖ Ask the grocer where the fruits and vegetables were grown. (He is not required to post this information.)

- ❖ Consider choosing fruits and vegetables that are in season and ones that are locally grown.
- ■ The FDA offers additional tips.
  - ❖ Most fruits and vegetables should be stored in the refrigerator.
    - — Exceptions
      - • Apples and bananas may be stored on your countertop.
      - • Store potatoes and onions at room temperature in a cool, dry place. But don't put them under the sink, because leakage from pipes can damage food.
    - — Any fruits and vegetables that have been cut, peeled, or broken apart should be refrigerated within two hours.
  - ❖ Use caution when serving sprouts because if eaten raw, they can be dangerous for children, the elderly, and anyone with a weakened immune system.
    - — Raw sprouts have been associated with Salmonella and E. Coli 0157:H7.
    - — Cooking sprouts significantly reduces the risk of illness.
  - ❖ Do not eat any fruit or vegetable that looks brownish, slimy, or dried out.
  - ❖ Buy only pasteurized fruit juices and cider.
    - — Why? Pasteurization kills harmful levels of bacteria.
    - — If you are unsure whether the product is pasteurized, bring it to a boil for a minute before cooling and drinking.
  - ❖ Before and after handling produce, thoroughly wash your hands with soap and warm water for at least twenty seconds. (For information on how to reduce pesticide residues on fruits and vegetables, see Chapter 5.)

Knowing How Long Food Will Keep

- ■ Care begins when the food is in the package.
  - ❖ If a product has a "use by" date, follow that date for optimal quality.
  - ❖ If a product has a "sell by" date, buy before the date expires and cook or freeze according to the following guidelines.
  - ❖ When freezing meat, poultry, or fish in original packaging longer than a month or two, overwrap it with airtight, heavy-duty foil, plastic wrap, or freezer paper or place the package inside a freezer bag.
- ■ To know how long to keep food in your refrigerator or freezer, heed the following guidelines, supplied by the USDA and FDA (3.11). Because the 0°F freezer tem-

perature keeps food safe indefinitely, recommended freezer storage times are for best quality.

- Fresh eggs in shell
  — Refrigerate four to five weeks.
  — Don't freeze.
- Hard-boiled eggs
  — Refrigerate one week.
  — Don't freeze.
- Cheese: Swiss, brick, or processed
  — Refrigerate three to four weeks.
  — Cheese may be frozen, but taste and texture will be affected.
- Tv dinners and frozen casseroles
  — Don't store in the refrigerator.
  — Freeze three to four months.
- Fresh ground beef
  — Refrigerate one to two days.
  — Freeze three to four months.
- Fresh steaks and roasts
  — Refrigerate three to five days.
  — Freeze six to twelve months.
- Fresh whole chicken or turkey
  — Refrigerate one to two days.
  — Freeze twelve months.
- Fresh chicken or turkey parts
  — Refrigerate one to two days.
  — Freeze nine months.
- Lean fish, such as cod
  — Refrigerate one to two days.
  — Freeze up to six months.
- Fatty fish, such as blue, perch, or salmon
  — Refrigerate one to two days.
  — Freeze two to three months.
- Hot dogs, opened package
  — Refrigerate one week.
  — Freeze one to two months (in freezer wrap).
- Hot dogs, unopened package
  — Refrigerate two weeks, but never more than one week after "sell by" date.
  — Freeze one to two months.

- ❖ Lunch meat, opened package
  - —Refrigerate three to five days.
  - —Freeze one to two months.
- ❖ Lunch meat, unopened package
  - —Refrigerate two weeks, but never more than one week after "sell by" date.
  - —Freeze one to two months.
- ❖ Leftovers: cooked meat and meat dishes
  - —Refrigerate three to four days.
  - —Freeze two to three months.
- ❖ Fried chicken
  - —Refrigerate three to four days.
  - —Freeze four months.
- ❖ Cooked chicken nuggets or chicken patties
  - —Refrigerate one to two days.
  - —Freeze one to three months.

Eating Away from Home

Picnic Basket Safety

- ■ Plan it.
  - ❖ Estimate the right amount of food to take. That way you won't have to worry about storage or safety of leftovers.
  - ❖ If you buy take-out food, plan to eat it within two hours of pick up; or buy it ahead of time and chill before putting it into the cooler.
- ■ Chill it.
  - ❖ Cook food in time to thoroughly chill it in the refrigerator before packing for the picnic.
  - ❖ Use an insulated cooler with sufficient ice or ice packs to keep food at 40°F or below. Pack the food directly from the refrigerator.
  - ❖ Don't put the cooler in the trunk; carry it inside the air-conditioned car.
  - ❖ When the day's temperature is higher than 90°F, discard any food that has been sitting out more than an hour.
- ■ Keep it safe.
  - ❖ At the picnic, keep the cooler in the shade. Replenish the ice if it melts.
  - ❖ Except when it's being served, the food should be kept in the cooler.
  - ❖ Use a separate cooler for drinks so that the one with perishable food won't be repeatedly opened and closed.

❖ Remember those good guys, *soap* and *water!* Servers and eaters should have clean hands. Take plenty of moist towels if no facilities for washing hands are available.

❖ Place leftovers promptly in the cooler after grilling or serving. Remember, any food left outside for more than an hour when the day's temperature is higher than 90°F should be thrown out.

Lunch Box Safety

■ Invest in an insulated lunch box to keep cold foods cold and hot foods hot.

■ It's fine to prepare the lunch the night before and store it unboxed in the refrigerator or freezer.

■ If the school doesn't refrigerate the lunches, include in the lunch box a small frozen gel pack or frozen juice box. The juice will serve two purposes: keeping the lunch cool and giving the child a cold drink. Tell your child to store his or her lunch box out of direct sunlight and away from other heat sources.

■ Foods that don't require refrigeration include fruits, vegetables, *hard* cheese, chips, bread, crackers, peanut butter and jelly, mustard, and pickles.

■ Foods like soup and chili need to stay hot. The USDA recommends that you use an insulated bottle stored in an insulated lunch box. Fill the bottle with boiling water, let it stand for a few minutes, empty it, and then put in the piping-hot food. The insulated bottle should be kept closed until the child is ready to eat (3.12).

■ Tell your child to promptly discard any perishable leftovers.

Restaurants

■ Inspect your child's meals. Send back any meat (especially ground), poultry, or fish that does not appear thoroughly cooked. Ask management how they ensure that all foods are cooked to their appropriate internal temperature. All cooked food should be served hot and all cold food, cold. When this is not done, it is likely that the food has not been held at the proper temperature.

■ Patronize only establishments that have records of good public health performance.

❖ If food preparation takes place in sight, check whether the kitchen is clean and there is no bare-handed contact with food.

❖ Check if any of the employees are certified or trained to handle food safely.

❖ If patrons and employees share the same restroom, check to see that there is hot running water, adequate soap, and paper towels or a hand dryer.

Mold: A Home-Grown Bad Guy

Bacteria aren't the only culprits that can sneak into your food. Mold can grow right under your nose.

- No matter how clean you keep your kitchen or refrigerator, mold will grow.
- When food is not stored properly or is kept too long, mold will grow.
- Discard any food that exhibits an uncharacteristic color, texture, or flavor.
- Don't taste it. Don't smell it. (Mold spores can enter your body through your nose.)
- Important note: Aflatoxins are by-products of common, naturally occurring mold growth on certain agricultural products such as wheat, cereals, corn, and peanuts. Aflatoxins have been found to cause liver cancer in animal species. Check carefully for any sign of discoloration or mold. A warm and humid climate provides favorable conditions for the development of the mold and the production of the toxin. Make sure that the above commodities are stored at home properly (in a dry, cool place) so that contamination does not occur at home.

When discarding food, place it in a bag first to avoid spreading the mold spores. Be sure to examine other items that the moldy product may have contacted. Clean the refrigerator or container that held the moldy product.

Safety Alert: Know When to Avoid These Foods

Honey
- Do not give honey to a baby under the age of one. Honey may contain bacterial spores that can cause infant botulism, a rare but serious disease that affects the nervous system of young babies.
- Do not add honey to your baby's food, water, or formula.
- Do not dip your baby's pacifier in honey.

Wild Mushrooms
Many common species of mushrooms are capable of causing poisoning or even death (3.13). Only an expert with specialized training can distinguish the edible kinds from the others. Serve only these mushrooms to your family:

- the ones you purchase in a grocery store or
- the ones you've raised at home from cultures bought from reputable sources.

For More Information

You may contact the USDA by writing to Food Safety Education Staff, Room 2932—South Building, 1400 Independence Avenue SW, Washington, DC 20250, or by calling their Meat and Poultry Hot Line, where there is recorded information twenty-four hours a day and the line is staffed M–F, 10 A.M.–4 P.M. EST, at (800) 535-4555, or, in the Washington, D.C., area, by calling (202) 720-3333. You may prefer to contact the USDA by faxing (202) 690-2859, or by E-mailing fsis.mphotline@usda.gov, or by visiting their website: www.fsis.usda.gov.

For more information on seafood products, as well as general food safety, contact the FDA's Food Information Line by writing to FDA's Center for Food Safety and Applied Nutrition, Outreach and Information Center Consumer Education Staff (HFS-555), 200 C Street SW, Washington, DC 20204, or for twenty-four-hour recorded information or to speak to staff personnel M–F, 10 A.M.–4 P.M. EST, by calling (888)SAFE-FOOD, or in the Washington, D.C., area, by calling (202) 205-4314, or by faxing (202) 401-3532, or by visiting their website: www.cfsan.fda.gov.

Parents and children alike may wish to visit the website: www.foodsafety.gov. This website is a gateway to government food-safety information. For children, it has activities that teach about food safety.

You may also wish to contact Safe Tables Our Priority (S.T.O.P.), a nonprofit organization composed of victims of food-borne illness, their families and friends, and concerned individuals and organizations who work toward preventing food-borne illnesses and death. To learn more and/or to join the group, write to S.T.O.P., P.O. Box 46522, Chicago IL 60646-0522, or call (800) 350-STOP (7867), or E-mail feedback@stop-usa.org, visit their website: www.stop-usa.org.

For more information on preparing nutritious meals for your family and to receive the USDA food guide pyramid for adults and children, contact the USDA by writing to Center for Nutrition Policy and Promotion, 1120 20th Street NW, Suite 200N, Washington, DC 20036, or by calling (202) 418-2312, or by faxing (202) 208-2322, or by visiting their website: www.usda.gov/cnpp.

4

Knowing What's in Your Tap

Mother used to ask:
"What's wrong with drinking plain tap water?"

As parents we should be concerned about the safety of our tap water. This is particularly true if there are infants in the house, for they drink more fluids per pound of body weight than anyone else and their immature systems may be more vulnerable to microbial contaminants.

Public drinking water in the United States is generally safe. What protects U.S. public drinking water systems from harmful contaminants? It is the Safe Drinking Water Act (SDWA), passed in 1974, and its amendments, passed in 1986 and 1996.

The Environmental Protection Agency (EPA) has issued drinking water standards, or maximum contaminant levels (MCLs), for more than eighty contaminants. These standards limit the amount of each contaminant allowed to be present in drinking water.

U.S. public water suppliers are required to perform water quality monitoring to ensure that the water remains free from unsafe levels of contamination. Utilities are required by law to notify customers when water fails to meet applicable standards. The EPA has also issued secondary drinking water standards concerning the taste, odor, color, and certain other aesthetic qualities of drinking water which, although they may be undesirable, are not considered to pose a health risk. The EPA recommends these guidelines to states as reasonable goals, but states are not legally required to comply. However, some states have adopted their own enforceable regulations.

According to the EPA's "1996 National Public Water System Annual Compliance Report and Update on Implementation of the 1996 Safe Drinking Water Act Amendments," 86 percent of Americans are served by water systems with no reported violations of health standards, and most violations that did occur were in the very smallest systems (4.1).

Experts agree that you are more at risk for contaminants in your water if it comes from a private water supply or from a smaller water system that may not have enough funds to hire trained specialists or make necessary improvements. *Private water supplies* are defined as those coming from private wells or those serving fewer than twenty-five people or having fifteen or fewer service hookups. These are not regulated by drinking water standards. Individual homeowners in these situations must take steps on their own to test and treat their water as necessary to avoid any possible serious health effects.

Contaminants Sometimes Found in Drinking Water

Microbial Pathogens (Bacteria and Parasites)

Sources: more common in lakes and rivers contaminated with human and animal fecal waste

Symptoms: diarrhea, nausea, vomiting, and/or stomach cramps

Most at risk: infants, the elderly, and those who are immune-compromised (HIV and AIDS victims, among others). I recommend that pregnant women take precautions as well.

History: you may remember seeing Cryptosporidium in the headlines when this microorganism made 400,000 ill with gastrointestinal illness and killed more than a hundred in Milwaukee in 1993. According to the EPA and the Centers for Disease Control and Prevention (CDC), it is very resistant to disinfection, and even well-operated water treatment systems cannot ensure that drinking water will be completely free of this parasite.

What to Do

- The most effective way to kill Cryptosporidium and other microbial contaminants is to boil the water.
    - ❖ Bring the drinking water to a rolling boil for one minute.
    - ❖ Immediately remove it from the heat source.
    - ❖ Let it cool before serving.
- Another alternative: buy bottled water from a quality source.
- You can also purchase a filter.
    - ❖ Two kinds of filters:
        - —POU (point of use) systems treat water at a single tap.
        - —POE (point of entry) systems treat water used throughout the home.

❖ When purchasing,
   —look for a POU device that specifies it is equipped with an "Absolute" one micrometer filter; or
   —find a POU device labeled as certified by NSF under ANSI/NSF standard 53 for "Cyst Removal." This filter may not protect you from organisms smaller than Cryptosporidium (4.2).

■ Remember to boil water that is used to make ice cubes.

Nitrates

Sources: ground and surface water in rural areas contaminated with animal waste; runoff from nitrogen-based fertilizer
Most at risk: infants

❖ When the nitrate level is above the national standard, it can react with the hemoglobin in the infant's blood to produce an anemic condition known as "blue baby." If the condition is untreated, it can be fatal (4.3).
❖ Until you are sure your water is safe, do not drink it if you are pregnant.
❖ Do not give your baby any nitrate-contaminated water or any food or formula that contains nitrate-contaminated water.

What to Do

❖ Boiling does not remove nitrates. The EPA recommends that you *do not boil* the water for extensive periods because doing so will only increase the nitrate concentration. Remember: to kill microbial pathogens, you need only bring the water to a rolling boil for one minute.
❖ Buy bottled water from a quality source.
❖ Or invest in a home-treatment device.

Trihalomethanes (THM)

Sources: THMs are formed when chlorine (the chemical used to disinfect water) combines with naturally occurring organic matter, such as decaying leaves (4.4).
Health consequences: Although some studies have linked THMs to bladder and rectal cancer, more research is needed to show a definitive cause and effect.
Most at risk: possibly fetuses

❖ A recent study of 5,144 pregnant women found that women who drank five or more glasses of cold tap water a day containing at least 75 parts per billion (ppb) of THMs were at greater risk of miscarriage than women with less exposure (4.5).

❖ The current federal level for THM is 100 (ppb), however, the MCL will soon be reduced to 80 ppb.

What to Do

❖ Don't panic! However, pregnant women may want to err on the side of the baby's safety.
— Some experts recommend using a carbon activated filter if you are pregnant and your water supply contains THM levels consistently at or above 75 ppb (4.6).
— Another option is drinking bottled water.
❖ To reduce the risk of inhaling THMs, reduce your shower time and maintain good ventilation in your bathroom (4.7).

Three Substances with Long Résumés

■ Radon, a radioactive gas found in certain types of rock
  ❖ It can seep into groundwater.
  ❖ People can be exposed by drinking it or while showering or washing dishes.
  ❖ Indoor air pollution by radon is usually more of a health concern. (See Chapter 11.)
■ Lead (See Chapter 9.)
■ Pesticides, including herbicides, insecticides, and fungicides: Those most at risk for having pesticides in their tap water are those living in active farming communities. (See Chapter 5.)

Investigating Your Water Supply

If You Are on a Public Water Supply

■ Contact your local water utility. The phone number is listed on your water bill.
  ❖ Ask where your drinking water comes from.
  ❖ Ask how your water is treated and what contaminants are tested.
  ❖ Request that they send you a copy of their Municipal Drinking Water Contaminant Analysis Report (4.8).
    — They are required by law to provide this information to you through the issuance of an annual Consumer Confidence Report.
    — Make sure to take particular note of any violations.
    — This report may be available on-line at www.epa.gov/safewater/dwinfo.htm.

—What that report won't tell you is what is happening between the treatment plant and your home. Lead and copper may leach from plumbing and pipes.

■ You still need to test for lead and copper. If your water has a blue-green tinge or if your fixtures are stained blue-green, you may suspect high copper levels. See "Getting It Tested" (page 33) to find out how to go about having your water tested.

■ Call your state water agency or state Department of Environmental Health; ask what contaminants they test for and request a copy of their analysis.

■ If you are having a water quality problem, contact your local water utility to have the matter investigated. They are required to investigate consumer complaints. If you are not satisfied with their findings, call your local health department.

If You Are on a Private Water System

■ Contact your state and local health department and your cooperative service extension agent.
  ❖ Ask about groundwater problems in your area.
  ❖ Look at past, present, or potential problems.
■ Testing
  ❖ Some local health departments test private water for free or a fee.
  ❖ You can contact your state laboratory certification office for a listing of certified drinking water laboratories in your state. (See "For More Information" at the end of this chapter.)
  ❖ The EPA recommends that private water supplies be tested at least once a year for
    —nitrates,
    —total dissolved solids, and
    —coliform bacteria, the presence of which (although it is generally harmless) may indicate other contamination.
  ❖ You may need to test more frequently and for more potential contaminants if a problem is suspected.
  ❖ Well water should be tested for lead. This is particularly important if you have lead pipes, soldered copper joints, or brass parts in the pump.
  ❖ Additional testing should be performed if certain conditions or nearby activities exist by your well, such as
    —intensive agriculture,
    —a dump,
    —a landfill,
    —a factory,

—a gasoline service station, or

—a dry-cleaning operation.

❖ Your state and local health department and the cooperative service extension agent can provide guidance on what specific contaminants should be tested.

Getting It Tested

Some suppliers will test free of charge. If that's not the case, have your water tested by a state-certified laboratory. To get the names of state-certified labs nearest you, call your state laboratory certification office or the EPA Safe Drinking Water Hot Line (see "For More Information," at the end of this chapter).

I recommend that you do not have your water tested by a company trying to sell you a water treatment device. Why? They have a vested interest in the test results. If the results from the lab indicate that you do have serious problems, it may be a good idea to get a second opinion from a different lab before spending money on an elaborate water treatment device. If your water is contaminated and you are on a public water supply, notify your water utility and local and state health department.

Finding the Right Water Treatment

There is no public agency that tests or approves home water-treatment devices, nor can one unit eliminate every kind of drinking water contaminant. To find a quality product and one that is certified to remove the specific contaminants found in your drinking water, contact NSF International, an independent, not-for-profit organization that tests and certifies home water-treatment units for health-related contaminants and aesthetic effects, or the Water Quality Association (WQA), an independent, not-for-profit organization that classifies units according to the contaminants they remove and lists units that have earned its approval. (See "For More Information," at the end of this chapter.) Note: WQA does not test or evaluate units for health-related contaminants, only for aesthetic effects such as hardness and chlorine.

Do your homework and shop around. Believe it or not, you can spend from $20 on a pitcher to $1,000 for an under-the-sink unit. Why should you invest in a costly water treatment unit that does more than you really need?

Maintenance Is a Must

■ All products require periodic maintenance or replacement.

❖ A poorly maintained filter could be worse for your health than actually drinking the water without the filter.

—It can cause the contaminants to begin flowing back into the water.

—It can act as a breeding ground for bacteria.

- Carefully follow the manufacturer's instructions. Some experts recommend that filter cartridges be changed at minimum every six months.
- If you are not inclined to keep up with the maintenance, it may be a good idea to consider purchasing a maintenance contract from the dealer.

Bottled Water

Bottled water is regulated as a food by the Food and Drug Administration (FDA), which imposes quality standards that are equivalent to the EPA's drinking water standards. Is it any safer than the water from your own tap? According to the EPA, bottled water is not necessarily any safer than your local drinking water (4.9). The Natural Resources Defense Council concurs. After a four-year review of the bottled water industry, the organization concluded that there is no assurance that bottled water is safer than tap water (4.10).

The quality of bottled water varies among brands, not only in price, but in quality, because of differences in the source of the water used and company practices (4.11). Check with the individual bottler of your favorite brand to find out how their water is treated, and request a copy of their annual water analysis. You can also contact the International Bottled Water Association (IBWA), the trade association representing the bottled water industry. (See "For More Information," at the end of this chapter.)

As with foods, to avoid bacterial contamination, refrigerate bottled water after opening.

Remember that using a home water-treatment device or drinking bottled water is just a temporary solution. It does not solve the problem. As parents and community members, we must support efforts to upgrade the supply of safe drinking water and to protect water supplies from industrial and agricultural pollution. Remember also to do your part at home to compost, recycle, and properly dispose of hazardous material.

For More Information

For information on evaluating filtering devices, contact the NSF International (formerly known as National Sanitation Foundation) by writing to P.O. Box 130140, Ann Arbor, MI 48113-0140, or by calling (800) NSF-MARK [673-6275], or by faxing (734) 769-0109, or by visiting their website: www.nsf.org.

For information about firms that produce and sell equipment and services, contact the Water Quality Association by writing Consumer Affairs Department, 4151 Naperville

Road, Lisle, IL 60532-1088, or by calling (800) 749-0234, or by visiting their website: www.wqa.org.

To get information on finding a certified lab in your area, contact ACIL (formerly the American Council of Independent Laboratories) by calling (202) 887-5872, or by visiting their website: www.acil.org.

Reach the EPA's Safe Drinking Water Hot Line, which is staffed M–F, 9 A.M.–5:30 P.M. EST, by calling (800) 426-4791, or by visiting their website: www.epa.gov/safewater.

For a list of state certification officers, visit this website: www.epa.gov/safewater/faq/sco.html.

You may also wish to contact Clean Water Action by writing to 4455 Connecticut Avenue NW, Suite A300, Washington, DC 20008-2328, or by calling (202) 895-0420, or by visiting their website: www.cleanwater.org.

Or contact the Natural Resources Defense Council by writing to 40 W. 20th Street, New York, NY 10011, or by calling (212) 727-2700, or by visiting their website: www.nrdc.org.

To speak to a staff member of the International Bottled Water Association (IBWA) M–F, 9 A.M.–5 P.M. EST, call (703) 683-5213. To receive information on bottled water sent to you by mail, contact the IBWA hot line by calling (800) WATER-11 [928-3711], or by visiting their website: www.bottledwater.org.

For information on the uses and releases of chemicals in your state, contact EPCRA (Emergency Planning and Community Right-to-Know Act) by calling their hot line M–F, 9 A.M.–6 P.M. EST: (800) 535-0202, or by visiting their website: www.epa.gov/epaoswer/hotline/.

Private well owners may wish to contact the national Farm*A*Syst/Home*A*Syst Program, an organization that provides fact sheets and worksheets to help farmers and residents assess pollution risks and develop management plans geared towards their circumstances, by calling (608) 262-0024 or by visiting their website: www.uwex.edu/farmasyst and www.uwex.edu/homeasyst.

5

Taking Care with Pesticides

Mother used to say:
"If it can kill a bug, it can make you sick."

*P*esticide is a generic name for a whole class of chemicals intended to prevent, control, eliminate, or mitigate any pest. These include

— *insecticide* (kills insects),
— *herbicide* (kills unwanted plants and weeds),
— *rodenticide* (kills rodents), and
— *fungicide* (kills fungi).

Pesticides Are Poison

Pesticides are designed to be toxic. It shouldn't surprise anyone that a poison that kills one organism will harm others as well. Some pesticides can cause cancer, central nervous system damage, and respiratory illnesses and have other adverse health effects in humans and animals (5.1). They have also been shown to have toxic effects on human reproductive, endocrine, and immunological systems (5.2). Moreover, the long-term health effects of many pesticides are still unknown.

Children Are Most at Risk

Children eat proportionately more food—particularly fruits and vegetables—than adults. They also drink more fluids and breathe more air relative to their body weight than adults do.

Children are caught in a giant squeeze play. On one hand, they have higher metabolic rates and therefore absorb higher concentrations of toxins from the environment. On the other hand, their defense systems have not fully developed, so they are less able to fight off the poisons! In adults, the liver and kidneys detoxify and excrete foreign substances, as well as act as a barrier to absorption of toxins (5.3). Because children's brains and nervous and immune systems are still developing, they may be particularly vulnerable to poisons.

Unfortunately, our children may be exposed to a variety of pesticides from a variety of sources, such as

— residues found in food and drinking water,

— chemicals sprayed in the garden and on lawns, and

— indoor use of bug and insect sprays in homes and schools.

In Our Food

Mother used to say:
"Wash it before you eat it!"

Who's in Charge?

The Environmental Protection Agency (EPA) regulates pesticide sale and use and determines acceptable pesticide levels (called *pesticide tolerance*) on food. The U.S. Department of Agriculture (USDA) and the U.S. Food and Drug Administration (FDA) both monitor foods for pesticide residues. The FDA is responsible for enforcing these tolerances on all foods except meat, poultry, and certain egg products, which are monitored by the USDA.

You can significantly lower your family's exposure. Experts suggest a number of ways to reduce pesticide residues in the food your family eats.

For Fruits and Vegetables, Go Organic!

■ Look for the "certified organic" label on produce.

  ❖ General definition

    — Grown in soil without the use of synthetic pesticides

    — Grown in soil without the use of synthetic fertilizers

    — Grown in soil that has had no synthetics added for at least three years prior to harvest

  ❖ Enforcement

    — Farmers and processors must keep detailed records of methods and materials used in growing or processing organic products.

    — All methods and materials are periodically inspected by a third-party certifier (5.4).

  ❖ Standards

    — Organic laws now vary from state to state.

—The USDA is presently developing national standards. When they go into effect, all agricultural products labeled *organic* will have to be in compliance with the U.S. law.

❖ No guarantees

—There is no guarantee that "certified organic" foods are completely free of synthetic pesticides and fertilizers.

—Factors such as air pollution, drifting spray from neighboring conventional farms, and persistent pesticides that have remained in the soil for years can all contribute to minimal residues (5.5).

❖ Cost: Organic can be a lot more expensive than conventionally grown fruit, but it's worth the price.

▪ Test results are in.

❖ *Consumer Reports*, in 1997, tested 1,000 pounds of unrinsed peppers, apples, peaches, and tomatoes for more than 300 pesticides.

❖ Their conclusions after testing organic, green-labeled, and conventional produce for pesticide residues: 25 percent of the organic, 55 percent of the green-labeled, and 77 percent of the conventional produce contained residues.

❖ Overall, organic produce was also found to have the least toxic residues (5.6).

▪ Environmental impact

❖ Even critics of the organic movement agree that organic farming is better for the environment.

—Organic farming utilizes crop-rotation methods, natural pesticides, and natural fertilizers (such as manure and compost), all of which help keep the soil nutrition rich.

—Conventional farming pollutes both land and water with pesticide runoff. It degrades topsoil and uses nonrenewable energy resources (5.7).

❖ Conventional farming techniques may be harmful to the farm workers who must work with toxic chemicals.

▪ Find organic produce.

❖ Ask for it.

—If your local grocer does not carry organic food, ask him or her to do so.

—The more we demand it, the more we will see it stocked on our supermarket shelves.

❖ Drive a little farther.

—It is worth the drive to shop at stores that stock a large variety of organic food.

—Look for locally grown produce.

❖ Grow your own chemical-free produce in your backyard garden.

- Choose organic baby foods.
    - ❖ Organic baby food is now available at major supermarkets. (See what asking will do?)
    - ❖ The brands
        - —Gerber's Tender Harvest
        - —Earth's Best
        - —Organic Baby
    - ❖ If you don't use certified organic baby food:
        - —Call the telephone number listed on the label of your favorite baby food.
        - —Learn how they are reducing pesticide-residue levels in their products.

Taking Care with Other Foods

Look for . . .

- Organic beef
    - ❖ Raised without antibiotics
    - ❖ Raised without growth hormones
    - ❖ Raised without synthetic chemicals
- Organic dairy products
    - ❖ The cow is fed a diet of only certified organic feed.
    - ❖ Milk products are produced without the use of antibiotics or hormones.
- Organic chicken
    - ❖ Fed only certified organic feed
    - ❖ No antibiotics have been administered.
    - ❖ Note: Presently, federal regulations prohibit the use of hormones to any poultry in the United States.
- Organic eggs
    - ❖ Produced from hens fed only certified organic feed
    - ❖ No antibiotics administered
    - ❖ No hormones administered

Contrasts and Comparisons

- Just for the taste of it
    - ❖ My family and friends think, hands down, that organically grown produce tastes better.
    - ❖ There is no scientific evidence that organic food is more nutritious than produce that is conventionally grown.

- This is not a beauty contest.
  - That perfect looking produce, without a flaw, may have gotten that way because of the use of pesticides and wax.
  - I have noticed lately that organic products are getting closer to that "flawless" look that general shoppers seem to prize, although that should not be a criterion when choosing produce.

Conventionally Grown Produce

- Buy produce in season. Not only is it less expensive but it is less likely to have been treated with fungicides and other preservatives.
- Buy from local growers.
  - This helps you avoid buying foods shipped over long distances or stored for long periods of time.
  - Produce is likely to be fresher than anywhere else in town.
  - You can quiz the producers themselves on the farming methods used.
  - You will also be giving support to the local farmer.
- Join a community-supported agriculture farm.
  - Local growers provide shares of seasonal fruits and vegetables to members.
  - Call (800) 516-7797 for farms in your area.
- Avoid foods that are waxed.
  - The wax coating won't rinse off with water.
  - It can trap pesticide and fungicide residues inside.
  - If the fruit is waxed, your best option is to peel the fruit.
  - Your local supermarket is required by federal law to post signs naming the products that are waxed.
  - Commonly waxed products are apples, avocadoes, and cucumbers.

Preparing Fresh Produce and Meat

- Carefully and thoroughly wash and scrub all fruits and vegetables (including organically grown).
  - Peel fruits and vegetables whenever possible.
  - Discard outer leaves of lettuce and other leafy vegetables, where the most residue is likely to be.
  - Under running water (which has an abrasive effect), thoroughly scrub all produce with a soft brush. Note: It is recommended not to wash produce with household soap; soap residues are very difficult to completely rinse off and most soaps are not meant to be consumed.

- ❖ Be aware that scrubbing will not remove pesticide residues that have been absorbed into the produce before harvest.
- ❖ A freshness tip: The best time to wash and cut up the produce is just before you are ready to eat it.
- ❖ Some pesticides break down or are reduced by cooking, so when appropriate, cook or bake food (5.8).
- ❖ Experts recommend that you eat a variety of food from a variety of sources. This will give you a better mix of nutrients and reduce the likelihood of exposure to a single pesticide.
- ▪ Meat, chicken, and fish
  - ❖ Be aware that pesticides tend to accumulate in the fatty tissues of animals.
    — Trim the fat from meat and poultry.
    — Remove the skin from chicken and fish.
    — Discard the fat in broths and pan drippings.
  - ❖ Contact your local health department or Environmental Protection Agency to find out if fish and game restrictions exist in your area because of pesticides or other chemicals.

Don't Just Skip It!

Don't even think about not serving fruits and vegetables to your family for fear of consuming pesticide residues. Fruits and vegetables should be a vital component of every child's healthy diet. Studies have shown that a diet low in fat and high in fiber is important in reducing the risk of cancer, as well as other diseases, which certainly outweighs any of the potential risks.

What's the Government Doing?

In 1996, the Food Quality Protection Act was passed into law. This edict stipulates that the level of allowable pesticide residues in raw and processed foods (pesticide tolerance) is determined with infants' and children's vulnerability in mind. When determining a safe level for a pesticide in food, the EPA must explicitly account for all infant and child exposures to other pesticides and toxic chemicals that share a common toxic mechanism (affect the body in the same way). Furthermore, the determination of what is safe must include noncancer risks such as neurotoxic effects and reproductive development.

The EPA is in the midst of reexamining approximately 9,700 existing pesticide tolerances by August 2006. Meanwhile, ensure the protection of your family by following the guidelines in this chapter.

In the Yard and Garden

Mother used to say:
"Rolling in the grass will make you itchy!"

Some of my favorite childhood memories were made right in my own backyard. My sisters and I would roll and play on the grass (I don't remember any itchiness!), climb the trees, and run and play with the dog. That's what being a child is all about. I want my children to enjoy the same simple pleasures.

Consequences of Keeping Bugs at Bay with Toxins

Unfortunately, your child's engaging in those simple pleasures may expose him or her to hazardous substances. The EPA reports that when crawling on the ground or floor, children may encounter contaminated dust and soil, lead paint, household and garden chemicals, and other substances that may be hazardous to their health.

Having pesticides stored in your home puts your children at greater risk for poisoning. Each year, according to the EPA, more than 100,000 children directly ingest pesticides. Here, again, we can use our common sense. This stuff is poison! The Florida Poison Information Center warns that many of these chemicals are as toxic to us and our children as they are to the bugs we wish to eliminate. Depending upon what type of pesticide is involved, ingesting or inhaling even small amounts may result in illness, especially for children (5.9).

For that reason, it is imperative that we store and lock away all pesticides. It is also important to keep the products in their original containers, so that what we see is what we get. (See Chapter 8.)

Possible Link: Pesticides and Children's Cancer

A 1995 study published in the *American Journal of Public Health* has found a possible link between home pesticide use and certain childhood cancers (5.10). According to the study, children whose yards were treated with chemicals were four times more likely to develop soft tissue sarcomas (cancer of the muscles and connective tissues) than children with untreated lawns. According to the authors, one of the yard chemicals most likely to have been used in the study population was Diazinon. Incredibly enough, Diazinon is approved for use on residential lawns, even though it is banned for use on golf courses and sod farms because it is toxic to birds.

What's a Parent to Do?

Although the results of this study are not conclusive, we as parents should be concerned enough to want to reduce or eliminate pesticides.

Because there are so many effective, less toxic alternatives, why take risks? Your family, pets, and any wildlife that venture onto your property will have a healthier place to live because of your precautions.

Prevention Is Paramount: Nonchemical Pest Elimination

Pests seek out shelters that provide them with food and moisture, so if you don't want to play the perfect host, eliminate their favorite places.

- Cut off their water supply.
    - Repair leaky faucets.
    - Repair all water leaks and structural problems.
    - Don't let water accumulate anywhere around the home.
    - Reduce humidity in your home.
    - Don't leave any water trays under your plants or under the refrigerator.
- Eradicate their food supply; start with the kitchen.
    - Don't leave any food out overnight (including pet food).
        — Store food items in tightly sealed containers.
        — Sweep up crumbs. (They are banquets to ants and roaches.)
        — Mop up spills promptly (especially after the children eat).
    - Designate the kitchen or dining room as the only place where your family eats or drinks. This makes it less likely that you will have crumbs or spills throughout the house. (Don't allow the children to snack in their bedrooms.)
    - Clean up promptly after eating.
        — Wash dishes.
        — Empty garbage.
        — Clean kitchen garbage pail.
    - Store garbage outdoors in tightly closed cans, with no food or attractants around.
- Eliminate their hiding places. (Don't play hide-and-seek with bugs.)
    - Don't keep more newspapers, paper bags, and boxes than necessary.
    - Keep clutter down to a minimum. (That's a tough one when kids are around!)
    - Remove stacks of reading material from the bathroom.

- ❖ When shopping:
    - — Look inside paper bags or boxes for pests before bringing them into your home.
    - — Better yet, take your own canvas bag to the store to carry purchases home.
  - ❖ Keep the family pets clean; bathe them often.
  - ❖ Vacuum often.
- ■ Plug up their entryways.
  - ❖ Install screens on all drains, doors, and windows.
  - ❖ Caulk and seal openings and crevices.
  - ❖ Block all passageways through the floor.
  - ❖ All doors should fit flush (no gaps) to the side, top, and bottom.
  - ❖ Keep sink plugs over drains.
  - ❖ Do not leave garage or other doors open.
    - — They're a tempting invitation to rodents, snakes, and stray animals.
    - — A gap or hole large enough to put a pencil through is large enough for a mouse to squeeze through. A rat can chew and enlarge such a hole.
  - ❖ Securely cover attic vent openings with a strong metal grate with holes no larger than a quarter-inch, just big enough so that air can circulate.
- ■ Clean up around the outside of the house.
  - ❖ Remove all debris from around the house perimeter:
    - — Stored wood, i.e., firewood
    - — Boxes
    - — Garbage
  - ❖ Clean up animal droppings.
  - ❖ Pet food left outside will attract and feed many pests.
  - ❖ Destroy diseased vegetation.
  - ❖ Rake leaves.
  - ❖ Make sure rain water properly drains away from your property.
  - ❖ Don't leave any pails or buckets outdoors that can collect water.
  - ❖ Use fine gravel around the immediate perimeter of the house instead of mulch. Mulch is organic matter, which attracts pests and provides them with attractive harborage. (Gravel should be 5–6 inches deep and 12–24 inches wide.)
  - ❖ Keep your lawn and garden healthy with proper care and maintenance.

Tips from a Pro for Particular Pests

Jerry Goodman, a pest control operator in Miami who practices Integrated Pest Management and has more than twenty years of experience successfully battling bugs, offers these tips if preventive measures don't work:

- Moths—pheromone scent traps help monitor and trap moths. Cedar blocks or chips can also help to repel them. (Make sure to clean all garments before storing in the closet.)
- Cockroaches
  - ❖ If you see a roach or two, you can step on it. They may have just come in with your grocery bags and have not set up a colony yet.
  - ❖ Boric Acid Bait Stations—read and carefully follow manufacturer's directions.
    — Important note: Boric acid is harmful if swallowed.
    - This product is considered to have a lower toxicity than many pesticides, but people and pets should not ingest it.
    - Place only in areas that are inaccessible to children and pets.
  - ❖ Boric acid powder
    — It can be purchased in the pest-control department of hardware stores and home and garden centers. (Don't use boric acid for roach control if the container does not say it can be used for this purpose.)
    — Request that your pest-control operator use a blue-tinted product that can't be mistaken for edible items such as flour or sugar.
    — To use, read and carefully follow label directions exactly.
    — Place or inject the product only in hidden areas, such as wall voids, cracks, and crevices where roaches hide.
    - Apply it only in areas that are inaccessible to children and pets.
    - Never leave it exposed on countertops, and never leave it exposed near food.
    - When using a broom or vacuum, make sure the boric acid is not kicked back into the air.
    — My grandmother lived in an apartment in New York City, where roaches run rampant. She successfully kept them at bay with nothing more than boric acid. (Of course, her kitchen was always meticulously clean!)
- Ants
  - ❖ Wash away ants you see in the home with a soapy dishrag.
  - ❖ An effective way to prevent ants from entering the home in search of food is through the use of exterior baiting. However, different types of ants prefer different baits (e.g., sugar, fat, protein, or carbohydrates). Look for hydramethylnon (minimally toxic) or boric acid bait stations by checking label ingredients. Liquid sweet baits can be placed in special holders, which are child-resistant. (Remember, child resistant does not mean childproof.) Read

and carefully follow manufacturer's instructions. Baits should always be placed out of reach of children.

❖ Don't plant flowering plants closer than six feet from your home because they attract aphids that attract sweet feeding ants. Also, don't allow any plants or trees to touch structure because this provides an attractive highway into the home.

■ Fleas

❖ A most important defense: Eliminate fleas from your lawn or grounds.

—This may keep your pet from becoming infected in the first place. Your pet, then, won't bring them into your home.

—Consider introducing beneficial *nematodes* (microscopic worms) into the lawn and soil. (They can be ordered from sources such as gardening catalogs, magazines, and Hydro-Gardens, which is listed at the end of this chapter.)

❖ Pet care as a deterrent

—Groom your pet often, or daily if fighting an existing problem, with a flea comb. Drop fleas caught in the comb in a pan of soapy water.

—Incorporate brewer's yeast into your pet's diet, but consult your veterinarian for the amount to administer. Proper dosage varies with the pet's weight.

—Use an herbal collar.

—Keep your pet healthy.

• A healthy diet is an absolute must.

• Regular visits to the veterinarian are essential.

• Some experts believe that a healthy animal is less vulnerable to fleas. Whatever the case, your pet's good health is in the best interest of your entire family.

❖ Cleanliness is the key.

—Regularly shampoo pet bedding, rugs, carpets, and furniture coverings.

—Vacuum often—everywhere the pet has gone.

—Bathe your pet and his or her sleeping areas regularly. Use soap, not detergent. Detergent can be a skin irritant to pets and will remove too many natural oils from their coat, leaving them with a bad hair day! (Remember, cats detest baths!)

❖ One method of treatment for serious fleas infestations is using diatomanceous earth (DE).

—How it works

• DE is the crushed remains of *diatom*—a prehistoric algae with a glasslike skeleton.

• It punctures the insects, especially their breathing system, causing them to dry out.

- When an insect walks through DE, it is something like our walking over broken glass.
— The purchase
    - Purchase the agricultural type of DE (from fresh water sources, not salt water), which can be found in the pest-control or lawn-care departments of hardware stores and home and garden centers.
    - Do not get the type sold for use in swimming pools because it contains free silica, which can be harmful to humans.
— Before application: Thoroughly vacuum the carpet to reduce the flea population. Just prior to vacuuming, put two or three tablespoons of cornstarch into the vacuum bag. This creates a mini dust storm; the tiny particles of the cornstarch will clog fleas' breathing holes.
— The application
    - Carefully follow the label directions.
    - Use adequate ventilation and avoid breathing DE dust.
— Precautions
    - Wear a dust mask when applying, sweeping, and vacuuming.
    - Keep children and pets off the carpet and out of the area until you have vacuumed well.
    - Carefully dispose of your vacuum bag after each use because flea eggs can still hatch in the bag. In addition, DE contained in the bag can become airborne.
- Rats and mice
    - Consider getting a cat to prevent rodents.
    - Use traps. Place traps in areas out of sight and reach of children and pets.
- Dry-wood termites
    - Using heat
        — This method should be applied only by professionals.
        — Heat will kill the termites in all areas that are properly heated.
        — The procedure consists of using equipment that gradually warms wood sections of the structure to 130°F, then holds the temperature for about sixty minutes to eliminate all stages of wood-destroying insects. Because insects can't sweat or tolerate heat as mammals do, they soon die from dehydration. (Heat also kills mold, mildew, and dust mites.)
    - Using sodium borate
        — This product protects bare wood (such as in attics) from wood decay and future attacks by termites.
        — When a new home is being built, all the wood can be effectively pre-treated with sodium borate. This will not only greatly extend the life of

the wood, but it will give the home positive, long-term protection from termites and all other wood-destroying organisms.

Toward Having a Bug-Free Yard

- Test the soil.
  - ❖ Develop healthy soil by making sure it has the right pH (acidity/alkalinity balance), nutrients, and texture.
  - ❖ Test the soil for lead.
    - — Home testing kits are available at most garden centers.
    - — Your county extension agent might provide testing.
- Let grass grow.
  - ❖ Most types of grass should be allowed to grow to around two and one half to three and one half inches.
  - ❖ Weeds have a hard time taking root and growing when grass is fairly long (5.11). (However, if grass is too long it offers ticks and snakes very attractive hiding places.)
- Choose grass and plants with care.
  - ❖ Select a grass that grows well in your climate.
  - ❖ Choose plants that have low requirements for water, fertilizers, and pesticides (5.12).
  - ❖ If you have pets or children under six years of age, buy flowers and plants that are nontoxic.
- Water deeply but not often.
  - ❖ Apply about an inch per week in ordinary circumstances.
  - ❖ For hot climates, apply an inch every three days (depending on rain frequency).
  - ❖ Consult with your county extension agent to find the recommended lawn care regimen for your area.
- Pull weeds.
  - ❖ Lawn weeds can be pulled up by the roots.
  - ❖ Parents can make a contest of this endeavor.
    - — Let the kids see who can pull the most weeds. (In my family, I always won!)
- Battle bugs the less toxic way.
  - ❖ UDSA recommendations (5.13):
    - — Nondetergent insecticidal soaps
    - — Hot-pepper sprays and/or hot pepper and wax sprays
    - — One teaspoon liquid soap in a gallon of water

— Used dishwater

— Forceful stream of water to dislodge insects

❖ Environmental strategies

— Import predators, such as ladybugs, ground beetles, lace wings, and beneficial nematodes.

— Do good planning and research before using such methods.

• Consult a good home-gardening guide.

• Check with your county extension service office.

▪ Consider the integrated approach.

❖ Integrated Pest Management is recommended by the EPA.

❖ What it is and how it is used

— An effective strategy for controlling pests, combining a variety of methods

• Prevention, such as sanitation and structural repair

• Mechanical measures, such as traps and pulling weeds by hand

• Biological controls, such as using beneficial predators

• Other measures based on knowledge of the pests

— Uses regular monitoring to determine if and when treatments are needed, such as sticky traps to monitor insect activity

— Toxic chemicals are sometimes used, but only in extreme cases. Even then, the least toxic effective agent is used.

❖ Check with your child's school.

— Ask what pest-control methods they use.

— Request that they use Integrated Pest Management.

If You Must: Using Poison Anyway

If you decide to use pesticides, please take the necessary precautions to protect your family, yourself, and the environment. Remember to use pesticides as a last resort. When you use them, select the least toxic pesticide, buy only pesticides that are pre-mixed (to avoid exposure to concentrated products), and the smallest amount necessary to do the job. If you are pregnant avoid all contact with pesticides.

▪ Follow these guidelines for using pesticides.

❖ Read the pesticide label and carefully follow all the directions.

❖ Mix or dilute outdoors.

❖ While using the chemical,

— wear protective clothing, including gloves; and

— don't eat or smoke.

- ❖ Cleanup
  - —Wash all protective clothing separately from the rest of the family wash.
  - —Take a bath or shower immediately after applying the chemical.
- ❖ More is not better!
  - —Don't change the recommended amount.
  - —You can harm yourself and your family if you do so.
- ■ Exercise caution when spraying indoors.
  - ❖ Keep area well ventilated.
  - ❖ Remove from the area
    - —children (a perfect time to send them to their grandparents' for a visit),
    - —pets (including birds and fish),
    - —plants, and
    - —toys and playthings.
  - ❖ Cover the furniture.
  - ❖ Take particular care in the kitchen.
    - —Remove food, dishes, pots, and pans from areas to be sprayed.
    - —Never spray food-preparation surfaces with pesticides.
  - ❖ After the spraying's over, do not return until after the time prescribed on the label (I recommend doubling that time).
- ■ When lawns are sprayed—whether it is you or your neighbor who uses pesticides on the lawn and garden—you and your family must take precautions.
  - ❖ Shut your family in.
    - —Bring your family and pets indoors.
    - —Shut your windows and doors.
    - —Carry in toys and playthings, even those usually left outside.
  - ❖ The American Academy of Pediatrics (AAP) says your child should not play on a treated lawn until
    - —the lawn has been watered twice, and
    - —the odor of pesticides has gone away.
  - ❖ Never spray or dust on a windy day because the wind can carry the spray to a neighboring property.
  - ❖ Never let your child near any chemically treated area that has not completely dried.
    - —Family members and guests should wipe their feet on the front doormat and leave their shoes at the door.
    - —Toxins may be carried into your home on the soles of shoes, where it can settle into your carpet, a place where young children play or crawl.

❖ Spray notification
  —Request that your neighbors or their lawn and tree service companies notify you twenty-four to forty-eight hours prior to application.
  —Laws requiring notification
    • There is no federal law requiring notification.
    • Your community may have Chemical Registers and Notification laws.
    • Check with your state Department of Agriculture or Department of Health.
  —Learn if and when lawns, trees, etc., at the parks where your children play are chemically treated.
  —Better yet, convince your neighbors and your area's parks system of the necessity to implement Integrated Pest Management techniques.
❖ Proper disposal
  —Never dispose of unused pesticides down the sink, into the toilet, or on the ground.
  —Check with your city or county to locate household hazardous waste drop-off sites.
  —Dispose of excess pesticides at those waste-collection centers.
■ Hire a certified pest control operator.
  ❖ When to do it
    —When your problem is widespread
    —When you have wood-destroying pests, such as termites
    —When you are too busy or not inclined to do this type of work yourself
  ❖ How to do it
    —Make sure the company and service person are qualified. (A requirement anytime you hire anyone!)
      • Ask to see his or her license.
      • Ask for references.
      • Inquire about experience. What types of insect problems has this person previously treated?
      • Contact your state Department of Agriculture to find out about its pesticide certification and training program.
    —Look for a pest-control operator who practices Integrated Pest Management.
  ❖ Be informed about the product.
    —Ask to see the label of the product that the operator will be using.

—And read the product's material safety data sheet.
- This tells you the active ingredients (chemicals) in the product.
- Precautionary warnings are listed here.

❖ Request that chemical pesticides be used only as a last choice for controlling pests.

❖ For additional information on the products the pest-control operator plans to use, call

—your state Department of Agriculture,

—the local EPA office, or

—the National Pesticide Telecommunications Network Hotline (See "For More Information" at the end of this chapter.)

■ Registration is no guarantee.

❖ Every pesticide sold legally in the United States is registered by the EPA.

❖ Such registration does not guarantee safety.

For More Information

To learn more about nonchemical pest-control methods or organic gardening, call your county cooperative extension office, listed in the telephone book under state or county government, or visit a local gardening center or nursery.

To learn more about pesticides, contact the National Pesticide Telecommunications Network, seven days a week, 9:30 A.M.–7:30 P.M. EST, by calling (800) 858-7378, or by visiting their website: www.ace.orst.edu/info/nptn/.

To order your free copy of "Citizen's Guide to Pest Control and Pesticide Safety" and "Healthy Lawn, Healthy Environment," contact the National Service Center for Environmental Publications and Information by writing to P.O. Box 42419, Cincinnati, OH 45242-2419, or by calling (513) 489-8190 or (800) 490-9198.

To discover the least toxic methods for pest management, contact Bio-Integral Resource Center by writing to P.O. Box 7414, Berkeley, CA 94707, or by calling (510) 524-2567, or by faxing (510) 524-1758, or by visiting their website: www.igc.org/birc/.

To learn more about pest-control methods from Jerry Goodman, cited in this chapter, contact A Safe Pest Eliminator, Inc., by writing to 11338 SW 158th Place, Miami, FL 33196, or by calling (305) 447-7152.

To order beneficial nematodes or beneficial insects, you may contact Hydro-Gardens, Inc. by writing to P.O. Box 25845, Colorado Springs, CO 80936, or by calling or faxing (888) 693-0578 or (719) 495-2266, or by visiting their website: www.hydro-gardens.com.

You may contact the Alternative Farming Systems Information Center at the National Agricultural Library, U.S. Department of Agriculture, by writing to 10301 Baltimore Avenue, Room 304, Beltsville, MD 20705-2351, or by calling (301) 504-6559, or by faxing (301) 504-6409, or by visiting their website: www.nal.usda.gov/afsic/.

To learn more about the dangers of pesticides and what can be done about their misuse, contact the National Coalition Against the Misuse of Pesticides by writing to 701 E. Street SE, Suite 200, Washington, DC 20003, or by calling (202) 543-5450, or by faxing (202) 543-4791, or by visiting their website: www.ncamp.org.

To obtain more information on pesticides and other toxic chemicals in your food and water, contact the Environmental Working Group by E-mailing: info@ewg.org, or by visiting their websites: www.ewg.org and www.foodnews.org.

You may also contact the Children's Health Environmental Coalition. CHEC is working to decrease children's chronic health and developmental problems linked with common toxic substances. The group's National Environmental Childproofing Campaign aims to educate parents regarding new pollution prevention tactics that limit exposure to toxins in food, water, air, and consumer products and services in homes. They hope to empower parents by increasing their knowledge and giving them confidence to address environmental health problems in schools and communities. Contact CHEC by writing to P.O. Box 1540, Princeton, NJ 08542, or by calling (609) 252-1915, or by faxing (609) 252-1536, or by E-mailing chec@checnet.org, or by visiting their website: www.checnet.org.

To learn how to treat head lice without using pesticide treatments contact the National Pediculosis Association by writing to P.O. Box 610189, Newton, MA 02461, or by calling (781) 449-NITS [449-6487], or by faxing (781) 449-8129, or by visiting their website: www.headlice.org.

For more information on battling head lice contact the American Head Lice Information and Resource Center by writing to 215 Lexington Avenue, Cambridge, MA 02138, or by calling (888) DIE LICE (343-5423), or by faxing (617) 864-3445, or by visiting their website: www.headliceinfo.com.

You may also wish to contact Mothers & Others for a Livable Planet. Founded by Meryl Streep in 1989, it is a national non-profit consumer education organization working to promote consumer choices that are healthy, safe, and environmentally sound for families and communities. For membership information, contact Mothers & Others for a

Livable Planet by writing to 40 W. 20th Street, New York, NY 10011, or by calling (212) 242-0010, or by faxing (212) 242-0545, or by visiting their website: www.mothers.org.

To order a wide range of organic food, contact Diamond Organics by writing to P.O. Box 2159, Freedom, CA 95019, or by calling (888) 674-2642, or by faxing (888) 888-6777, or by E-mailing shop@diamondorganics.org, or by visiting their website: www.diamondorganics.com.

You may also order from Walnut Acres Organic Farms, by writing to Walnut Acres Road, Penns Creek, PA 17862, or by calling (800) 433-3998, or by faxing (570) 837-1146, or by E-mailing customerservice@walnutacres.com, or by visiting their website: www.walnutacres.com. In addition, you may order from Eco-Organics USA, by writing to P.O. Box 13133, Jersey City, NJ 07303, or by calling (888) ECO-ORGANIC [326-3784], or by faxing (201) 333-8825, or by E-mailing info@eco-organics.com, or by visiting their website: www.eco-organics.com.

6

Making Good Luck Happen
Perils to Avoid

Mother used to say:
"Don't let the baby play with that! She'll strangle!"

Strangulation

"Aw, Mom. She just wants to play!"

Mother was right. Even a pretty necklace that attracts Baby's attention can be deadly. Strings and cords, too, can somehow move from Baby's toes and fingers to her neck. When tied around your child's neck, a necklace, string, or cord can get caught on a crib, playpen, doorknob, stationary piece of furniture, or playground equipment, causing a strangulation hazard. Any such item can also get tightly twisted around the child's neck. Think about every item in your home that has a string, cord, or ribbon attached and keep it safely away from your child and her crib.

- Never
  - ❖ tie pacifiers, necklaces, toys, or other items around a child's neck; or
  - ❖ attach anything with ribbon or string to a child's clothing; or
  - ❖ leave strings and cords of any kind near an infant.
- Remove
  - ❖ bibs or other clothing tied around a child's neck before putting the child in a crib; or
  - ❖ drawstrings from the hoods and necks of older garments. These can lead to injury or death if they get caught on cribs, playground equipment, or bus doors. (The Consumer Product Safety Commission [CPSC] worked with industry to eliminate neck drawstrings from children's outerwear, as of 1995.)
- Follow CPSC recommendations that waist and bottom drawstrings should measure no more than three inches from where strings extend out of the garment.
- At the playground, make sure your child does not wear necklaces, scarves, garments with drawstrings, oversized clothing, or any outer attire with emblems or buttons that could get snagged on equipment.

- A bicycle helmet saves lives when used for bike riding, but it should be removed when the child gets off to play, especially on playground equipment, for the strap poses a strangulation hazard.

Hazards in Surprising Places

Window Cords

A study published in the *Journal of the American Medical Association* (JAMA) shows that most strangulation deaths from window cords happen when children are in places their parents think are safe: in a crib or in a child's bedroom (6.1). According to the study, there are two common ways children strangle: (1) when infants in cribs near windows get tangled in looped cords while sleeping or playing; and (2) when toddlers try to look out a window or climb on furniture and fall or jump, getting caught in the window cords.

These deaths are silent. A child in this circumstance cannot cry out for help. Safeguard your child in the following ways:

- Don't allow her to play with drapery or window blind cords.
- Do not put his crib or bed near a window, drapery, or window blind cords.
- Do not keep furniture such as chairs, benches, tables, toy boxes, or a bookcase near a window, drapery, or blind cords.
- Cut the loops on two-corded horizontal blinds and attach separate tassels to prevent entanglement and strangulation.
- Install a permanent tie-down or tension device to vertical blinds, continuous loop systems, and drapery cords, for they need looped cords to function. To obtain free tassels and tie-down devices, call the Window Covering Safety Council listed at the end of this section.
- Keep all window-covering cords and chains out of reach of children.
- The CPSC offers recommendations for buying new window coverings:
  - ❖ When ordering new coverings, specify that you want a short cord.
  - ❖ Ask for safety features to prevent child strangulation.
  - ❖ When installing window coverings, adjust the cords to their shortest possible length.

The Window Covering Industry has recently agreed to a voluntary standard that eliminates all loops on miniblind cords and requires the use of a tensioning device on the continuous loop cords that are used primarily in vertical blinds. They are now available at your local window-covering retailer.

The Crib

Putting your baby in a new crib that meets current safety standards is much safer than placing her in a used crib. So think twice before buying second hand (or accepting hand-me-downs). According to the CPSC, each year about fifty babies suffocate or strangle as a result of their becoming trapped between broken crib parts or in older cribs of unsafe design.

- If you do buy or accept secondhand:
  - ❖ Make sure the product meets current national safety standards (use a crib built after 1991), that it has never been recalled, and that it includes manufacturer's instructions.
  - ❖ Never compromise safety for savings.
  - ❖ Periodically inspect for missing hardware, loose threads and strings, holes and tears, chipped or peeled paint (6.2). Not a bad idea for products you've received new, as well!

If the old crib you have does not meet the checklist guidelines listed here, destroy it and replace it with a safe crib.

- Safety checklist
  - ❖ A sturdy crib, with no broken, loose, missing, or improperly installed hardware
  - ❖ Slat space no more than $2\frac{3}{8}$ inches apart (If you can pass a soda can between the slats, they are too far apart.)
  - ❖ Corner post extensions less than $\frac{1}{16}$ of an inch (If greater, they may cause entanglement with clothing or a necklace.)
  - ❖ For a canopy bed, the extensions may be larger if they are at least 16 inches high.
  - ❖ No cutouts in the head and footboards
  - ❖ Mattress must fit tightly so that two adult fingers cannot fit between the edge of the mattress and the crib side. (An infant can suffocate if his head or body becomes wedged between the mattress and the crib sides.)
  - ❖ A mattress support that does not easily pull apart from the corner posts (so a baby cannot get trapped between mattress and crib)
  - ❖ No cracked or peeling paint (Cribs built before 1978 may contain lead-based paint.)
  - ❖ No splinters or rough edges
- Safety tips while using any crib
  - ❖ Never use thin plastic dry-cleaning or trash bags as mattress covers.
  - ❖ Make sure crib sheet fits securely. (It can be pulled up by the child and become a strangulation hazard.)

❖ Use bumper pads when your child is an infant.
  — The pad should fit around the entire crib, with at least six ties.
  — To prevent strangulation, trim off excess length after tying.
❖ Remove bumper pads when the baby can pull up to a standing position.
❖ Remove mobiles and crib gyms that are strung across the crib (or playpen area)
  — when your child is five months old, or
  — as soon as your child can push up on his or her hands and knees, or
  — whichever of the above two comes first.
❖ Always lock the side rail in its raised position when you place your child in the crib.
❖ As soon as your child can stand up, adjust the mattress to the lowest position.
❖ Do not keep pillows, soft bedding, comforters, or plastic materials in the crib when your baby is put in the crib. This is a precaution to prevent suffocation, which kills about 900 infants each year.
❖ Remove toys from child's crib when he is sleeping or unattended.
❖ Mobiles and hanging crib toys should be out of your child's reach. Do not hang anything near the crib with a ribbon or string longer than seven inches.
❖ When your child is thirty-five inches tall, he or she has outgrown the crib and can use a bed.
❖ Put your healthy baby on his back to sleep. See the section on Sudden Infant Death Syndrome (SIDS) in this chapter to learn more about putting your baby safely to sleep in the crib.
❖ Don't sleep with your baby or put the baby down to sleep in an adult bed. This puts her at risk of suffocation and strangulation.

Always "think safety" when purchasing any children's product and look for the Juvenile Products Manufacturers Association (JPMA) certification label.

Staying Up-to-Date on Recalled Products

Recalled products are those that have been found to pose a threat of injury or death. Any time you buy a new product that comes with a registration card, do not delay in filling it in and mailing it to the manufacturer. This allows the company to notify you if there's a recall. Check your entire home, as well as your children's day care or school, to make sure that no recalled products are being used. Even if your child uses only new nursery equipment and toys, recalls can occur at any stage of a product's life cycle. What you buy today could be recalled tomorrow. Make sure you are kept up to date about future recalls and corrective actions. To stay current on this matter, don't rely on the news media to keep you informed. Parents, schools, and day care centers can receive recall information free by fax, E-mail, or regular mail. Call the CPSC hot line or visit their website to sign up for this service.

- Invest in a baby monitor.
  - ❖ Keep the monitor on at all times when the child is alone in the nursery.
  - ❖ Get a portable unit so you can carry it with you when you go from room to room.
  - ❖ A new baby monitor on the market enables you to not only hear your child, but to see him as well.
- Remember, nothing takes the place of you, physically, checking on your child to make sure everything is fine.

For More Information on Strangulation Hazards

To obtain free safety tassels or tie downs, call the Window Covering Safety Council at (800) 506-4636, or visit your local window covering retailer.

For safety information on window cords or on product recalls, call the CPSC at (800) 638-2772 or visit their website: www.cpsc.gov. You may also call the above number to request "The Safe Nursery," a free publication with ideas to help avoid injuries from nursery furniture and equipment.

For a free copy of the JPMA brochure "Safe and Sound For Baby: A Guide to Juvenile Product Safety Use and Selection," send a stamped, self-addressed business-size envelope to JPMA Public Information, 236 Route 38 West, Suite 100, Moorestown, NJ 08057, or visit their website: www.jpma.org.

Contact Kids in Danger, a nonprofit organization dedicated to protecting babies and young children from dangerous juvenile products, by writing to P.O. Box 146608, Chicago, IL 60614-6608 or by visiting their website: www.kidsindanger.org.

Choking

Mother used to say:
"Don't give that thing to the baby! He'll put it in his mouth!"

Infants and toddlers are curious beings and will put anything in their mouths. According to the National SAFE KIDS Campaign, choking is a leading cause of unintentional death of children. Children ages three years and under are at the greatest risk (6.3). Food, small objects, balloons, and small toys or parts are usually the culprits.

Food

Knowing What Not to Serve

- These foods can choke your child.
  - ❖ Popcorn and nuts
  - ❖ Whole grapes and raisins
  - ❖ Raw carrots and celery
  - ❖ Hard candies
  - ❖ Hot dogs
  - ❖ Peanut butter (Any sticky food can pose a choking hazard.)
    — Do not spoon-feed it to your child.
    — Serve it in a thin layer on a sandwich.
    — Always serve it with a beverage.
- Consult your pediatrician about when it's appropriate to serve any of these foods.
- A child under age six should never be served hard, round foods.
- The American Academy of Pediatrics (AAP) recommends you not give your child nuts until she has reached the age of seven.
- Trust your instincts. If you have any doubts about whether your child is ready to eat a certain type of food, do not serve it.

Preparing Your Child's Meal

- Cut or break the food into small, angular pieces so they won't lodge in the child's throat.
- Cut vegetables into small strips rather than circles. (Round or cylindrical objects can fit snugly in the windpipe and completely block the flow of air.)
- Remove pits, skin, and seeds.
- You may prefer to use a food processor or blender to puree table foods to make them soft enough for your baby to chew.
- Take care when serving a hot dog:
  - ❖ Remove the peel.
  - ❖ Slice it lengthwise.
  - ❖ Cut it into small, bite-sized pieces.

Staying Alert in Restaurants and Stores

- Be watchful in restaurants.
  - ❖ Food that is brought to the table can be a choking hazard.
    — Peanuts, popcorn, and other "freebies" that are meant for older children and adult munchers.

— Even food that is ordered may cause a hungry toddler to choke as he quickly shovels it into his mouth.

❖ After cutting your child's food into bite-sized pieces, cut up your own, too, if your child is likely to reach over and grab food off your plate.

■ Small items can be grabbed at the check-out station in restaurants and other places of business where there are "impulse items" displayed.

❖ Hard candy is frequently available at the cashier counter, and a child can grab it without your noticing.

❖ Other small items on display can just as quickly go into the child's mouth.

Taking Care in the Car

■ Any aged child should eat only soft foods while riding in a car.

■ An unexpected bump or sudden swerve could result in choking. Getting to the child would be difficult, especially if the only adult in the car is the driver.

Teaching Table Manners for Safety

■ Always supervise your child during a meal.

■ Teach these rules for eating.

❖ Sit upright.

❖ Eat slowly.

❖ Take small bites.

❖ Chew all foods thoroughly.

■ Behavior to avoid when food is in mouth:

❖ Walking, running, or playing

❖ Talking, laughing, or giggling

■ For the infant: Never prop up your baby's bottle. Hold your baby during bottle feeding. An infant fed with a propped-up bottle is at risk for choking, tooth decay, and ear infections. Moreover, you wouldn't want to miss out on this important time for snuggling and bonding with your baby!

Nonfood Items Might Go in the Mouth

Taking Care with Common Items Around the House

■ Regularly and carefully inspect your home for small objects.

❖ Floors and carpet; underneath beds, furniture, and cushions

❖ Purses and pockets

■ What to look for:

❖ Coins, small batteries, small balls, marbles, crayon pieces, keys, jewelry, paper clips, buttons, pop can tops

- ❖ Plastic bags, wrappers
- ❖ Nails, tacks, screws, safety pins
- ❖ Removable rubber tips on door stops
- ❖ Bar soap (Instead, use liquid soap.)
- ❖ Items on child's clothing
  - —Use Velcro instead of buttons.
  - —Avoid jeweled decorations that the child can pull off.
  - —Avoid plastic labels or decals. (Pull them off and properly discard.)

Inspecting Pacifiers

- ■ Use a commercially manufactured pacifier for your child.
  - ❖ Don't make one from a bottle top and nipple.
  - ❖ Check it frequently for holes and tears.
- ■ Specifications for a safe pacifier
  - ❖ The guard or shield should be large and firm enough not to fit into the child's mouth.
  - ❖ The unit should have ventilation holes in case it does, somehow, get into the child's mouth.
- ■ As with any other item, the pacifier should not be tied around the child's neck. (For infants, avoid buying toys with strings or cords.)

Monitoring Teething Items

- ■ Teethers, rattles, and squeeze toys should be large enough that they cannot become lodged in the child's mouth.
- ■ Make sure these toys are of sturdy enough construction that they will not come apart, enabling a piece to get into the child's mouth.

Keeping Balloons Away

- ■ According to the CPSC, more children have suffocated on uninflated balloons and pieces of balloons than on any other type of toy.
- ■ This is an issue not just for small children.
  - ❖ "Balloon-related deaths are more common among children ages three and older than among younger children" (6.4).
  - ❖ Keep balloons away from children under eight years of age.
- ■ Safety tips
  - ❖ Keep children from blowing up balloons.
  - ❖ Supervise any play with an inflated balloon.

❖ Immediately discard deflated and broken balloon pieces.

❖ Choose Mylar balloons (shiny, metallic) over latex.

Toys Just Ought to Be Fun

In 1997, an estimated 140,700 children were treated in U.S. hospital emergency rooms after toy-related incidents; thirteen children died (6.5). With careful selection of our children's toys and teaching and reinforcing proper use and appropriate behavior, along with adult supervision, we can greatly reduce potential risks to our children.

Making the Purchase

- Buy only age-appropriate toys.
    ❖ A toy labeled for children three years and older should be kept away from children under the age of three for *safety's* sake. This is not a matter of how "smart" the child might be.
    ❖ These toys may have small parts, such as small balls, marbles, and balloons.
- Heed the warnings.
    ❖ Read all safety information on the product package.
        — "The Child Safety Protection Act requires choking hazard warning labels on packaging for small balls, balloons, marbles and certain toys and games having small parts that are intended for use by children ages 3–6. . . . This act also bans any toy intended for use by children under age 3 that may pose a choking, aspiration, or ingestion hazard" (6.6).
    ❖ Even if a toy has no warning label, inspect it for a possible choking hazard if your child is under three.
        — Small detachable parts, product accessories
        — Security of eyes, nose, and mouth of stuffed toys
        — Well-sewn seams of stuffed animals and cloth dolls (Stuffing or pellets inside can pose a choking hazard.)
- Buy only when you see these labels.
    ❖ "Flame retardant/flame resistant" (fabric products)
    ❖ "Washable/hygienic material" (stuffed cloth toys and dolls)
    ❖ Underwriters Laboratories "UL" or Electrical Testing Laboratories "ETL" (electric toys)
    ❖ American Society for Testing Materials "ASTM D-4236" (household art materials, including crayons and paint sets)
        — This label means the product has been reviewed by a toxicologist.
        — If it is necessary, cautionary information will be included with this label.

- Purchase a small parts tester from your local toy store. If a toy can fit into the cylinder, keep it away from children under the age of three years and from any child who still puts toys in her or his mouth.
- Avoid buying toys with long strings or cords for infants and young children.
- Purchase toys of known quality (durable and well constructed) from a toy company that has earned a good reputation.
- Promptly discard plastic bags and other packaging material.
- Toys to avoid
  - For children under eight, avoid toys with sharp edges and points and electrical toys with heating elements.
  - For children of all ages, avoid toys that include propelled objects. These can be turned into weapons.
    — Do not allow the child to play with adult lawn darts (Cpsc banned lawn darts in 1998.) or other hobby or sporting equipment that has sharp points.
    — Arrows and darts for use by children should have cork tips, rubber suction cups, or other protective tips. Always be sure these are secure.
  - Do not purchase a toy gun that looks real.
- Limit the noise.
  - Using toys that produce loud noises such as toy caps, noise-making guns, or sirens can produce sounds at noise levels that can injure a child's hearing.
  - Check the noise level before purchasing; exercise discretion.
  - Remember that infants may hold toys close to their ears; test squeaky toys, as well.
  - When using any loud-noise toy, make sure your child follows the directions for safe use.

For More Information About Choosing Toys

General information on toy safety, including consumer tips on selecting age appropriate safe toys and toy safety publication, is available by contacting the Toy Manufacturers of America, Inc., by writing to 1115 Broadway, Suite 400, New York, NY 10010, or by calling (877) 4TOYSAFETY or (212) 675-1141, or by faxing (212) 633-1429, or by visiting their website: www.toy-tma.org.

Toy Tips for Young and Old

Using Toys Safely

- Check toys frequently for broken, ripped, or loose parts. If the toys cannot be repaired, promptly discard them.

- Be familiar with directions and safe use of every toy in your home.
- Remember these tips about toys in the crib.
    - ❖ Remove toys from the child's crib when he or she is sleeping or unattended.
    - ❖ Remove crib gyms and other crib toys that are strung across the crib or playpen area when the child begins to push up on hands and knees or at five months of age, whichever occurs first.
    - ❖ Do not hang toys in cribs and playpens with long strings, ribbons, or cords.
- Share the experience. Supervise your child while she is playing; enjoy this wonderful time.

Removing and Storing Toys

- Bring toys in from outside to avoid rust.
- Do not place your child's toys or games in a high place—such as the top shelf of the bookcase. Heavy items belong on a low shelf.
- Teach the child to put toys away after each use in a safe place where
    - ❖ they will not fall; and
    - ❖ they will not be tripped over.
- Teach older children to store their toys out of the baby's reach.
    - ❖ Explain why this is necessary.
    - ❖ Make sure they have properly done so.
    - ❖ Exercise caution when purchasing a toy for an older sibling, keeping in mind that a younger child could get it.
- The toy chest
    - ❖ The best choice is one without a lid or one with a lightweight, removable lid.
    - ❖ If you choose a chest with a hinged lid, follow these CPSC recommendations:
        - —Use a toy chest with a lid that will stay open in any position to which it is raised, so that it will not fall unexpectedly.
        - —Just in case your child climbs inside, make sure the chest has ventilation holes and that the lid of the toy chest does not have a latch.
        - —Check for smooth and finished edges.
        - —Inspect the chest periodically to ensure that the support device that holds the lid is functioning properly.
        - —If you already own a chest with a freely falling lid, remove it or install a spring-loaded lid support.

Entrapment Alert: Enticements That Aren't Toys

Look around your entire home, including the attic, garage, basement, and the recreational vehicle for items such as filing cabinets; latch-type clothes dryers, refrigerators, and freezers; combination washer-dryer units; camper ice boxes; picnic coolers; and storage chests. Your child may think any one of these is a great hiding place during a game or a cozy place to curl up to take a nap.

Suffocation deaths occur in such places when children crawl inside and cannot escape. The tight-fitting gasket on most appliances cuts off air to the child; the insulated construction of the appliances prevents anyone from hearing the child's cries for help.

- Childproof old refrigerators and other appliances that are to be discarded or are in storage.
    - The surest method is to take off the door and leave in the shelves.
    - Keep children away from any currently used item that may present an entrapment hazard by locking the door to the room where it is kept.
- Warn your child about the dangers of playing inside any such item. As a backup, put a lock on the item.
- If a child is missing, these places should be among the first places to check.
- Don't forget the car and the trunk of the car. Entrapment anywhere in a closed car, especially the trunk, is extremely hazardous and can be deadly. (See Chapter 17, "Rules of the Road" for more information on car safety.)
    - Keep doors and trunk of your car always locked.
    - Keep your keys out of sight and reach of your children.
    - Always double check carefully when leaving your car to make sure that no child is still inside. (Your little one could be under the seat picking up a toy when you think he has run into the house.)
    - The rear fold-down seat should be kept closed to help prevent access into the trunk from inside the car.
    - Never leave the trunk open. (If you are bringing in packages that require more than one trip, close it each time. You may get distracted inside the home, and an open trunk is an invitation for a child to climb inside.)
    - Never leave your child unattended in a car, even for a few minutes.
    - Warn your children never to play in the trunk or anywhere else in or around the car.
- Just in case:
    - Show your child how to disable the driver's door lock.
    - Ask your car dealer about having your car retrofitted with an internal trunk release mechanism.

Many of the victims who get into old appliances are four to seven years of age and even older children are playing in car trunks! Do not assume your child knows better. Remember that kids don't just sit there for very long. They need to be properly supervised, always. You never know—*literally!*—what they will get into next.

Prepare for Choking Emergencies

Lifesaving advice: All parents and caregivers should take a first aid and CPR course. It is one of the best investments of time you will ever make.

Important note: The following are brief first-aid procedures for the conscious choking victim. This is not meant as a substitute for completing a first aid and CPR course taught by certified instructors. The first-aid procedures to use when a victim is unconscious go beyond the scope of this book.

- If the child is conscious and is able to speak, cry, or cough
  - ❖ Keep her calm.
  - ❖ Let her cough.
  - ❖ Do not interfere; she may cough up the foreign object.
  - ❖ Contact pediatrician for further advice.
- If the child cannot cough, speak, make noise, or breathe; is coughing weakly; or is making high-pitched noises.
  - ❖ Have someone else call 911.
  - ❖ Start first aid while waiting for medical assistance.

First-Aid Procedures for the Choking Infant

If the infant is conscious, take the following steps.

- Lay the infant face down on your forearm and support his head and neck.
- Hold the infant so that his head is lower than his chest.
- With the heel of your hand, administer five quick back blows between his shoulder blades.
- If that doesn't work, carefully turn the infant on your forearm face up (keeping Baby's head lower than his chest), or rest on a firm flat surface.
- Using the tips of two fingers, give five chest thrusts on his breastbone, just below the nipples.
- Repeat the above steps if necessary.

First Aid Procedures for the Choking Child or Adult (Heimlich Maneuver)

For a child over one year of age and adults who are conscious, take the following steps.

- Stand behind the victim and reach around her.
- First place the thumb side of your fist slightly above the victim's navel and well below the lower tip of the breastbone.
- Then place your other hand over the fist and give up to five quick thrusts, inward and upward into the victim's abdomen.
- Repeat thrusts if necessary.

Save-Yourself Heimlich

If something lodges in your air passage and you are alone or with your small child, you can administer the Heimlich maneuver to yourself. There are two ways to do it.

- Abdominal Thrusts
  - Make a fist with one hand.
  - Place the thumb side on the abdomen above the navel, below the lower tip of the breastbone.
  - Grasp the fist with the other hand, then press inward and upward toward the diaphram with a quick motion.
- If thrusts are unsuccessful, quickly press upper abdomen over any firm surface. (Be sure it does not have a sharp edge.)
  - The back of a chair
  - The side of a table
  - A porch railing
  - A kitchen sink

For More Information About Choking Hazards

To obtain these free publications on toy safety, "For Kids' Sake: Think Toy Safety" or "Which Toy for Which Child—A Consumer's Guide for Selecting Suitable Toys," or to report an unsafe product or get other assistance, contact the Consumer Product Safety Commission (CPSC) by writing to Washington, DC 20207, or by calling (800) 638-2772 or TTY (800) 638-8270, or by visiting their website: www.cpsc.gov.

For information on safeguarding refrigerators and freezers, contact the CPSC or contact the Association of Home Appliance Manufacturers (AHAM) by sending a self-addressed, stamped envelope to Entrapment, 1111 19th Street NW, Suite 402, Washington, DC 20036, or by calling (202) 872-5955, or by faxing (202) 872-9354, or by visiting their website: www.aham.org.

For information about classes on first aid and CPR, contact the local Red Cross or visit their website: www.redcross.org. Local hospitals, fire departments, and other organizations may also offer classes on first aid and CPR.

For information on choking hazards and toy safety contact the National SAFE KIDS Campaign by writing to 1301 Pennsylvania Avenue NW, Suite 1000, Washington, DC 20004-1707, or by calling (202) 662-0600, or by faxing (202) 393-2072, or by visiting their website: www.safekids.org.

Sudden Infant Death Syndrome

Although old wives cautioned against letting babies sleep on their back lest they get flat heads, this is one time that listening to such tales could be hazardous to your baby's health. Read on for an explanation.

While Sudden Infant Death Syndrome (SIDS) may not always be preventable, we can most certainly take precautions. SIDS, sometimes known as crib death, is the sudden, unexplained death of an infant under one year of age. This medical disorder takes the lives of 3,000 babies each year in the United States. The cause of SIDS is still unclear. However, recent studies have found defects in some SIDS infants in a region of the brain that may control sensing of carbon dioxide, breathing, and arousal during sleep (6.7). SIDS is more common among premature and low birth-weight babies, and among twins and triplets. SIDS is more frequent during winter months, and boys are at higher risk for SIDS than girls. Since 1992, when physicians first recommended that infants be positioned on their backs to sleep, the rate of SIDS has dropped more than 43 percent, the equivalent of saving more than 2,000 babies a year.

Tips to Reduce the Likelihood of SIDS for Nighttime or Nap Time (6.8)

- *Always* place your healthy baby on his back to sleep.
- Use a firm, tight-fitting mattress in a crib that meets current safety standards.
- Remove from the crib any pillows, quilts, comforters, sheepskins, and other soft bedding items and toys. In addition to increasing SIDS risk, any of these can pose a suffocation hazard.
- Consider using a sleeper as an alternative to a blanket on colder nights; use light pajamas in warmer weather.
- If using a blanket, put baby with his feet at the foot of the crib. Tuck a thin blanket around the crib mattress, only as far as the baby's chest.
- Make sure your baby's face and head remain uncovered during sleep.
- Do not place baby on a waterbed, sofa, soft mattress, pillow, or other soft surface to sleep. Bedding that bunches up around baby's face and head can block airways, causing potentially dangerous rebreathing of stale air.
  Note: If your baby suffers from certain health conditions, or if she frequently spits up, it may be necessary to put her, instead, on her stomach. Check with your pediatrician about what sleeping position would be best for your child.
- Do not overheat your baby, especially if he already has a fever.
  - ❖ Keep the temperature in his room at a level you find comfortable.
  - ❖ Promptly remove your baby's outerwear (jacket, sweater, and hat) when indoors, in cars, or in stores to keep your baby from being overheated.

- No smoking anywhere near your baby! Women who smoke cigarettes during or after pregnancy put their babies at increased risk for SIDS. (For information on secondhand tobacco smoke, see Chapter 11.)
- Educate caregivers.
  - ❖ Inform your infant's sitter and any friends or relatives who may watch the baby of the guidelines for reducing the risks of SIDS.
  - ❖ If your baby goes to day care, make sure the employees there are aware of these guidelines.

Research has shown there is an increased risk of SIDS when a baby who routinely sleeps on her back is then put on her stomach to sleep. Continuity of care is an essential component of SIDS risk reduction. Put the baby on her back during nighttime and naptime at home and everywhere (6.9).

Other Ways to Maximize Your Baby's Health

- Seeing the pediatrician
  - ❖ Make sure your child has regular checkups.
  - ❖ Follow her immunization schedule.
  - ❖ If your baby seems ill, contact the pediatrician immediately.
- Breast-feeding: Breast milk contains nutrients and antibodies that are needed to help keep your baby healthy (6.10).
- Preventive measures during pregnancy
  - ❖ Do not smoke while pregnant.
  - ❖ Do not drink alcohol or take any drugs not prescribed specifically for you by your physician after you become pregnant.
  - ❖ Go for frequent medical checkups.
  - ❖ Eat nutritious meals.

Get Some Sleep Yourself

When your baby starts to turn over from his back to his stomach, at about five months of age, you needn't stay up all night checking on him. Put him down to sleep on his back on a firm mattress without soft bedding or toys and try to get some sleep yourself! You can now sleep a little easier knowing that SIDS most often occurs in infants two to four months of age. Ninety percent of SIDS victims are under six months of age (6.11).

Ignore "Old Wives"

Don't be concerned that back-sleeping might cause your baby's soft head to flatten. The American Academy of Pediatrics says that you need only make sure your infant spends some waking time on her stomach while she is being watched (6.12).

For More Information About SIDS

Contact the Back to Sleep Campaign, which is staffed M–F, 8 A.M.–8 P.M. EST, by writing to NICHD/Back to Sleep, 31 Center Drive, Room 2A 32, MSC 2425, Bethesda, MD 20892-2425, or by calling (800) 505-CRIB [2742], or by faxing (301) 496-7101, or by visiting their website: www.nih.gov/nichd/.

Centers for Disease Control (CDC) National Immunization Hot Line specialists are available M–F 8 A.M.–11 P.M. EST. To ask question about immunizations, call (800) CDC-2552; to learn about immunization schedules, vaccine-preventable diseases, referrals, and publications, call (800) CDC-SHOT [232-7468]; in Spanish, call (800) CDC-0233. The CDC website for this information is www.cdc.gov/nip.

Contact the Sudden Infant Death Syndrome Alliance by writing to 1314 Bedford Avenue, Suite 210, Baltimore, MD 21208, or by calling the twenty-four-hour SIDS Information and Referral Hot Line at (800) 221-SIDS [7437], or by faxing (410) 653-8709, or by visiting their website: www.sidsalliance.org.

Contact the National SIDS Resource Center, staffed M–F, 8:30 A.M.–5 P.M. EST, by writing to 2070 Chain Bridge Road, Suite 450, Vienna, VA 22182, or by calling (703) 821-8955, or by faxing (703) 821-2098, or by visiting their website: www.circsol.com/sids/.

Shaken Baby Syndrome

Mother used to say:
"Never, ever shake a baby."

What Mother used to say now has the weight of both the medical establishment and the social services legal network behind it. Injuries that occur when a young child's head is whiplashed back and forth during shaking is referred to as "Shaken Baby Syndrome" (SBS). When a British nanny stood trial in the shaking death of an eight-month-old boy, the event underscored to the world the need for public education on the dangers of shaking a baby. No one should shake a baby.

Possible Results of Shaking, Throwing, or Jerking a Baby

- A wide range of serious injuries might occur such as
  - brain damage,
  - retardation,
  - learning disabilities,
  - speech disabilities,

- ❖ behavior problems,
- ❖ seizures,
- ❖ broken bones, or
- ❖ blindness.
- ▪ Death

Why Is Shaking So Damaging?

Babies can be so easily injured when shaken because their neck muscles aren't strong enough to support their heavy heads. Consequently, when they are shaken, the head flops back and forth causing serious damage. The rapid movement of the head from shaking can result in the brain's being bruised from slamming against the inside of the skull, causing the blood vessels to tear away and blood to pool inside the skull (6.13).

Each year, thousands of babies either die or suffer permanent injuries as a result of being severely shaken. The vast majority of SBS cases occur before the infant's first birthday, and the average age of the victim is between three and eight months of age. However, children as old as five are vulnerable to injury as a result of being shaken.

In most cases of shaken baby syndrome, the episode was triggered by a crying baby. In frustration over not being able to get the baby to stop crying, a parent, relative, or babysitter shook the baby.

Know How to Prevent SBS

All healthy babies fuss and cry. It is normal, a fact of life. And with each cry, the reasons may change.

Reasons for the Baby's Crying

- ▪ The baby is uncomfortable.
    - ❖ The baby is hungry.
    - ❖ The diaper needs to be changed.
    - ❖ The baby is tired.
    - ❖ The baby is too cold or too hot.
    - ❖ The baby needs an extra burp.
    - ❖ The baby's gums hurt because a tooth is coming through (teething).
    - ❖ The baby has a fever.
- ▪ The baby simply wants to be held.

It is important to realize that the baby is not crying to irritate or annoy you. Most times, you can easily figure out what the child wants and can successfully calm him down by responding to his immediate needs. For those other times, here's my top-ten list of ways to calm a crying baby. It worked for my mom, and she handed down this advice to me.

Ten Ways to Calm a Crying Baby

1. Take her for a drive in the car or for a ride to the park in her stroller.
2. Vacuum the entire house. Babies like the noise, and your house will never be so clean!
3. If the baby is still small enough, put him inside a snug pouch that attaches to you and walk around the house with him.
4. Put on the stereo; take her in your arms and dance to the classics.
5. Hold him in your arms and sing softly.
6. Rock her in a rocking chair.
7. Give him a pacifier. If he's teething, give him a cool teething ring.
8. Lay the baby face down across your lap and gently rub her back. (Do this while the baby is awake and you are closely watching her.)
9. Wrap the baby snugly in his favorite baby blanket while you hold him in your arms.
10. It is OK, after tending to the baby's immediate needs such as feeding or diapering, to simply put the baby back into her crib and leave the room. My husband or I would peek into the baby's room every ten minutes or so to check to see if everything was OK.

In addition, experience has taught me that as a parent, the calmer I am around my children—no matter what their age—the calmer *they* are. And like everything else in life, the constant crying by your baby will, truly, pass.

Time-Out!

Know when it's time to take a time-out. When you feel frustrated, angry, or stressed out—before you lose control—it is important to calm yourself down. Put the baby in her crib and take some time out for yourself, away from the baby. Here are some suggestions.

Ways to Take a Time-Out

- Have a trusted adult come by and watch the child for a while.
- Telephone a friend, relative, or a member of a support group and chat for a while.
- Engage in an activity that you find relaxing:
  - ❖ Read.
  - ❖ Exercise.

- ❖ Take a warm bath.
- ❖ Play your favorite music.
- ❖ Clean the house.

What worked for me was developing a strong support system among my friends. We met weekly at one of our homes or at a restaurant to compare our children's milestones and complain about how tired we were. We laughed and cried a lot! I learned early not to be afraid to ask for help.

Spread the Word

Start spreading the word now! Tell your spouse, the child's siblings, the baby-sitter, your friends and family, and anyone else who has contact with your child: shaking a baby, even if it is done playfully, can cause him great harm.

For More Information about SBS

For information on Shaken Baby Syndrome contact the National Information Support and Referral Service on Shaken Baby Syndrome, a service of the Child Abuse Prevention Center, staffed M–F, 8 A.M.–5 P.M. MST, at 2955 Harrison Boulevard, Suite 102, Ogden, UT 84403, or by calling (888) 273-0071, or by faxing (801) 393-7019, or by visiting their website: www.capcenter.org.

Contact Child Help USA, which is staffed twenty-four hours, seven days per week, for information, referrals, and assistance in a crisis by calling (800) 4-ACHILD [422-4453], or by visiting their website: www.childhelpusa.org.

Ask your pediatrician or call the local hospital where your baby was born for the names of parent support groups in your area. In addition, you can join the local Y. It's a great way to meet other new parents and take some classes.

7

Preventing Burns

Mother used to say:
"Don't touch that! It's hot!"

In the Bathroom

Getting into Hot Water

Any family member could receive a serious burn from scalding water coming from the faucet of a sink or while taking a bath or shower. However, children are particularly vulnerable because they have thin skin. The risks of severe scalding can occur with temperatures over 120°F. In fact, scalding water kills about 100 people in this country each year. Water with 140°F temperature will produce third-degree burns on a child in about three seconds!

The first measure in protecting the family is to make sure your water heater thermostat is set at 120°F or lower. It takes about five minutes to receive a third-degree burn from a temperature of 120°F. At least this gives you some reaction time to move away. Water at 120°F will still get your clothes and dishes clean.

You can call your local electric company (for electric water heaters) or your local gas company (gas water heaters) for assistance in adjusting the thermostat. They may offer this service free of charge. If you live in an apartment building, contact your landlord. If your efforts to lower the thermostat fail or if you want to offer your family additional protection, install antiscald devices on the tub faucets and other bathroom fixtures. These devices shut off the water before it reaches a temperature that could harm your child.

- When filling the bath,
  - ❖ start with cold water, then
  - ❖ add hot water.
  - ❖ Turn off the hot water first.

Doing it this way, you can reduce the likelihood that the water will get too hot and that your child will get burned from a hot metal faucet.

Out of sight, out of mind. When placing your child in the tub, position her with her back facing the faucet. If she doesn't see the faucet, she won't be tempted to play with it.

Testing the waters. Always check the water temperature before a young child gets into it. A safe and comfortable temperature of the water is near the child's own body temperature, around 98°F. The temperature should not exceed 100°F. Check the water temperature by moving your hand through the water for several seconds. Make sure the faucet is completely turned off before your child enters.

Always be there. Constant adult supervision is always required while your young child takes a bath or shower. Never leave, even for a moment. Your not being there could result in the unattended child's scalding or drowning. (For additional tips to prevent drowning, see Chapter 16.)

Wherever you go. When you are in a public restroom or staying as a guest at a hotel or in the homes of friends or relatives, make sure to always check the temperature of the water before your child's hands or body hit the water. If your child stays at day care, make sure the management has taken the necessary measures to prevent scalding.

Getting Burned by Beauty

Safety Tips About Grooming Appliances

- Keep such items as hot rollers, curling irons, and hair dryers out of the reach of your children.
- Never leave grooming appliances unattended, and make sure your child is safely away from the area
  - while using them;
  - after use, while they are still hot; and
  - even when they are cooling down.
- If your teenager is using a curling iron, instruct her to take care to keep the iron away from her eyes and face.
- Purchase only electrical appliances with the certification mark of a recognized testing lab, such as Underwriters Laboratories (UL) or Electrical Testing Laboratories (ETL).

Safety Tips When Ironing Clothes

- Follow the same safety precautions as with grooming appliances.
- Keep children away from the immediate area while ironing clothes.
- Never leave an iron unattended, and properly secure it safely after it has cooled.

In the Kitchen

Burner Basics

- Remove stove knobs when the stove is not in use or install a knob cover.
- Keep children away from the stove at all times.
- Keep children off the floor in the kitchen while anyone is cooking. Put them in their crib, playpen, or high chair in the kitchen, but safely away from the cooking area.
- While cooking
  - ❖ Use the back burners.
  - ❖ Turn pot handles to the rear of the stove.

When I did volunteer work at a hospital, my most memorable experience was meeting an adorable boy named Stevie, a seven-year-old burn victim who had sustained third-degree burns when he went over to check on the cooking spaghetti. He had pulled on the pot handle and the pan tipped over onto him. Children often do not think of the consequences of their actions. Stevie simply wanted to tip the pot to see if the pasta was ready. What a cruel lesson he—and the adults in his family—learned.

Table Talk

- Place all items in the center of the table, especially hot foods or drinks.
- Do not set anything hot near the edge of a counter.
- Keep all cords from dangling over the edge of counters from slow cookers, coffeepots, and anything else that could contain hot liquids.
- Avoid tablecloths or place mats. With one tug on a cloth or mat, a child can easily pull hot foods or beverages onto himself.
- Don't hold or carry a child while holding a hot beverage or hot food.
- Invest in a spill-resistant mug to use for your hot beverages. Look for a mug that has a cover over the spout that one must actively slide open or press down in order to release the liquid.

Microwave Safety

Do not heat your baby's bottle in the microwave. In fact avoid or use extreme caution while warming up anything in the microwave. Because the microwave oven does not heat evenly, it is important—to avoid hot spots—to thoroughly shake up the baby bottles, stir beverages, and mix food and let it stand before serving. You cannot tell how hot an item is by touching the outside of the container, so sample it before giving it to your child! If you choose to microwave in spite of these warnings, follow these guidelines.

Microwaving Baby's Hard Plastic and Glass Bottles

Use microwave-safe bottles and follow these safety recommendations (7.1):

- Make sure to carefully follow manufacturer's guidelines for operation and use.
- First remove cap and nipple.
- Heat a refrigerated eight-ounce bottle for thirty seconds on high.
- Let stand for a minute.
- Shake and test the temperature by squirting a few drops on your inner wrist to see if the temperature is just right before serving it to your child.
- Test the bottle the same way when you warm it under the hot water tap.

What Bottles Not to Microwave

- Bottles with disposable inserts should not be heated in the microwave.
- "Hot spots in milk heated in these bottles may weaken the seams, causing the plastic to burst and spill hot milk on the baby" (7.2).
- Instead, place the bottle under hot water for a few minutes.

Microwaving Baby's Food

- Do not heat solid baby foods in their jars. The center heats up to dangerously high temperatures while food in other parts of the jar that are close to the glass stay cool.
- Instead, transfer the food to a dish.
  - ❖ A four-ounce dish of solid food cooked on high power will take approximately fifteen seconds.
  - ❖ Before serving,
    — stir,
    — let stand thirty seconds, and
    — taste test to see if it's lukewarm before serving to the baby (7.3).
    - • For microwave cooking, do not use take-out containers or cold storage containers such as margarine tubs which can warp or melt from hot food, possibly causing chemical migration (7.4).

- To avoid the potential of any plastic particles melting into food while cooking in the microwave, it's best to use glass or ceramic glass cookware that is approved for use in microwave ovens (7.5).

Keeping Children Away

- Do not let your child remove hot food or beverages from the microwave.
- Do not let your child remove plastic coverings or product coverings from food you have removed from the microwave.

Summertime "Hot" Spots

The Playground

Hot metal playground equipment can burn your child's delicate skin. Check for hot surfaces before allowing your children to play on or near them.

The Car

Park your car in a garage or shaded area. If you must park in the sun, keep children's seats covered with a light-colored towel or blanket. Make sure to check the metal and vinyl before placing your child into a seat.

The Beach

(See Chapter 15 and follow "sun sense" guidelines to protect your child from over-exposure to the sun.) Make sure your children wear sandals or footwear while walking on or near beaches.

The Barbecue

Read and always carefully follow manufacturer's instructions that accompany the grill. Make sure children are carefully supervised keeping them at least three feet away from a hot grill. Just in case adult supervision is ever distracted, teach children never to touch coals even if they appear to be cool because they stay hot long after they have turned from red to gray. (Please see Chapter 11 on carbon monoxide.)

Hot Lights and Electricity

Halogen Torchère Floor Lamps

Use halogen torchère floor lamps only with extreme caution. Their tubular halogen bulbs get extremely hot; they differ greatly from regular bulbs. In fact, the Consumer

Product Safety Commission (CPSC) reports that these lamps have been responsible for twelve deaths and more than 200 fires. What to do?

- Keep a protective wire or glass guard over the bulb.
  - ❖ Lamps made since 1997 have this feature.
  - ❖ See "For More Information About Halogen Lights" following, on how to receive a free guard.
- Use a bulb of 300 watts or less.
- Keep the appliance far away from children, drapes, bedding, and everything else that is flammable.
- Always turn off the lamp when leaving the room.

Outdoor Floodlights

Children are curious, and they examine by touching. Remember Mother's admonition: "Don't touch it! It's hot!" My own daughter, Laura, ran over to touch an outdoor floodlight. Fortunately I was close by and caught her just in time.

For More Information About Halogen Lights

For a complete listing of retail stores that offer free wireguards for torchère floor lamps using halogen light guards, call (800) 985-2220.

Speaking of Electricity

Don't Mix Electricity and Water

- Install ground fault circuit interrupters (GFCIs) if you do not already have them.
  - ❖ Have a qualified electrician do the work.
  - ❖ Have the devices installed in the outside outlets as well as those in the bathrooms, kitchen, and garage.
- Why do you need GFCIs?
  - ❖ The GFCI can protect anyone in your family from receiving a severe or fatal electric shock if an electrical appliance falls in the water.
  - ❖ This sensitive device will automatically shut off the electricity flow when it detects electricity entering a body and grounding the flow.
- The National Electrical Code has required GFCIs in
  - ❖ outdoor receptacles since 1973,
  - ❖ bathroom receptacles since 1975,
  - ❖ garage outlets since 1978, and
  - ❖ receptacles in crawl spaces and unfinished basements since 1990 (7.6).

- Portable GFCIs that plug into electrical outlets are available for purchase at hardware stores.
- To avoid any potential risk, I recommend that no electrical appliance ever be used in the bathroom or around water sources.

Getting Unplugged

- Always unplug appliances immediately after each use. Even if the switch is off, the appliance is still electrically live if it is plugged in.
- Store the appliance safely out of the reach of your child.
- Never place or store any appliance where it can fall or be pulled into the bath or sink.
- Make sure appliance cords do not dangle and are tied up so that your child cannot pull the appliance down on herself.

For an Extra Margin of Safety

Use hair dryers with built-in shock protection. (The voluntary standard has required built-in GFCIs in hair dyers since 1991.) Such a dryer has a larger-than-usual, rectangular-shaped plug at the end of the cord.

Lessons About Water and Electricity

- For the child
  ❖ Don't touch an electrical appliance when you are wet.
  ❖ If an appliance falls into the water, get an adult.
- For the parent: never pull an appliance out of the water until you are absolutely certain that the appliance is unplugged.

Something Else to Chew On

- There are voluntary standards for electric cords, so look for the mark of recognized testing labs such as UL (Underwriters Laboratories) or ETL (Electrical Testing Laboratories) when you buy cords. Keep out of the reach of children.
- Tie loose electrical cords up out of the way of curious hands.
- Children can bite into the cord or put the junction between the cords in their mouth and receive a mouth burn.

When a Coverup Is a Good Thing

- Make sure you cover all electrical outlets, when they are not in use, with items such as outlet covers that plug in place or those that screw over the switchplate. (Make sure the outlet covers are not choking hazards.)

- These can prevent your child from putting his tiny fingers or sharp objects into them.

Home Heaters
- Use only with a guard around the heating element.
- Keep away from children and their play area.
- Do not leave a heater and a child alone together in a room.
- Refuel kerosene heaters outdoors, never in the house
- Fuel-burning appliances produce carbon monoxide. (Please see Chapter 11.)

Fireworks

Serious burns can occur when children play with firecrackers and sparklers. Each year thousands of fireworks-related injuries are treated in hospital emergency rooms. Even though sparklers may appear harmless to you, they burn at high temperatures and can easily ignite your little one's clothing. I strongly recommend that because the private use of fireworks is so dangerous that you celebrate July 4 by taking your family to a professional fireworks show. If you do decide to use fireworks of your own, follow fireworks laws in your locale, exercise extreme caution, and follow fire safety procedures in Chapter 12 along with these important safety tips (7.7).

- Do not allow your children to play with fireworks, and teach them to leave the area if their friends are using them.
- Read and follow the product instructions and warnings.
- Before lighting fireworks, carefully check to see that children and spectators are out of range; instruct others to do the same.
- Keep a bucket of water nearby—just in case.
- Never try to relight fireworks that have not fully functioned.
- Never shoot fireworks in metal or glass containers.
- Light fireworks on a smooth, flat surface, away from the house and away from any flammables.
- Grab and dispose of burned-out sparklers in a bucket of water as soon as the sparks have finished flying. Be careful! They remain very hot.

What to Do If Your Child Gets Burned
- If a burn is extensive or severe, or if there is an electrical burn, call 911. Your child needs urgent medical treatment.
- Contact your pediatrician for all burn injuries, even ones that appear minor.

First Aid for Minor Burns or Scalds

■ Immediately immerse the affected area under cool running water.
- ❖ Continue doing this as long as the child will let you. (Aim for about fifteen minutes.)
- ❖ This stops the heat from further damaging the skin.
- ❖ For scald burns: Make sure to remove all hot wet clothing including the child's diaper, and cool the area immediately with water.

■ Treat the burn with care.
- ❖ Do not use ice.
- ❖ Do not use ointments, greases or fats, lotions, or powders.
- ❖ Do not break any blisters.
- ❖ You can cover the burn with a large, loose gauze dressing or clean cloth.

For More Information About Electricity and Fireworks Safety

For more information, contact the CPSC by writing to U.S. Consumer Product Safety Commission, Washington, DC 20207, or by calling (800) 638-2772, or by visiting their website: www.cpsc.gov.

You may also contact the National Council on Fireworks Safety, Inc., by writing to 4804 Moorland Lane, Suite 109, Bethesda, MD 20814, or by calling (301) 907-7998, or by visiting their website: www.fireworksafety.com.

For More Information About Preventing Burns

Contact the Burn Prevention Council by writing to 5000 Tilghman Street, Suite 215, Allentown, PA 18104, or by calling (610) 481-9810, or faxing (610) 481-8913, or by visiting their website: www.burnprevention.org.

8

Watching Out for Poisons

Mother used to say:
"Don't put that in your mouth! It might be poison!"

Preventive Steps

Poison control centers across the nation report that every year nearly a million children under the age of five are exposed to potentially poisonous medicines and household chemicals. Particularly prone to unintentional poisoning are toddlers, twelve months to three years of age. They are at a stage of their development in which they explore, touch, and taste everything.

My family learned that lesson when I was pregnant with our daughter, Laura, and our son, Adam, was three. While I was in the bathroom with morning sickness, the toddler found some of my father's heart medication, which Dad had hidden. When I returned to the room, I saw Adam holding pills in his hand. Because I didn't know for sure whether he had taken any of the pills, we had to rush him to the emergency room. After being monitored for nearly six hours, he was released. Thank goodness, he hadn't ingested any, but we all really learned a lesson about locking up poisonous products. It is not enough to just hide them!

Out of Sight, Away from Little Hands
- Identify and store all potentially harmful products in locked cabinets or cabinets secured with safety latches.
  - ❖ Out of sight
  - ❖ Out of reach
- Extend your antipoisoning strategy to include the highest shelf, for a child can climb up to reach just about anything.
- Teach your children to always ask permission before eating and drinking anything.

- Store harmful products away from food.
  - ❖ Never put harmful products in a refrigerator or pantry.
  - ❖ Keep all products in their original containers and properly re-close any child-resistant packages.
  - ❖ Never transfer these products to a milk jug, two-liter soda bottle, or cup.
    - —A family member could ingest the substance thinking it was something else.
    - —The labels on the original containers will assist medical caregivers or personnel at poison control centers in the event of a poisoning.

Caution: Pills Can Look Like Candy

The same rules that apply to household products apply to medicines, vitamins, and supplements. It is alarming that supplements containing iron have been a leading cause of pediatric poisoning for children under age six in the United States. Although iron supplements are safe for adults who follow label instructions, ingestion of only a few of them can be lethal to young children (depending on the amount of iron per tablet and the weight of the child).

Simply putting these items on a high shelf in the kitchen or in the bathroom "medicine cabinet" is not safe. Instead, follow these guidelines.

- Keep medicines, vitamins, and supplements in a locked cabinet out of the reach of children.
- Don't put them in your purse, where children can easily get them.
- Securely close child-resistant caps after using a medication and promptly return the item to its place after using it. This includes aspirin, diet pills, and vitamins. Be sure your pharmacist puts all your medications in child-resistant packaging. (This is the law!) You must realize, though, that these closures are *child resistant*, not childproof. They buy you only some extra seconds.
- Discard all expired and unlabeled medicines by flushing them down the toilet; then, rinse the container thoroughly before discarding.
- Never call medicine *candy.*
- Don't take medicines in front of children because they tend to imitate adults.
- Never let children play with medicine bottles.
- Never give medication in the dark. You may reach for the wrong medicine or give an inaccurate dosage.

When giving medicine to children

- Always check with the pediatrician first.
- Carefully follow directions for dosage on the label (based on weight and age).

- Do not give more without contacting the doctor.
- Use the measuring dispenser that comes packaged with the child's medication.

Poisons That Lurk in Good Guys' Guise

It isn't so much that some poisons pretend to be good guys. In reality, the products are good when used as intended. They are useful to us. However, they are also poison, and we must handle them carefully. Just as we take precautions with fire—which is necessary to warm our home and cook our food—we must take care as well that little hands don't get too close to poison, bringing harm to the child.

Handling Household Products

Many common household products that we use to keep our homes sparkling clean are toxic. If we use these products incorrectly, we are endangering the health of our family and the air quality in our homes. If we store them improperly, an unintentional poisoning may result. If we dispose of these products incorrectly, they can pollute our drinking water. All cleaning products should be kept out of the reach of children.

- Choose the product carefully.
  - At the store, select the least toxic product you can find.
  - Avoid purchasing products labeled "Danger" or "Poison"; they typically are the most hazardous.
  - Use water-based products whenever possible.
  - When you must buy products containing hazardous substances, buy only the amount you expect to use, and use it only when necessary.
- Use the product safely.
  - Read labels and follow directions carefully before use.
  - Wear protective equipment, such as gloves, as recommended by the manufacturer.
  - Never mix cleaning products or chemicals unless directions indicate you can safely do so, especially ammonia and bleach, which produce a toxic gas.
  - Use products in a well-ventilated area. Open windows and use a fan to circulate the air toward the outside.
  - Close the lid as soon as the product is used.
  - Do not reuse empty household cleaning product containers.
  - Store all cleaning products (even less toxic ones) in a locked cabinet or cabinet secured with safety latches.

❖ Purchase household cleaners in child-resistant packaging and properly reclose it.

■ Practice preventive measures.

❖ Wipe up spills when they first happen. (The cleanup is tougher after the spill has had time to set.)

❖ Use liners to catch spills.

❖ Air out the house to avoid using air fresheners.

❖ Don't smoke or eat while using cleaning products.

Making Your Own

The most toxic of the household products found in the home are the corrosive or caustic cleaners. These contain lye and acids, and they are found in drain cleaners, oven cleaners, and toilet-bowl cleaners that are acid based. These are the most dangerous cleaning products to have around the house because they can burn skin, eyes, and internal tissue at the slightest contact.

My grandmother and mom used homemade products to keep their homes clean. The Environmental Protection Agency (EPA) (8.1) and the North Carolina Cooperative Extension Service (8.2) offer some recipes to use as alternatives to caustic products:

Homemade Cleaning Products

Instead of:	Use:
Drain cleaner	A plunger or plumber's snake
Oven cleaner	Steel wool and baking soda
	For tough stains, add salt.
	Clean spills as soon as oven cools.
	Don't use for self-cleaning oven.
	Don't use for continuous-cleaning oven.
Toilet-bowl cleaner	Toilet brush and baking soda or vinegar
	This will clean but not disinfect.
Glass cleaner	1 tablespoon vinegar in 1 quart water
	Spray on and use newspaper to wipe dry.
Furniture polish	1 teaspoon lemon juice, 1 pint mineral or vegetable oil
	Wipe on furniture and wipe off.
All purpose cleaner	4 tablespoons baking soda, 1 quart warm water
	Apply with sponge. Rinse with clear water.

Even with these products, safe storage is required. Make sure you properly label your homemade cleaning products. Note on the label the exact ingredients and the purpose for which the product should be used. In a month or two—*trust me!*—you will not remember what is in that unlabeled (or incorrectly labeled) container. More important, your child can ingest the contents, thinking it is something else. Remember: never put homemade products in a milk jug, cup, or two-liter soda bottle.

Use only those recipes obtained from reputable sources. Please don't just concoct brews in your kitchen. Save your creativity for bedtime stories. If you have any questions about mixing products together, call the product manufacturers to find out if they recommend the mixture or if there are hazards associated with using their products in this manner (8.3).

Recognizing Dead Ringers

Many poisonous products in your home are literally dead ringers for foods and drinks that our children commonly eat. Even an older child or an adult can easily make a mistake and unintentionally ingest such products, so take extra care to store them away after use. Some examples follow:

- Chocolate laxatives that look like candy bars
- Pills that look like candy
- Clear lamp oil that looks like bottled water
- Colored lamp oil that looks like mouthwash
- Motor oil in a can that looks like a soda pop can

Poisonous Plants

Some of the plants you have in and around your home for beautification may be toxic. (See Appendix C for a list of poisonous plants.) Children, attracted to a plant because of its color or shape, may put parts of it in their mouths, perhaps swallowing it. These symptoms may occur when this happens:

- Skin, eye, and mouth irritation
- Breathing problems
- Allergic reactions
- Stomach or other pain
- Vomiting
- Diarrhea

I recommend that you purchase only nontoxic plants when you have children under the age of six. Toxic plants outside the home should be either removed or fenced in. Inside the home, keep all plants on a high shelf or hang them from the ceiling, but still keep an eye out for fallen leaves. Even in the case of nontoxic plants, a child can choke on a leaf.

Be Ready for an Emergency

Call your nearest poison control center or local cooperative extension service agent for a list of common poisonous plants that grow in your geographical region.

- Always identify a plant before purchasing it, and learn the plant's botanical and common names.
- Keep a list of or put labels on all plants. Knowing the exact name of a plant can help the poison control center prescribe the correct treatment if the child ingests part of it.

If the poison control center recommends that your child must be treated in an emergency room or doctor's office, take part of the plant, seeds, or berries with you.

Reinforce with your children the rule that they should not eat or put into their mouths any leaves, stems, flowers, twigs, wild berries, mushrooms, or any parts of shrubs or garden or ornamental plants. Keep an eagle eye on your child after rainy weather, when wild mushrooms are abundant.

Alcohol

Keep alcohol away from children. Children are much more sensitive to the toxic effects of alcohol than adults. Alcohol can cause drunkenness, low blood sugar, seizures, and even death. Keep out of the reach of your children any alcohol-laced products:

- Mouthwash—read the label. (I was shocked to see that the alcohol content of these products varies significantly with different brands. I found they range from 0 percent to 20 percent.)
- Perfumes, colognes, or aftershave
- Vanilla extract and lemon extract
- Cough and cold medications
- Rubbing alcohol
- Windshield-washer fluid
- Antifreeze

First-Aid Tips and Emergency Measures

Be Prepared

- Be ready to reach poison control quickly.
  - ❖ Prominently post the telephone number of the nearest poison control center, which can be found in the front section of your telephone book, near or on every phone in your home.

❖ Check with the poison control center; they may be able to provide free phone stickers or magnets on request. (For a complete list of emergency phone numbers you should post near your telephone, see Appendix A.)

■ Check with your local poison control center to see if they recommend keeping activated charcoal on hand. This product absorbs poison. Use it only upon specific advice of your doctor or the poison control center.

■ Keep syrup of ipecac on hand.
  ❖ Purchase it in a drugstore; no prescription is necessary.
  ❖ Use it to induce vomiting if the poison control center recommends it.

■ Before inducing vomiting, call the poison control center or your pediatrician.
  ❖ Some items—such as caustic liquids and petroleum solvents—should not be thrown up, for they can do more harm to tissue as they pass by again and they can also cause chemical pneumonia if aspirated into lungs.
  ❖ Do not follow antidote instructions on product labels without checking first with the poison control center. (Depending on the age of the particular product, it may contain antidote instructions that are no longer recommended.)
  ❖ It's best to call the poison control center before calling your doctor, so you won't be waiting for a call back.

Immediate First Aid

■ If poison is swallowed:
  ❖ Check your child's mouth and carefully remove any remaining poisonous material.
  ❖ Call the poison control center before administering anything by mouth.
  ❖ Call as soon as you suspect a poisoning; do not wait until symptoms are displayed.
  ❖ Bring ingested product (or container) with you if you must visit the emergency room or doctor's office.

■ If poison gets into the eye:
  ❖ Flood eye with lukewarm (never hot) water.
  ❖ Pour the water from a large glass held three to four inches from the eye, or take the child into the shower and rinse the eye under a gentle stream of water.
  ❖ Continue for at least fifteen minutes.
  ❖ Call your nearest poison control center.

■ If poison gets on the skin:
  ❖ Remove any contaminated clothing and flood skin with cool water for fifteen minutes.
  ❖ Wash gently with soap and water, then rinse.
  ❖ Call your nearest poison control center.

- If poison is inhaled:
  - ❖ Immediately bring the person into fresh air.
  - ❖ Provide resuscitation if necessary.
  - ❖ Open doors and windows wide.
  - ❖ Call your nearest poison control center or pediatrician.
- If the situation appears life threatening, call 911. In all other cases, call poison control, where specialists can assess the severity of the situation.

Poison Patrol

Use this checklist to keep common household items out of your child's reach.

Throughout the House

- ☐ cigars, cigarettes, butts, ashes, and matches
- ☐ plants
- ☐ plant food
- ☐ batteries
- ☐ older repainted toys (Lead paint was banned in 1978.)
- ☐ lead paint chips
- ☐ broken plaster

In the Kitchen

- ☐ window and counter cleaners
- ☐ dishwasher products, detergents, soaps
- ☐ oven cleaners
- ☐ drain cleaners
- ☐ ammonia
- ☐ cleanser and scouring powder
- ☐ carpet and upholstery cleaner
- ☐ furniture polish
- ☐ pet products, such as flea and tick collars and powders
- ☐ vitamins and medications, including aspirin

On the Table

- ☐ green potatoes or potato sprouts (Don't eat them. They contain a toxin called solanine, which can cause gastrointestinal illness.)
- ☐ table salt (As little as half a teaspoon to an infant or a tablespoon to a toddler can cause damage to his central nervous system.)

In the Bathroom

- ☐ cosmetics
- ☐ all grooming products
- ☐ baby powder
- ☐ shampoos
- ☐ hair straighteners and relaxers
- ☐ hair dyes
- ☐ hair removers
- ☐ creams
- ☐ nail polish and polish remover
- ☐ deodorants
- ☐ perfumes, colognes, aftershave
- ☐ suntan lotions
- ☐ mouthwash
- ☐ fluoride toothpaste (Ingesting large amounts [most or all of the tube] may cause symptoms of fluoride toxicity. Use a pea-sized amount of toothpaste for children under six.)
- ☐ medications, both prescriptive and over-the-counter, including aspirin, vitamins, and iron pills
- ☐ rubbing alcohol
- ☐ jewelry cleaner
- ☐ toilet-bowl cleaners
- ☐ disinfectants
- ☐ room deodorizer

In the Garage, Basement, Storage Areas

- ☐ pest-control products
- ☐ weed killers and fertilizers
- ☐ gasoline and car care products such as motor oil, windshield washer solution, and antifreeze[1]
- ☐ turpentine, paints, and paint thinner
- ☐ pool supplies
- ☐ kerosene

---

[1]Antifreeze alert: the main ingredient in many major antifreeze brands is ethylene glycol, which is very toxic. Antifreeze has a sweet taste. Children or pets will drink large amounts of it if it is left out in open containers or if it is spilled on your driveway.

There is a less-toxic alternative. I recommend that you purchase what I use: antifreeze that is formulated with propylene glycol. It does not contain the sweet taste that is prominent in conventional antifreeze.

☐ art and hobby supplies
☐ glues and adhesives
☐ charcoal lighter

In the Laundry Room

☐ soaps and detergents
☐ bleach
☐ fabric softeners
☐ stain remover

In Closets

☐ mothballs
☐ shoe polish

In Bedrooms

☐ aspirin and other medicines
☐ perfumes, colognes
☐ room fresheners

In Purses

☐ cosmetics
☐ aspirin and other medicines

Try to poisonproof places your child frequently visits, such as your office or the homes of grandparents, other relatives, and friends. Check as well at the nursery or day-care center for potentially poisonous items, including poisonous plants on the grounds where the child has access. As always, closely supervise your child.

Take-Home Hazards

Don't bring your work home with you. If parents are exposed to hazardous materials in the workplace, such as pesticides, lead, asbestos, mercury, dust, and infectious agents, they may inadvertently carry these hazardous materials home on their clothes, hair, tools, and vehicles.

Take the following preventive measures to protect your family members (8.4).

■ Store your street clothes in a separate area of the workplace to prevent possible contamination.

- Handle contaminated clothing with care.
  - ❖ Leave the clothing at work and ask your employer to wash it.
  - ❖ If your employer will not wash the contaminated clothing and assigns that task to you, launder it separately from the rest of the family wash.
- Do not let your child visit your workplace.
- Reduce your own exposure in the workplace.
- Do not bring home any hazardous materials or contaminated items (such as your tools) from your workplace.

Work Carefully with Hazardous Materials at Home

- Separate the work area from the living areas.
- Prohibit children from entering and seal off the work area.
- Properly store and dispose of toxic substances and hazardous materials.

For More Information

For more information about take-home hazards, contact the National Institute for Occupational Safety and Health (specialists available M–F, 9 A.M.–4 P.M. EST) by calling (800) 356-4674.

For more information on poisons in the home, call your nearest poison control center. The number can be found in the front section of your telephone book. Or you can visit the website of the American Association of Poison Control Centers, www.aapcc.org, which maintains a directory of poison control centers as well as other useful information.

To receive the free pamphlet "Clean and Safe: The Facts About Using Household Cleaning Products Effectively and Safely," a four-page guide to safe use and storage of household cleaning products and what to do in case of emergency, contact the Soap and Detergent Association by writing 475 Park Avenue S, New York, NY 10016, or by faxing (212) 213-0685, or by E-mailing order@sdahq.org, or by visiting their website: www.sdahq.org.

To receive the free pamphlets "Prevent Poisoning and Death With Iron-Containing Medicine" and "Poison Lookout Checklist," contact the Consumer Product Safety Commission (CPSC) by writing to Washington, DC 20267 or by calling (800) 638-CPSC [2772].

For more information on alternatives to hazardous household cleaners, contact the Washington Toxics Coalition by writing to 4649 Sunnyside Avenue N, Suite 540 E, Seattle, WA 98103, or by calling (800) 844-SAFE [7233] or (206) 632-1545, or by faxing (206) 632-8661, or by E-mailing info@watoxics.org, or by visiting their website: www.watoxics.org.

For information on environmentally responsible products, packaging, and materials, contact Scientific Certification Systems (SCS), an independent organization certifying manufacturers' environmental claims. You may request a complete list of products with certified claims or more information about SCS's certification requirements by writing to 1939 Harrison Street, Suite 400, Oakland, CA 94612, or by calling (510) 832-1415, or by faxing (510) 832-0369, or by visiting their website: www.scs1.com.

To order a wide variety of environmentally friendly household products, contact Harmony/Seventh Generation Mail Order Catalogs by writing to 360 Interlocken Boulevard, Suite 300, Broomfield, CO 80021, or by calling (800) 869-3446, or by faxing (800) 456-1139, or by visiting their website: www.gaiam.com.

For more information about reducing hazardous waste, contact the EPA Office of Solid Waste by writing to 401 M Street SW, Washington, DC 20460, or use their Resource Conservation and Recovery Act hot line, M–F, 9 A.M.–6 P.M. EST, by calling (800) 424-9346, or by visiting their website: www.epa.gov/epaoswer/hotline.

9

Staying Ahead of Lead

Mother never said anything about
"getting the lead out."
That was Dad's line.

Despite the Consumer Product Safety Commission's (CPSC's) ban of lead paint for consumer use in 1978, lead continues to lurk in our children's environment more than two decades later, and it remains a serious health risk to our children. It shows in the statistics. In the United States, approximately 900,000 children ages one to five years have blood-lead levels exceeding the threshold for concern (9.1).

Lead does not break down naturally, so it poses problems until it is actually removed from the environment. You may have lead in your home (in paint, dust, soil, food, or drinking water) without even knowing it because you can't see, taste, or smell it. Even children who appear healthy can have dangerous levels of lead in their blood.

According to the U.S. Environmental Protection Agency (EPA), "Fetuses, infants, and children are more vulnerable to lead exposure than adults since lead is more easily absorbed into their growing bodies, and the tissues of small children are more sensitive to the damaging effects of lead" (9.2). Moreover, children have higher exposures because they often put their hands and other objects—which can have lead dust on them—in their mouths.

Prevention is the key to protecting your child. Parents must identify and control sources of lead exposure and take prompt action to receive care and treatment so that the effects of lead exposure can be limited. Pregnant women should limit their exposure to lead because lead can pass through their bodies to their babies.

Where It Comes From

One place lead is *not* is in pencils. The writing tip is made of graphite, not lead, and there is no lead in the paint covering the pencil. That's a good thing for me and my children! I always chewed on my pencils, and I think it's a family trait.

The primary sources of lead poisoning in children today are

— lead-based paint and
— lead-contaminated dust.

Eighty-three percent of private housing and 86 percent of public housing built prior to 1980 contain some lead-based paint, the EPA reports (9.3).

Lead-based paint that is in good condition is usually not a hazard. Problems occur when the paint peels or flakes off into chips or lead dust or when remodeling, renovation, or repainting is performed improperly, without safeguards to control lead dust. Children don't have to ingest paint chips to be poisoned; lead-contaminated dust on little hands reaches mouths when children do what comes naturally: put their hands in their mouths. The best defense is to limit your child's exposure.

Check the Paint in Your Home

The EPA recommends these actions if you suspect that your home has lead paint:

- Regularly wash floors and high wear and tear areas such as window frames, window sills, doors, and doorframes.
  - Use a mop or sponge with a solution of water and an all-purpose cleaner.
  - Clean up paint chips using a wet sponge or rag (9.4).
- Wash your younger children's hands before meals, nap time, and bedtime.
- Teach your older children to wash their hands before meals, nap time, and bedtime.
- Keep the area where your children play as clean and dust-free as possible.
- Wash toys and stuffed animals, bottles, and pacifiers often, especially after they fall on the floor.

  In addition, if you suspect that lead-based paint has been used in your home or if you plan to remodel or renovate, get your home professionally tested.

- The EPA recommends that you do not rely on home test kits because studies show the kits are not reliable enough to tell the difference between high and low levels of lead (9.5).

  Note: While consumer spot-test kits that give instantaneous results by color changes are not as reliable as laboratory tests, many consumers find them helpful as an initial screen for the presence of lead.

  - Two types of professional testing
    — *Risk assessment* determines if lead hazards are present and makes recommendations for how they can be controlled.

—*Lead inspection* reveals the presence of lead content of every surface in your home, but it will not tell you whether the paint is a hazard or how you should deal with it.

❖ As of March 2000, federal law requires risk assessors and inspectors to be certified.

■ Do not attempt to remove lead paint yourself.

❖ Hire a professional with special training (a certified lead-abatement contractor).

❖ Improper removal can increase your health risk by spreading even more lead dust around your home.

❖ Move out of the home while abatement is being performed.

■ Follow lead safe practices in repainting, remodeling, and other projects. Contact the National Lead Information Center Clearinghouse, listed at the end of the chapter, for guidelines.

■ For a list of certified lead inspectors, risk assessors, and certified abatement contractors in your area, contact the National Lead Service Providers' Listing Systems, the National Lead Information Center's Clearinghouse, or your state environmental agency or health department. (See "For More Information" at the end of this chapter.)

If you are planning to buy or rent a home built before 1978, be aware that federal law requires sellers and landlords to make full disclosure regarding known lead hazards to potential buyers or renters.

Check the Soil Around Your Home

Soil very close to the home may be contaminated from exterior lead paint. Homes built near roads and highways may also contain contaminated soil from years of exhaust fumes from cars and trucks that, in the past, used leaded gasoline. If your soil is contaminated with lead, take these precautions:

■ Make sure everyone removes his or her shoes before entering the house.

■ Encourage your child to play in other areas (in lead-free sand or grassy areas).

■ To keep your child from playing in the contaminated area,

❖ plant bushes around the house; and

❖ apply pine bark mulch, gravel, or grass sod as a protective layer.

■ Try to keep the child from eating dirt.

■ Cover bare soil areas.

■ Make sure the child's hands are thoroughly washed after playing outdoors.

■ Don't plant any home gardens or serve any food that is grown in soil that contains lead.

Test the Water

Lead may be present in your household drinking water. In old homes, the pipes themselves may contain lead. In homes built before 1988 lead solder was probably used in
your plumbing. Leaded brass faucets were phased out between 1996 and 1998. Call
the EPA's Safe Drinking Water Hot Line or call your local health department or sup-
plier to find out about testing your water. Testing to determine the presence of lead
in paint, dust, water, and soil is best done by trained professionals. However, you can
get mail-in kits from environmental laboratories for under $20.00. (Look in the Yel-
low pages under "environmental labs.") If your water has not been tested or if it contains levels of lead, take these precautions:

- Use only cold water for drinking, cooking, or preparing baby formula. It's a
  good idea to run the cold water for thirty to sixty seconds. (Hot water is likely
  to contain higher levels of lead.)
- Once you have flushed your tap, you can store the cold water in your refrigerator for later use.
- If you have not run any cold water for more than six hours, allow cold water to
  run until it becomes as cold as it will get (which may take up to two minutes or
  more) before using it for drinking or cooking. (You need not waste the water.
  You can use it for your plants or for washing clothes.) The more time water has
  been sitting in your home's pipes, the more lead it may contain.
- Clean faucet screens regularly to remove any captured solder particles.
- Consider purchasing a water filter that is certified for lead removal, or switch to
  bottled water of known quality for drinking and cooking. (See also Chapter 4.)

Check for Lead Hazards in Other Environments

Day-care centers and homes of family or friends that are visited often can also pose a
lead hazard. If such other homes or buildings were built before 1978, make sure the
paint is in good condition.

The CPSC has shown that equipment at many older school, park, and community playgrounds across the United States were painted with lead paint. Investigate playgrounds that your children frequent. Ask when the playgrounds were built, and look
for any signs of chipping paint or dust.

Research Your Purchases

Miniblinds. The CPSC has discovered that vinyl miniblinds from China, Taiwan,
Mexico, and Indonesia made before July 1996 may contain lead. Over time, the plastic deteriorates from exposure to sunlight and heat to form lead dust on the surface

of the blinds. Young children can ingest this lead by wiping their hands on the blinds and then putting their hands in their mouths. If you have miniblinds in your home, made before July 1996, it's a good idea to call the store where you purchased the blinds to determine if they are the hazardous kind. The CPSC recommends removing these blinds from homes where children ages six and younger are present.

Dishes. Some dishes, bowls, and mugs have lead in their glazes. Be especially careful when purchasing ceramic ware abroad. It may contain dangerous levels of lead in the glaze, which may be extracted by acid foods and beverages. Test for lead release or use it for decorative purposes only. Here are precautions to take:

- Use lead-free or lead-safe dishes, i.e., it meets California's Proposition 65 standards for lead. Most tableware in common use does not pose a lead hazard. However, if the amount of lead that can leach into food from your dishes is greater than Proposition 65 levels, your dishes may pose a potential health risk. (Ask the retailer or manufacturer if it meets those standards, or contact the Environmental Defense Fund, listed at the end of this chapter.)
- Never heat, microwave, or serve hot food or drinks in a lead-glazed bowl or mug.
- Do not store acidic foods such as fruit juices in suspect ceramic containers. Hot and acidic foods absorb the greatest amount of lead.
- Do not feed a baby from a lead crystal bottle.
- Never serve food on dishes designated only for decorative purposes.
- Never serve food to children on silver-plated items or on plates made from brass, bronze, or pewter.

Tin cans. Avoid purchasing foods stored in tin cans that are manufactured outside the United States. They may contain lead. The United States banned the use of lead solder cans in 1995.

Know What to Do If You Bring Lead Home from Work

If you are exposed to lead at work (e.g., radiation shops, steel work, painting, welding), you may be bringing it home with you on your hands and clothing.

- If possible, shower and change your clothing before coming home.
- Launder your clothing separately from the rest of your family's.
- Do not let your child visit your workplace. (See "Take-Home Hazards" in Chapter 8.)

Use similar precautions when engaging in hobbies involving lead exposure, such as refinishing furniture and making stained glass and jewelry. (See "Hobbies and Crafts" in Chapter 13.)

What It Can Do to You

The effects of lead poisoning are severe. Lead affects practically all systems in your body.

- At high levels, it may cause
  - ❖ convulsions,
  - ❖ coma, or
  - ❖ death (9.6).
- Lower levels of lead exposure can harm a child's
  - ❖ brain,
  - ❖ nervous system,
  - ❖ blood cells, and
  - ❖ kidneys.
- These effects may cause other problems, such as
  - ❖ learning disabilities,
  - ❖ slower development,
  - ❖ impaired hearing,
  - ❖ hyperactivity, and
  - ❖ behavior problems.

Lead levels are measured in micrograms of lead per deciliter of blood. The Centers for Disease Control and Prevention (CDC) warns: "Levels as low as 10 micrograms per deciliter (ug/dl), which do not cause distinctive symptoms, are associated with decreased intelligence and impaired neurobehavioral development" (9.7).

Because most children do not display any symptoms, the only way to know for sure if your children have elevated blood lead levels is to have them tested.

When to Test Your Child

First, know if your child is at risk. For example, your child is at risk if:
  - ❖ he lives in or frequently visits a home or child care facility built before 1950,
  - ❖ he lives in or frequently visits a home or building built before 1978 that has peeling or chipping paint or has been recently remodeled;
  - ❖ he has a sibling or friend who now has or once had lead poisoning,
  - ❖ any of the adults in the home work with lead.

If you feel your child has been exposed to lead, speak with your pediatrician or health department. A blood test can detect levels of lead in your child's body. If your child has an elevated blood lead level, your pediatrician should advise you about the care and precautions you need to take. Treatment can range from changes in your diet to medication or a hospital stay.

How to Lower Lead Levels: Healthy Diet

Encourage your child to eat regular nutritious meals at least three times a day, because lead is more readily absorbed on an empty stomach. Foods high in iron and calcium are part of a healthy diet and may help decrease absorption of lead. Make sure your child's diet contains plenty of these foods.

- For iron, children should eat
  - ❖ dried beans and peas;
  - ❖ raisins;
  - ❖ lean beef, pork, and poultry;
  - ❖ spinach and collard greens;
  - ❖ whole grains, fortified cereal, and breads;
  - ❖ tuna; and
  - ❖ eggs.
- For calcium, children should eat
  - ❖ milk, cheese, and yogurt; and
  - ❖ cooked greens.

For More Information

About Lead Poisoning

To learn how to protect your child from lead poisoning, contact the National Lead Information Center Clearinghouse by calling (800) 424-LEAD [5323], or by visiting their website: www.epa.gov/lead/.

For detailed answers, you may call and speak to a specialist M–F, 8:30 A.M.–6 P.M. EST. For a general information packet, including the brochures "Lead Poisoning and Your Child" and "Lead in Your Home: A Parent's Guide," you may call twenty-four hours a day, any day.

For a list of certified lead inspectors, risk assessors, and certified abatement contractors in your area who have received training from a state-accredited training provider, contact the National Lead Service Providers' Listing System by calling (888) LEAD-LIST [532-3547], or by visiting their website: www.leadlisting.org.

Visit the website of the Alliance to End Childhood Lead Poisoning: www.aeclp.org.

Visit the website of Housing and Urban Development (HUD) office of lead hazard control: www.hud.gov/lea.

About Lead in Your Drinking Water

To speak to a specialist about lead in your drinking water, receive a referral to certified labs, or order the free brochure "Lead in Your Drinking Water," call (M–F, 9 A.M.–5:30 P.M. EST) the EPA's Safe Drinking Water Hotline at (800) 426-4791.

About Lead in Consumer Products

Write the Environmental Defense Fund (EDF) for a free copy of "What You Should Know About Lead in China Dishes." It includes a shopper's guide. Send a self-addressed, stamped business-size envelope to Environmental Defense Fund Member Services, 1875 Connecticut Avenue NW, Washington, DC 20009.

You may also contact the EDF by calling (800) 684-3322 or by visiting their website: www.edf.org/pubs/brochures/leadinchina.

To request information on lead in consumer products, contact the CPSC (M–F, 8:30 A.M.–5 P.M. EST) by calling the CPSC hot line at (800) 638-2772 or TDD (800) 638-8270, or by visiting their website: www.cpsc.gov.

To receive further information on childhood lead poisoning, contact the Health Line of the National Center for Environmental Health, CDC, by calling (888) 232-6789.

Call your health-care provider or local health department about having your child's blood lead level tested.

10

Exercising Prudence with EMFs

Mother used to say:
"Just because you can't see it, doesn't mean it isn't there."

Because EMFs—electromagnetic fields, or electric and magnetic fields are both invisible and controversial, we must gather what information is available and be willing to exercise prudent avoidance. If there is no danger, we have erred on the side of caution. Most parents would choose that type of error over ignoring something that could possibly make their children ill.

The Source of EMFs

Electric and magnetic fields are emitted from devices that produce, transmit, or use electric power. Electric fields are produced by the presence of electrical charges. Magnetic fields are produced by the movement of these charges.

The Concern

There has been public and scientific concern regarding possible health effects of low-frequency EMFs that are produced by power transmission and distribution lines and electrical wiring, as well as from such appliances as computers, television sets, microwave ovens, and electric blankets. The focus in recent years has been on magnetic fields.

Some epidemiological studies have suggested that a link may exist between proximity to power lines and childhood cancers such as leukemia. Other studies have found no such link. At this point there is no consensus on the effects of EMFs on children's health (10.1).

Prudent Avoidance

While this debate is raging, parents want to stay on the safe side. Exposure to EMFs is detected by a gauss meter, which measures fields in units called milligauss (mG). (For more information, see "Measuring EMFs" on the following page.) Parents can exercise prudent avoidance by reducing personal exposure levels to 1 or 2 mG if it doesn't cost much to do so. Several EMF epidemiological studies have used 2 or 3 mG as cutoff points to define people as "exposed." Prudent avoidance, as applied to EMFs, means taking steps to avoid EMF exposure when it is reasonable and practical.

A significant feature of EMFs is the fact that the fields will rapidly weaken with distance. You can reduce your exposure significantly by increasing the distance between you and any EMF source. The precautions are fairly simple.

- Keep your distance.
  - Don't have electrical appliances at your bedside, by your head.
    — Alarm clocks
    — Answering machines
  - Move them away or replace such appliances with a windup or battery version.
  - Keep children away while you are using electrical appliances.
    — No one needs to stand vigil by the microwave oven and watch the food cook!
    — Turn off electrical appliances when not in use.
  - Until there is more research in this area, limit your children's use of a hand-held cell phone. You may wish to take this precaution to reduce exposure: use a hands-free headset to increase the distance between the phone's antenna and the user.
  - Have family members sit at least three feet from the TV screen.
  - If you need electric bedding for warmth, limit its use to warming up the bed. Turn off and unplug before sleeping
    — electric blankets,
    — electric mattress pads, and
    — water-bed heaters.
  - Have everyone sit an arm's length from the computer monitor, if possible and practical. (Don't move the monitor too far away, though—the children may strain their eyes and contort their postures to see it, both of which have their own adverse health effects!)
    — Low EMF models of video displays are available.

— Comforting note: If you are pregnant and must sit at a computer at work, you can rest a little easier knowing that recent studies have not found any relationship between video-display terminals (VDTs) and miscarriage (10.2). Moreover, a woman does not increase the risk of delivering a baby of reduced birth weight or delivering prematurely by working with VDTs (10.3).

▪ Facts to guide you
 ❖ EMF levels are highest at the side and back of the appliance, so position yourself and the appliances accordingly.
 ❖ Magnetic fields can penetrate walls, so don't, for example, place your television set against a wall that backs to where your child's bed is located.
▪ Places to avoid
 ❖ Do not allow your children to play near high power lines or transformers.
 ❖ Avoid activities near magnetic field sources.
▪ Measuring EMFs
 ❖ The tools and what they measure:
  — Gauss meters are used to detect magnetic fields.
  — Fields are measured in units called milligauss (mG).
 ❖ Whom to call:
  — Your local electric utility company may conduct field measurements in and around your home at no charge.
  — Your state health department or state department of environmental protection may be able to refer you to consulting firms that conduct field measurements although this is a very expensive option.
 ❖ Important areas of your home (or a prospective home) to measure:
  — Check those areas where your children spend the most time, such as their bedrooms and your backyard.
  — Note: Field-level measurements can vary in different parts of a room. (Accordingly, I placed my children's beds in a section of their bedroom that had the lowest reading.)
 ❖ You can purchase or rent a gauss meter.
  — Some larger health food stores carry them.
  — A list of manufacturers of gauss meters can be obtained from *Microwave News*. (See "For More Information" at the end of this chapter.)
  — You can order a meter from environmental magazines or scientific equipment journals.
  — Wherever you get your meter, be sure you learn how to take measurements properly.

❖ A personal example:
— Standing directly in front of the digital clock in my son's room, we obtained a reading of 28 mG.
— At six inches away the reading was 4 mG.
— At one foot away the reading was 1 mG.

For More Information

To make inquiries about possible health effects associated with exposure to electric and magnetic fields or to receive a free copy of the publication "Questions and Answers about EMF, Electric and Magnetic Fields Associated with Use of Power," call the National Institute for Occupational Safety and Health Hot Line (M–F, 9 A.M.–4 P.M. EST) at (800) 356-4674.

To obtain more information about EMFs, visit the Electric and Magnetic Fields Research and Public Information Dissemination Program at www.niehs.nih.gov./emfrapid/.

To order a current list of gauss meter manufacturers, send $1 to *Microwave News*, P.O. Box 1799, Grand Central Station, New York, NY 10163 or visit their website: www.microwavenews.com.

To receive an EMF newsletter, call (212) 517-2800, or visit their website: www.micro wavenews.com.

Researchers at Carnegie Mellon University have produced a series of non-technical brochures describing EMF health effects and how to measure and interpret EMF levels in your home. Available titles and single-copy prices are: "Fields from Electric Power," $6.50; "Measuring Power Frequency Fields (Part I)," $2.75; "What Can We Conclude from Measurements of Power Frequency Fields (Part 2)," $3.25. These publications can be obtained by sending a list of desired items, your name and address and a check payable to "Carnegie Mellon University" to EMF Brochures, Carnegie Mellon University, Department of Engineering and Public Policy, 129 Baker Hall, Pittsburgh, PA 15213-3890.

11

Making Sure Our Air Is Safe

Mother used to say:
"Breathe through your nose. Are you trying to catch a fly?"

Today's mother might say:
"Breathe through a mask. Without it you could die."

Radon

Radon is an invisible and odorless gas that occurs naturally from the breakdown of uranium. It can be found in soil, rock, and air. Breathed outdoors, this gas poses a minimal health risk, but when it becomes trapped in buildings, concentrations build up. Then it is cause for concern.

What Does Radon Do?

In the United States, radon is a leading cause of lung cancer, second only to cigarette smoking (11.1). The estimates range from 15,000–22,000 lung cancer deaths each year (11.2). Here's what takes place (11.3):

- When radon decays, it emits radiation and produces tiny radioactive decay products.
- When you inhale these radioactive decay products, they can get trapped in your lungs.
- As particles break down, they release small bursts of energy.
- This can damage the live cells lining the lungs.
- Years of this damage can lead to lung cancer.

Where Does Radon Hide?

It wasn't until 1984 that the dangers posed by radon received attention. (That's why Mom didn't warn us.) In Pennsylvania that year it was discovered that a nuclear plant worker was radon contaminated, and the source was not job related. The worker and his family were so contaminated with radioactive radon in their home that living there was as dangerous as smoking 280 packs of cigarettes a day (11.4).

Although the level of radon found in that home was extraordinarily high, a much lower level can pose a serious health risk to your family. Don't be lulled into a false sense of security because you live outside certain geographical areas—such as Reading Prong, which runs from eastern Pennsylvania through northern New Jersey and into New York.

- High radon levels exist
  - ❖ in every state in the United States and throughout North America; and
  - ❖ in approximately one out of every fifteen homes, according to estimates by the Environmental Protection Agency (EPA) (11.5).
- Radon does not discriminate. Any home can have a radon problem, including
  - ❖ old and new homes,
  - ❖ drafty and insulated homes, and
  - ❖ homes with or without a basement (11.6).
- Homes *more likely* to have *higher* levels are those built on uranium-rich soil.
- Basements and first floors are more likely to have the highest radon levels.
- It is also possible for your home to have an elevated radon level while a neighboring home does not.
- Routes of entry
  - ❖ Openings around water and gas pipes
  - ❖ Openings around sump pumps and drains
  - ❖ Cracks and holes in walls and foundation
  - ❖ Water supply
    - This is not likely to generate a dangerous level by itself.
    - If you have tested the air in your home and found a radon problem and your water comes from a well, you may want to contact a lab certified to measure radiation to have your water tested—especially if you live in an area that is known to have high levels of radon in water.
    - If you are on a public water supply, call them for more information.
    - In any case, for more information call the EPA Safe Drinking Water Hot Line: (800) 426-4791.

According to the EPA, your family's risk of getting lung cancer from radon depends mostly on how much radon is in your home, the amount of time you spend in your home, and whether you are a smoker or have ever smoked. Smoking combined with radon is an especially serious health risk (11.7).

How Can Radon Be Detected?
- Test your residence.
- Insist that your child's school be tested.

Because of the serious health threat posed by radon, the EPA recommends that all residences (except those above the second floor in multilevel buildings) be tested for radon. The EPA also recommends that testing be done in all schools. You should check with your local school board to determine if a periodic testing program is in effect. Better yet, call your state radon office to see what state environmental radiation standards and programs are in effect for schools.

The only way to truly know for sure if you have a radon problem is through testing. Fortunately, radon testing is very easy and inexpensive. There are presently a number of radon kits available on the market that you can purchase through mail order or at your local hardware stores. The price ranges from $10 to $30. Use detection kits that have passed the EPA's testing program or are state approved. You can perform your own test or you can hire a radon tester in your area who is state certified or proficient with a national radon program. Your state radon office can supply you with a list of testing kit companies and radon testers that have met those standards.

How Is Radon Measured?

The amount of radon in the air is measured in picoCuries of radon per liter of air (or pCi/l). Although the EPA says there is no known safe level of radon and that any radon exposure carries some risk, it has set 4pCi/l as the level at which action is recommended to reduce your home's radon level (11.8).

How Is Radon Removed?

Don't despair if elevated levels are found in your home. There are a variety of ways to lower radon levels.

- Radon levels in homes can be reduced by
  - preventing radon entry,
  - increasing the ventilation within the house by using fans or opening windows, or
  - removing radon and its decay products from the air.
- Hire a professional.

The EPA generally recommends methods that prevent the entry of radon. The costs for reducing radon levels typically range from $500 to $2,500, with an average cost of $1,200 to $1,500. Because reducing levels requires technical knowledge and special skills, the EPA recommends that you use a contractor who is trained to fix radon problems. Call your state's radon office and ask them to provide you with a list of contractors in your area who are state certified or proficient with a national radon program.

If you are building a new home in a place with a high radon potential, you should consider installing radon-resistant features during construction. The average cost to install radon-resistant features during new home construction is $350 to $500 (11.9).

For More Information About Radon

To receive assistance in contacting your state radon office or to order free publications, contact the EPA Indoor Air Quality Information Clearinghouse (IAQ INFO) M–F, 9 A.M.–5 P.M. EST, by calling (800) 438-4318, or by visiting the EPA website: www.epa.gov/iaq/radon/.

You may also receive free radon publications by calling the National Radon Hot Line operated by the National Safety Council at (800) SOS-RADON [767-7236]. To speak with a radon specialist M–F, 8:30 A.M.–5 P.M. EST, call (800) 55-RADON [557-2366].

If your home has elevated radon levels, call the Radon "FIX-IT" Line operated by the Consumer Federation of America Foundation at (800) 644-6999.

Carbon Monoxide

Carbon monoxide (CO) is a colorless, odorless, tasteless, and toxic gas created when fossil fuels such as oil, natural gas, wood, propane, or kerosene burn without enough oxygen for full combustion. Motor vehicle exhaust is also a source of this hazardous gas. It is not produced by electric appliances. Any fuel-burning appliance, vehicle, tool, or other device is a potential CO source. When appliances are kept in good working condition, they produce little CO. Malfunctioning, improperly used, or poorly vented appliances can produce fatal CO concentrations in your home.

CO Guidelines
- Perform regular maintenance and inspection on all fuel-burning appliances, especially before turning on the furnace in the fall.
- Use a CO alarm.
- Avoid running a car in a garage.
- Avoid using charcoal indoors.

According to the Consumer Product Safety Commission (CPSC), CO poisoning associated with using fuel-burning appliances kills more than 200 people each year and sends about 10,000 people to hospital emergency rooms for treatment (11.10).

Sources of CO Poisoning:

furnace	gas stove	lawn mower
gas water heater	gas dryer	snow blower
fireplace	kerosene or gas space heater	automobile
wood stove	charcoal grill	tobacco smoke

Health Effects and Symptoms

Co is deadly because when inhaled it combines with hemoglobin—the oxygen carrying pigment in red blood cells—to form a compound called carboxyhemoglobin. Carboxyhemoglobin interferes with the ability of the blood to carry oxygen from the lungs to body tissues, including vital organs such as the heart and brain, eventually causing suffocation. How quickly the carboxyhemoglobin builds up (and just how sick a person gets) is a factor of the concentration measured in parts per million (ppm) of co in the air, the length of exposure, and the size, age, and overall health of the person. Co poisoning can occur from inhaling small amounts of co over a long period of time or from large amounts inhaled in a short time. Unborn babies, infants, and people with anemia or a history of heart disease are more vulnerable to exposure to co.

- Breathing low levels of carbon monoxide can cause, excluding fever, flu-like symptoms:
  - Mild nausea
  - Mild headaches
  - Fatigue
  - Shortness of breath
- Symptoms at moderate levels include the following (II.II):
  - Nausea
  - Severe headaches
  - Dizziness
  - Disorientation
  - Confusion
  - Fainting
- Breathing higher levels of carbon monoxide can cause two things:
  - Loss of consciousness
  - Death
- Although many of the symptoms of co poisoning resemble other illnesses, such as flu or food-borne illnesses, become highly suspicious if the following occur:
  - Other family members experience similar symptoms.

- Symptoms occur only in the house.
- Symptoms decrease when you leave the house and reappear when you return.

Tell the doctor that you suspect CO poisoning. It can be diagnosed by a simple blood test.

Reducing Risk of Exposure: Prevention Is the Best Defense

- Never use the gas range or oven to heat a room.
- Make sure appliances are installed according to manufacturer's instructions and local code.
  - Most appliances should be installed professionally.
  - Follow manufacturer's directions for safe use and operation.
- Only a trained service technician can detect hidden problems and sources of carbon monoxide and correct them. Have a trained professional annually inspect the following:
  - Oil or gas furnace
  - Gas water heater
  - Gas range and oven
  - Gas dryer
  - Gas or kerosene heaters
  - Fireplace
  - Wood stove
  - Swimming pool heater
- Repair any leaks immediately.
- Make certain that the flues and chimneys are connected and in good working order and are not blocked.
  - Examine vents and chimneys regularly for improper connections and visible rust or stains.
  - When using a fireplace, open the flue for adequate ventilation.
- Keep gas appliances properly vented and never operate an unvented gas-burning appliance in a closed room.
- Choose properly sized wood stoves that are certified to meet EPA emission standards. Make sure all doors fit tightly.
- Install and use an exhaust fan vented to outdoors over gas stoves.
  - Never use a charcoal grill or hibachi inside the home.
  - Use the same precaution in a trailer or tent.
- Do not run any automobile or other fueled engine or motor indoors, even if the garage doors are opened. Most CO deaths related to motor vehicles in garages have occurred even though the garage doors or windows have been opened (11.12).

- Periodically have your car's exhaust system inspected.
  - ❖ Regularly check your exhaust pipe for any obstructions.
  - ❖ Look for any taillight cracks.
  - ❖ Make sure the trunk or hatchback is securely closed before driving.
  - ❖ After a heavy snowfall, inspect your automobile to ensure that exhaust pipes are cleared of snow before starting the engine.
  - ❖ Also check combustion appliances that vent to the outside to ensure that vents have not been damaged or blocked with snow.
- Never ignore these warning signs:
  - ❖ An unfamiliar smell or burning odor
  - ❖ A decreasing hot water supply
  - ❖ A furnace's inability to heat the house or its running constantly
  - ❖ Soot—especially on appliances and on the outside of the chimney or flue—indicating that an appliance is not operating properly
  - ❖ A persistent, yellow-tipped flame—indicating that the fuel is not burning efficiently
  - ❖ Increased condensation inside windows
- Use only battery-powered flashlights and heaters in places such as tents, trailers, and motor homes.

Installing CO Alarms

A CO alarm measures how much CO has accumulated and sounds an alarm before the gas reaches toxic levels. I do not recommend that you purchase CO detection cards, which change color when exposed to gas. They do not make a sound, and they won't be able to wake you while you are sleeping.

Discount and hardware stores sell CO alarms. They typically cost between $30 and $70. Select alarms that meet the requirements of the most recent Underwriters Laboratories (UL) 2034 Standard (11.13).

- Where to install the CO alarm (11.14)
  - ❖ In every sleeping area
  - ❖ On the ceiling at least fifteen feet from fuel-burning appliances.
- Read and carefully follow manufacturer's directions for placement, use, and maintenance.
- In addition to those you place in your home, have alarms installed in recreational vehicles and boats.

A CO alarm, however, should never be a substitute for the safe use and maintenance of fuel-operated appliances. Teach your child the difference between the alarm sounds of your CO detector and smoke detector.

Other Combustion Pollutants

- Nitrogen dioxide symptoms (Asthmatics are more susceptible to the effects of this pollutant.)
  - ❖ Eye, nose, and throat irritation
  - ❖ Impaired lung function and increased respiratory infections in young children
- Sulphur dioxide symptoms (Asthmatics are more susceptible to the effects of this pollutant.)
  - ❖ Low-level exposure: eye, nose, and respiratory irritation
  - ❖ High-level exposure: narrowing of lung airways

The preventive measures for these pollutants are the same as those for carbon monoxide.

For More Information About Carbon Monoxide

To receive the free brochure "The Senseless Killer," contact the CPSC by writing to Washington, DC 20207, or by calling (800) 638-2772, or by visiting their website: www.cpsc.gov.

For more information about reducing your risks for CO and other combustion gases and particles or to request the free brochures "Combustion Appliances and Indoor Air Pollution," "The Inside Story: A Guide to Indoor Air Quality," and "Protect Your Family and Yourself from Carbon Monoxide Poisoning," contact the EPA's Indoor Air Quality Information Clearinghouse by calling (800) 438-4318, or by visiting their website: www.epa.gov/iaq/.

Secondhand Tobacco Smoke

Advice for all parents:
Make your body and your home a smoke-free zone.

Known as environmental tobacco smoke (ETS), this air pollutant is more commonly called secondhand smoke. It refers to the smoke that is exhaled by a smoker, as well as the smoke that is given off from the burning end of a cigarette, cigar, or pipe. This mixture, set free in the air, contains more than 4,000 substances, 43 of which are known to cause cancer in humans or animals. Many of them are strong irritants (11.15).

According to the EPA, secondhand smoke is estimated to cause approximately 3,000 deaths each year from lung cancer in people who do not smoke. This kind of smoke hurts children especially because their lungs are more susceptible to harmful effects.

- Children whose parents smoke in their presence are more likely to experience the following:
  - Pneumonia, bronchitis, and other lung diseases
  - Reduced lung function and symptoms of respiratory irritation
    — Coughing
    — Excess phlegm
    — Wheezing
  - Irritation of the eyes, nose, and throat
  - More ear infections (because ETS leads to buildup of fluid in the middle ear)
- Other health implications
  - Secondhand smoke may affect the cardiovascular system.
  - Some studies have linked exposure to secondhand smoke with the onset of chest pain (11.16).
- The numbers—estimates by the EPA and American Lung Association (11.17)
  - Some 150,000 to 300,000 children under eighteen months of age get lower-respiratory-tract infections, such as pneumonia or bronchitis, from breathing secondhand smoke.
  - Of these, 7,500 to 15,000 must be hospitalized for the condition.
  - Some 200,000 to 1,000,000 asthmatic children have their condition made worse by exposure to secondhand smoke.
  - ETS may cause thousands of nonasthmatic children to develop the condition each year.

Consider the Health of Your Unborn Baby

If you are expecting a baby, quit smoking. Please. The impact of maternal smoking on fetal development is well documented. According to the Centers for Disease Control and Prevention (CDC), the harmful effects include the following (11.18):

- Stillbirth
- Premature birth
- Low birth weight
- Sudden infant death syndrome (SIDS)
- Higher rate of infant mortality

The longer you smoke during your pregnancy, the greater the risk. Quitting any time will help, but the sooner the better.

Even if you don't smoke, you and your children may be routinely exposed to secondhand smoke at work, home, or in other regularly frequented environments; try to protect your entire family by taking the following steps:

- Enforce a no-smoking policy in your home and car. That includes guests, babysitters, and workers. Remember, smoke doesn't just linger in the air; it also recirculates throughout the house by way of the ventilation system.
- Encourage all family members to quit. For assistance, seek advice from a doctor, who can refer you to a local smoking-cessation program.
- Enroll your child only in a smoke-free day-care center or school.
- Frequent restaurants and other places that prohibit smoking. At the very least, ask to be seated in the nonsmoking section.
- Ask your employer to ban smoking or restrict smoking to separate ventilated areas.
- Advice for smoking parents
  - ❖ Be a role model. Behave the way you want your children to behave.
  - ❖ Don't smoke around your children.
  - ❖ Don't be caught sneaking one.
  - ❖ Never smoke around anyone with asthma.

For More Information About Environmental Tobacco Smoke

To receive free educational material on smoking and lung disease and information on smoking-cessation programs in your area, contact the American Lung Association by writing to 1740 Broadway, New York, NY 10019, or by calling (800) LUNG-USA [586-4872], or by visiting their website: www.lungusa.org.

To request the free publications "Clearing the Air: A Guide to Quitting Smoking for Keeps," "What You Need to Know About Lung Cancer," and "Why Do You Smoke? Smoking Facts and Tips for Quitting," contact the National Cancer Institute by writing to P.O. Box 24128, Baltimore, MD 21227, or for twenty-four-hour information or to speak to a staff specialist M–F, 9 A.M.–4:30 P.M. EST, by calling (800) 4-CANCER [422-6237], or by visting their website: www.nci.nih.gov.

If you have a teenager who smokes and you want information on getting him to quit, contact the Office on Smoking and Health at the Centers for Disease Control and Prevention by writing to Mail Stop K-50, 4770 Buford Highway NE, Atlanta, GA 30341-3724, or to speak to a staff specialist M–F, 8 A.M.–5 P.M. EST, by calling

(770) 488-5707, or to order free publications or listen to recorded information on the CDC Smoking, Tobacco Health Line by calling (800) CDC-1311 [232-1311], or by visting their website: www.cdc.gov/tobacco.

For more information about cancer, contact the American Cancer Society, whose personnel are available twenty-four hours, seven days a week, by writing to 1599 Clifton Road NE, Atlanta, GA 30329-4251, or by calling (800) ACS-2345 [277-2345], or by faxing (404) 325-2217, or by visiting their website: www.cancer.org.

Asbestos

Mother used to say:
"If it ain't broke, don't fix it!"

Mom couldn't have been more right, especially when it comes to asbestos.

Asbestos is the name given to a category of natural minerals that separate into very strong, fine fibers that can only be identified with a special type of microscope. Until the 1970s, asbestos was a widely used commodity in a variety of products because it is fire resistant and strong and it insulates well. A ban on asbestos use and production was imposed by the EPA in 1989, to be implemented over a seven-year period. Many provisions of the ban were overturned by a federal court in 1991. However, many manufacturers have voluntarily limited their use of asbestos. Today, asbestos is most commonly found in older homes or buildings, especially those built before 1980.

Possible Locations of Asbestos in the Home

- Asbestos-asphalt shingles, asbestos-cement shingles and siding
- Artificial ashes and embers sold for use in gas-fired fireplaces
- Textured paint and patching compounds
- Cement sheet, millboard, and paper
- Vinyl floor tiles and vinyl sheet flooring, backing, and adhesives
- Stoves (Asbestos-containing sheets and millboards were used as insulation in and around wood-burning stoves.)
- Building insulation
- Boiler and furnace duct insulation, insulation on water or steam pipes, and insulation on heating and air conditioning ducts
- Door gaskets
- Soundproofing or decorative material sprayed on walls and ceilings (resembles popcorn)

- Plaster walls
- Spray-on fireproofing
- Older household products
  - Stove-top pads
  - Pot holders
  - Ironing-board pads
  - Hair dryers

Health Effects

Breathing in asbestos fibers can damage your lungs, although usually there are no immediate symptoms. Breathing in high levels increases the risks of several diseases:

- *Asbestosis,* a chronic lung ailment producing shortness of breath and permanent lung damage
- *Lung cancer,* responsible for the greatest number of asbestos-related deaths
- *Mesothelioma,* a rare type of cancer that attacks the thin membranes lining the chest and abdomen

The greater the exposure, the greater the risk of developing one of these diseases. These diseases may not appear until years after exposure.

Most people with asbestos-related diseases were exposed to elevated concentrations through working with asbestos products or from exposures through clothing or equipment brought home from such job sites. Another heartening note for parents is a 1995 *Consumer Reports* article stating there have been no reports of anyone getting an asbestos-related disease solely from exposure to home building materials (11.19).

When Is Asbestos a Problem?

The mere presence of asbestos in your home should not send you into a tailspin. In fact, it really all depends on its condition and its location. According to the EPA, intact and undisturbed asbestos materials generally do not pose a health risk. "Asbestos fibers must be released from the material in which they are contained, and an individual must breathe those fibers in order to incur any chance of disease" (11.20). Do not scrape, crush, cut, rip, or sand materials that contain asbestos. Demolition or remodeling often causes the release of asbestos fibers, if not done properly.

If It Ain't Broke, Don't Fix It!

"The best thing to do with asbestos material in good condition is to leave it alone. Disturbing it may create a health hazard where none existed before" (11.21) advises the EPA. If possible, the home owner should prevent such material from being damaged, touched, or disturbed. Inspect periodically for any damage or deterioration.

When to Call the Professionals

- Before having your house remodeled (especially before tearing into a plastered wall)
- Before moving into an older home
- If you suspect that there may be asbestos-containing surfaces

An accredited asbestos inspector can ascertain if asbestos-containing materials are present by spotting suspicious materials and having them tested. The inspector will also determine whether those materials need encapsulation, enclosure, covering, or removal. In the meantime, do not let your children play near damaged or deteriorating materials.

What to Do When Repairs Are Needed

If the consultant determines that you need someone to repair, remove, or clean up asbestos, you must use only a licensed asbestos contractor. Improper removal or containment can result in even more problems. It can release asbestos fibers into the air, increasing asbestos levels and endangering your entire family.

The best sources of names of accredited asbestos inspectors, asbestos-abatement contractors, and asbestos testing labs are

- local and state asbestos officials (who may be a part of the environmental protection, health, or labor departments),
- the asbestos coordinator in your region's EPA office, or
- call the EPA's asbestos ombudsman at 1-800-368-5888 to find appropriate telephone numbers.

Removal Is a Last Resort

The EPA recommends that because asbestos removal is a hazardous and expensive process, it should only be performed as a last resort. If the materials are not significantly damaged and are not likely to be disturbed, repairing the product is the appropriate remedy. These are the primary methods:

1. *Encapsulation:* spraying the material with a sealant to prevent fiber release
2. *Covering:* placing an impervious substance over or around the material
3. *Enclosure:* boxing the material in, dropped ceiling below piping, for example

However, if you are remodeling or if the asbestos material is damaged beyond repair, the removal of the asbestos-containing material may be required.

What the Schools Are Doing About It

The Asbestos Hazard Emergency Response Act (AHERA) was signed into law in 1986 to protect children and school employees from asbestos. This federal law requires that schools make sure asbestos is properly managed to ensure that the children and employees are not exposed. Periodic inspections are required by specially trained experts, and the results must be made publicly available. You can ask your school's asbestos program manager for the latest report. Peak years of installing asbestos in schools were from World War II until the late 1970s (11.22).

For More Information About Asbestos

To order the free publication "Asbestos in Your Home," contact the CPSC by calling (800) 638-2772, or by visiting their website: www.cpsc.gov.

For more information about asbestos in schools, contact the TSCA hot line, M–F, 8:30 A.M.–5 P.M. EST, by calling (202) 554-1404. Also, the EPA has an asbestos ombudsman to provide information on the handling and abatement of asbestos in the workplace and the home. Contact them M–F, 7:30 A.M.–4 P.M. EST, by calling (800) 368-5888.

For information about floor renovations, order the free booklet "Recommended Work Practices for Removal of Resilient Floor Coverings" by writing to Resilient Floor Cover Institute, 401 E. Jefferson Street, Suite 102, Rockville, MD 20850.

Another source of information is the product manufacturer. If you supply the manufacturer with a serial number or a product brand name, it can be verified whether the product contains asbestos.

For More Information

To receive free information and brochures on health effects of secondhand smoke; radon; carbon monoxide; combustion pollutants; biological pollutants such as mold, mildew, and dust mites; and formaldehyde, contact the EPA Indoor Air Quality Information Clearinghouse (IAQINFO) by writing to P.O. Box 37133, Washington, DC 20013-7133, or speak to an information specialist M–F, 9 A.M.–5 P.M. EST, by calling (800) 438-4318 or (703) 356-4026, or by faxing (703) 356-5386, or by E-mail-ing iaqinfo@aol.com, or by visiting their website: www.epa.gov/iaq/.

The National Hispanic Indoor Air Quality Hotline provides bilingual information about indoor air pollutants that consumers may find inside their homes, offices, or schools. Specialists are on duty M–F, 9 A.M.–6 P.M. EST. In Washington, D.C., call (202) 265-6388. Elsewhere in the nation, call (800) 725-8312.

12

Taking Steps to Fend Off Danger

Mother used to say:
"Stay away from fire or you'll get burned."

Fire Safety

Each year more than 4,000 people—1,000 of whom are children—die from home fires. You can eliminate most of the factors that can cause home fires by (1) removing potential fire hazards and correcting unsafe practices and (2) installing and maintaining smoke alarms. To further reduce your family's risk of fire-related injuries, two other steps are also important: (3) keeping on hand equipment to help fight and escape fires and (4) devising and regularly practicing an escape plan.

Removing Potential Fire Hazards and Correcting Unsafe Practices
- Clean outside your home. Keep your entire roof, gutters, and outside property areas of your home clean and free of debris (such as leaves and garbage) that could feed a fire.
- Keep all matches and lighters in a locked cabinet.
  - Teach your children that matches are not toys, but tools. Your children know that they should never use their dad's drill. That also goes for matches. Children as young as two years old are capable of lighting cigarette lighters and matches.
  - Purchase lighters designed with child-resistant features. The Consumer Product Safety Commission (CPSC) requires that all disposable lighters be child-resistant. Remember, however, this does not mean they are childproof.
- Never smoke in bed or when you are drowsy.
- Don't leave a lit cigarette unattended in the ashtray; always use deep, sturdy ashtrays.
- Make sure that cigarettes are properly extinguished before emptying the ashtrays. Even cigarette butts can ignite trash.

- Take extra care in the kitchen.
  - ❖ Never leave the stove unattended when cooking, especially when the burner is on a high setting. Particularly for late night feedings, use a timer to alert you that food is done.
  - ❖ Make it a habit to always turn off cooking and heating appliances immediately after use.
  - ❖ Do not store flammable and combustible items near the stove.
  - ❖ Never place or store pot holders, plastic utensils, rags, towels, or aprons near the stove. (Keep such items at least three feet away.)
  - ❖ Do not store any tempting treats or items that could attract children near or above any cooking units. (This will reduce the possibility that children will climb onto cooking equipment to reach appealing items.)
  - ❖ When cooking or when near a fireplace or open space heater, do not wear long, loose-fitting garments, for they are more likely to catch fire than short, fitted clothing.
  - ❖ If a fire starts in a frying pan, slide a lid over it and turn off the burner. If an oven fire occurs, quickly turn off the heat and close the oven door.
- Take care while storing flammable material.
  - ❖ Store flammable liquids such as gasoline, paint thinners, and kerosene in properly labeled, tightly closed, metal, safety-approved containers. These products should be stored outside the home in a locked shed or detached garage, in a well-ventilated area, away from any source of ignition, and out of the reach of children. Always fuel power mowers and other equipment outside.
  - ❖ Heed these safety guidelines to reduce the hazard of flammable vapors.
    — Gas water heaters should be installed so that the pilot light/flame is at least eighteen inches above the floor.
    — Keep all flammable materials and liquids away from gas-fired water heaters.
    — Make sure gas-fired water heaters are installed according to code requirements.
    — Never use gasoline to clean equipment or tools.
    — Use gasoline only as a motor fuel.
    — Store gasoline only in a tightly sealed, red container intended for gasoline (12.1).
- Position and use a space heater with caution.
  - ❖ Place any space heater at least three feet away from walls, upholstered furniture, drapes, bedding, rugs, and other combustible materials.
  - ❖ Read and carefully follow manufacturer's instructions regarding use of the heater.

- Be smart with your fireplace.
  - ❖ Inspect and clean your home's chimney and fireplace annually. Employ a professional chimney sweep for the job. Care is crucial, for creosote builds up in chimney flues and can cause a chimney fire.
  - ❖ Use a fireplace screen in front of any open flame.
- Use electric appliances and cords carefully.
  - ❖ Inspect electrical appliances and cords on a regular basis. Replace frayed extension cords and appliances that have worn or loose connections. Make sure cords have the mark of a recognized testing lab, such as Underwriters Laboratories (UL) or Electrical Testing Laboratories (ETL).
  - ❖ Do not overload electrical outlets.
  - ❖ Do not run electrical cords under carpeting or hang them from nails or doors.
- Take care with your dryer (12.2).
  - ❖ Check your dryer's exhaust duct (usually a tube that runs from the back of your dryer to a wall vent).
    - —If it's made of plastic, replace it with metal, which won't burn if lint lodges inside and catches fire.
    - —If the duct is metal but is crushed or bent, replace it. This will eliminate a place where lint could build up.
  - ❖ Carefully follow manufacturer's maintenance procedures.
  - ❖ Remove any obstructions around the exterior vent cap. Trim shrubbery to maintain at least twelve inches of clearance.
  - ❖ An additional reminder: do not leave home with your dryer running unattended.
- Don't take chances with your child's life.
  - ❖ Never leave young children home alone or unsupervised—not even for a few minutes.
  - ❖ Dress your children for bed in sleepwear that is made from flame-resistant materials.
    - —Look for garments made from 100 percent polyester, which is inherently flame-resistant and does not require chemical treatment.
    - —Sleepwear (larger than nine months, up to size 14) must be flame-resistant or snug-fitting to meet CPSC sleepwear requirements.
  - ❖ Do not put your children to sleep in loose-fitting T-shirts or other oversize clothes made from cotton blends. These garments can catch fire easily.
    - —Loose-fitting clothes stand away from the body, which makes contact with an ignition source more likely.
    - —Loose-fitting clothing allows an air space next to the body that helps keep the fire burning (12.3).

Installing and Maintaining Smoke Alarms

Smoke alarms are your family's first line of defense against fires. These alarms sound a loud alarm to warn you in time to escape from a fire. They can cut nearly in half your family's chances of dying in a fire.

The CPSC explains: "Many fire deaths and fire-related injuries are actually caused by smoke and gases. Victims inhale smoke and poisonous gases that rise ahead of the flames. Your family's survival depends on being warned as soon as possible. The longer the delay the deadlier the consequences" (12.4).

Because smoke alarms are required by law in many localities, check with your local codes and regulations before you purchase one. Some government codes require specific types of alarms. Make sure you purchase only those alarms that bear the mark of an independent testing lab such as Underwriters Laboratories (UL).

- Choosing a smoke alarm
    - ❖ Battery-operated smoke alarms start at less than $10 and can be purchased at your local discount or hardware store.
    - ❖ Electrically powered smoke alarms with battery backup systems are excellent choices for your safety protection. These alarms are hardwired into your home's electrical system. They should be installed by a qualified electrician.
- Installing the smoke alarm
    - ❖ Read and carefully follow the manufacturer's instructions.
    - ❖ Place each alarm either on the ceiling or six to twelve inches below the ceiling on the wall.
    - ❖ Place alarms away from air vents, windows, doors, fireplaces, or high air flow. Do not place in a corner where the ceiling meets the wall.
    - ❖ Install an alarm in every sleeping area and on every level of your home (including the basement—near the furnace if it is located there).
    - ❖ It is best to install an individual smoke alarm in each bedroom.
    - ❖ If your smoke alarm is subject to nuisance alarms, relocate it or use one with a "hush button," which quickly stops nuisance alarms caused by smoke or steam.
- Maintaining the smoke alarm
    - ❖ All the smoke alarms in the house must be in working order if they are to save lives. Test each one monthly, whether battery operated or hardwired.
    - ❖ Replace batteries twice per year, when you change your clocks from daylight savings to standard time.
        - — If remembering to change a battery isn't your forte, consider using smoke alarms powered by lithium batteries that last up to ten years.

—Never remove a battery from the smoke alarm to use even temporarily in another battery-operated item, such as in your child's toy.
❖ Clean the alarm regularly to keep it dust free.
❖ Replace the alarm every ten years.

Keeping on Hand Equipment to Help Fight and Escape Fires

■ Fire extinguishers
 ❖ Purchase multipurpose extinguishers.
 ❖ Install fire extinguishers in the kitchen, basement, and workshop area. Put them in plain view but out of reach of your children.
 ❖ Take the time to learn how to operate the equipment before an emergency strikes.
 ❖ Use the extinguisher only for small, confined fires. While you are extinguishing a small fire, have other family members exit the home and telephone the fire department.
■ Automatic fire sprinkler systems
 ❖ Consider purchasing such a system because it will attack a fire in its early stages by spraying water on the area where it detects a fire.
 ❖ It is least costly to install the system when a house is under construction, but it can also be installed in an existing home.
 ❖ Used in conjunction with smoke alarms, such a system is extremely effective in protecting your family from fire.
■ Escape ladders
 ❖ Purchase a noncombustible ladder that bears the mark of an independent testing lab.
 ❖ Make sure the ladder can support the heaviest person in the home.
 ❖ Store the ladder close to a window. In the event of a fire, one hooks the ladder on the window sill, throws it down, and climbs out.
 ❖ Become totally familiar with the manufacturer's instructions on how to safely use the ladder. Make sure every family member knows how to use it properly, but do not actually practice the drill of climbing down from a second floor window (or higher) to avoid falling while practicing.

Devising and Regularly Practicing an Escape Plan

■ Map out at least two escape routes from every room. One way out is the door; the second way out may be a window.
 ❖ Always keep these routes clear.

- ❖ Be sure that windows designated as fire exits have not been painted or nailed shut.
- ❖ Be sure that windows or doors with security bars are equipped with quick-release devices.
- Practice your escape route with all family members at least twice a year. Because a house filled with smoke can frighten and disorient family members, it is critical to have an emergency plan that everyone in the family understands.
  - ❖ Sound the smoke alarm as part of the practice session.
  - ❖ Conduct your fire drills at night because that's when the most deadly fires occur.
- If you live in an apartment building, take the stairs, not the elevator.
- Decide in advance which parent will be responsible for helping each young child out of the house.
- Designate a place outside the home where family members will meet, such as beside a lamppost. This will allow you to be sure that everyone is safe.

Teaching Your Children Essential Fire Survival Skills

(Recommended by the National Fire Protection Association)
- Get out fast and stay out.
  - ❖ Don't take time to change clothes.
  - ❖ Don't hide!
  - ❖ Meet at the arranged outside meeting place.
  - ❖ Never go back inside a burning home to retrieve possessions (such as a favorite toy or a family pet). Never go back.
  - ❖ Call the fire department's emergency telephone number from a neighbor's home.
- Stop, drop, roll.
  - ❖ If your clothes catch on fire, *stop. Drop* to the ground right where you are. *Roll* over and over to smother the flames.
  - ❖ Cover your face with your hands.
- Touch a door with the back of your hand before opening it.
  - ❖ If the door is warm, do not open it. Use an alternative exit.
  - ❖ If the door is cool, open it slowly and proceed with caution. Move quickly to the nearest exit.
- Crawl on the floor *under* the smoke, where the air is safer to breathe.
- You can also cover your nose and mouth with a damp towel or shirt to protect your lungs from toxic fumes.

Explaining the Firefighters' Role

- Explain to your child that firefighters need to wear protective clothes to keep them from getting burned. They use equipment to help them breathe, protecting them against smoke inhalation.
- Explain that although firefighters may look like aliens from another planet when they come to fight a fire, because of their clothing and equipment, they will be there to help protect the family.
- Take your child to visit your local fire station or arrange for a firefighter to visit your child's school.

Knowing What to Do If You Are Trapped in a Burning Building

- Close all the doors between you and the fire.
- Line the doors with towels or clothing—ideally, they should be damp—to keep the smoke out.
- If there is a phone in the room, call 911 or the fire department.
- If there is no phone in the room, go to the window and signal for help.

Applying These Rules Everywhere

The rules and guidelines provided here should be applied everywhere your children visit. Make a game of having each child apply the rules to the school, library, movie theater, and friends' homes. Make sure your child knows at least two ways to get out of any building. Teach your child to be fire smart.

For More Information on Fire Safety

Contact your state or local fire marshal or fire department for guidelines on how to prevent fires and how to install smoke alarms.

The nonprofit National Fire Protection Association (NFPA) is the official sponsor of Fire Prevention Week, commemorated each October. You can contact NFPA by writing to One Batterymarch Park, Quincy, MA 02269-9101. If you have technical questions, the staff is available M–F, 8:30 A.M.–5 P.M. EST. You may reach them by calling (617) 770-3000 or faxing (617) 770-0700. You can order publications by calling the NFPA's customer service line (800) 344-3555. You may also wish to visit their websites: www.nfpa.org and www.sparky.org, which is informational and fun for the kids.

To order publications from the U.S. Fire Administration (USFA), which is part of the Federal Emergency Management Agency (FEMA), contact their Publications Center by writing to 16825 S. Seton Avenue, Emmitsburg, MD 21727, or use their twenty-four-hour recorded hot line by calling (301) 447-1660, or speak to staff personnel M–F, 8:30 A.M.–5 P.M. EST, by calling (301) 447-1189 or visit their website: www.usfa.fema.gov.

Gun Safety

Mother used to say:
"Every gun is a loaded gun."

In 1997 approximately twelve children aged nineteen and younger were killed every day in America in gun homicides, suicides, and unintentional shootings (12.5). Many more were wounded.

According to the American Academy of Pediatrics, "your child is in more danger of being shot by himself, his friends, or a family member than of being injured by an intruder" (12.6). The Academy's recommendation is this: remove all guns from places children live and play.

Preventing Access

As a parent, choose not to keep a gun in your home. If you absolutely must have a gun, make sure you keep it under lock and key. Literally. If you keep a gun at home, follow these safety guidelines, which, all experts agree, can save lives.

Store Gun Components Out of Reach

- Always store every gun out of reach and sight of children.
  - The firearm should be stored unloaded and securely locked away in a
    — locked gun cabinet,
    — locked safe, or
    — locked gun vault.
  - Ammunition should be locked away in a separate location.
- Make sure your child does not have access to the keys.

Use a Child Safety Lock

- Install trigger locks and/or other safety devices to prevent the unauthorized use of a firearm.
  - Make sure each gun lock is made of metal and comes from a reputable company. Never use a lock with plastic parts.
  - Do not use a trigger lock on a loaded gun, which can discharge even with the lock on.

■ Don't think it is just older children you need to protect. National SAFE KIDS says that children as young as three are strong enough to pull the trigger (12.7).

Quiz Your Friends

■ Because nearly half the homes in America have firearms, ask the parents of your children's friends and relatives—anywhere your children may visit—if they own a gun and how it is stored.

■ Don't allow your child to visit there unless you are certain that the gun is stored unloaded and securely locked away.

■ Gun owners may be legally required to either store loaded firearms in a place that is inaccessible to children or to use a device to lock the gun. A growing number of states and cities have passed child access prevention (CAP) laws.

Teach Kids This Message

■ If you find or see a gun,
   ❖ stop,
   ❖ don't touch it,
   ❖ get away, and
   ❖ tell a trusted adult (12.8).

■ Follow the same guidelines if you see any other kind of weapon or dangerous instrument, such as a syringe.

■ Every child, from preschoolers to teens, should be taught that guns and other weapons can hurt and kill people.

Understanding the Difference

Teach your young child the difference between a toy gun and a real one. National SAFE KIDS says that before age eight, few children can reliably distinguish between real and toy guns or fully understand the consequences.

Children watch TV and movies and see people using guns. Explain to your child that the gun in the story is not real and the people are just pretending to be shot by the gun. Help your child understand that in real life, guns do kill people.

The Myth of Gun Security

Guns kept in the home for self-protection are twenty-two times more likely to be used to kill a family member or friend than to kill in self-defense (12.9). Moreover, the presence of a gun in the home triples the risk of domestic homicide in the home (12.10) and increases the risk of suicide by fivefold (12.11).

Effective Ways to Protect Your Family Against Intruders

- Be familiar with your neighborhood.
  - ❖ Know your neighbors so you can recognize who belongs in the neighborhood and who doesn't.
  - ❖ Be familiar with the vehicles your neighbors drive.
  - ❖ Establish an informal network of neighbors who inform each other when a strange vehicle will be making pickups or deliveries in the neighborhood.
- Keep your windows and doors locked.
- Get a dog whose bark can scare away intruders. Consult a veterinarian regarding the best dog for your family.
- Invest in a home security system.
- Organize and/or become involved in a neighborhood watch program.

Being Wary of Other Shooting Weapons

BB guns and pellet guns should also be kept out of children's hands. According to National SAFE KIDS, in 1997 nearly 10,700 children aged fourteen and under were treated in hospital emergency rooms for nonpowder-gun-related injuries (12.12).

For More Information About Firearm Safety

Contact the Center to Prevent Handgun Violence by writing to 1225 Eye Street NW, Suite 1100, Washington, DC 20005, or M–F, 9 A.M.–5 P.M. EST, by calling (202) 289-7319, or by faxing (202) 408-1851, or by visiting their website: www.cphv.org.

Contact the Eddie Eagle Gun Safety Program by writing to NRA Community Services Program, 11250 Waples Mill Road, Fairfax, VA 22030, or M–F, 8:30 A.M.–5 P.M. EST, by calling (800) 231-0752, or by faxing (703) 267-3993, or by visiting their website: www.nra.org.

Contact Communities Addressing Responsible Gun Ownership (CARGO) by writing Dan DeCoursey, Director, P.O. Box 460222, Ft. Lauderdale, FL 33346, (954) 467-8979 or by visiting their website: www.projectcargo.org.

13

Playing It Safe

Mother always said:
"Keep your hands on the handlebars
and the wheels on the ground!"

Bicycles

Was mother's advice enough? Each year in the United States, an estimated 900 people, including more than 200 children, are killed in bicycle-related incidents. The Consumer Product Safety Commission (CPSC) reports that of those deaths, about 60 percent involve a head injury. In addition, more than 500,000 people require hospitalization for bicycle injuries (13.1). The most severe injuries are those that can cause permanent injury to the brain. Many of these deaths and injuries can be prevented through proper education and training. It is recommended that children under the age of ten should be properly supervised by an adult and not be allowed to ride in the street. Even after they have attained that age, be sure they have repeatedly demonstrated that they have the skills and judgment to justify their new privileges. (See Chapter 18.)

The Right Bike

- Choose a bike that fits the child's size today, not one that he or she will grow into later. A bike that is too big (or too small) will be harder to control.
- Bring the child to the bike store to actually try it out before purchasing.
- Choose a bicycle that suits the rider's ability and kind of riding.
- Check hand and foot brakes for fast, easy stops without instability or jamming. Coaster brakes are recommended for your child's first bike since they are much easier to coordinate than a hand brake.
- Avoid slippery plastic pedals. Look for rubber-treated or metal pedals.
- Shop at a reputable bike shop and find a knowledgeable salesperson to assist you in selecting a bicycle and helmet for your child.

The Right Helmet

A bicycle helmet reduces the risk of serious head injury by 85 percent (13.2). No safety rule is more important than making sure all family members wear a helmet every time they ride a bike. No excuses—not even from teenagers or spouse. It shouldn't take too much convincing. Helmets made today are lightweight, well ventilated, and a lot more comfortable than they have been in the past, and they come in a variety of cool styles and colors. And they are inexpensive. The price starts around $15 in retail stores. Although safety is the reason for wearing a helmet, there is the added incentive in many states and local jurisdictions, where the law requires bicycle helmets.

After March 1999, all bicycle helmets made or imported to the United States must meet a uniform safety standard issued by the CPSC. If you purchased a helmet before that date, as long as it states it meets one or more of the voluntary bicycle helmet standards—such as those set by the American Society for Testing and Materials (ASTM), Snell, or the American National Standards Institute (ANSI)—you do not need to buy a new helmet (13.3).

- The purchase
  - Do not purchase a helmet that is not made specifically for bike riding.
  - Bring your child with you to ensure that you have the proper size helmet for his head.
  - Have your child select the color and style of her helmet, which will make it much more likely that she will wear it.
  - If a helmet is involved in a crash, it should be replaced. Even invisible cracks can greatly reduce its effectiveness in preventing injuries (13.4). Some manufacturers will replace helmets free of charge, so contact the manufacturer if your helmet has been involved in a crash.
- The fit
  - The helmet should be worn squarely on top of the head, covering the forehead.
  - The straps should be adjusted so that the two side straps form a *V* around the ears.
  - The straps should be tight when the chin strap is buckled, but not uncomfortable. You should be able to slide a finger between the wearer's chin and the strap.
  - The helmet should have a snug, but comfortable, fit and should not be able to slide down over the child's eyes. It should not rock forward and back or from side to side.
  - You can use extra padding that comes with the helmet to ensure proper fit. This padding can be removed as your child's head grows.

- ❖ Initially, plan to spend at least fifteen minutes adjusting your child's helmet to ensure the proper fit. Check periodically for correct fit.
- ■ Special consideration for toddlers
  - ❖ All children should wear a bicycle helmet whether they are riding bicycles, tricycles, or are passengers on a parent's bicycle.
  - ❖ Under CPSC's new standard, bicycle helmets for children ages one through five come down lower around the back of the head than helmets for older persons, thus providing more coverage and additional protection.
  - ❖ Toddler helmets are lightweight because a toddler's neck is not strong enough for a regular helmet.
  - ❖ Do not put a child under the age of one in a helmet; she does not have the neck structure to wear one. Never carry a child under the age of one on your bicycle, either in a bicycle seat, a trailer, or any other carrier.
- ■ The safe ride
  - ❖ Regular maintenance and inspection of the bicycle are essential for safe riding.
  - ❖ A great idea would be to take your child to a good bike shop and have them show you both how to check the bicycle to make sure it works properly.
  - ❖ Install a basket or rear carrier on your child's bike so she won't be trying to balance books or other items on the handlebars or in her hands as she rides.
  - ❖ Equip every bicycle with pennant-shaped flags and a horn or bell. Being visible and audible are important parts of avoiding collisions.
  - ❖ Use a properly mounted bicycle child seat or trailer when transporting your children.
- ■ What to wear
  - ❖ Properly fitted helmet, worn every time (making sure the helmet straps are always fastened): teach children to remove helmets before they go off to play, especially on playground equipment. The helmet poses a strangulation hazard.
  - ❖ Bright, fluorescent clothing for daytime riding. Do not allow your child to ride at dawn, dusk, or night. (See "When to Ride" below.)
  - ❖ Cycling gloves (providing protection in case of a fall)
  - ❖ Leg clips or rubber bands to keep pants from tangling in the chain
- ■ What not to wear
  - ❖ Loose clothing, a book bag, or anything else that can catch in the pedal or wheels
  - ❖ Head phones (keeping the wearer from being able to hear what is going on around him)
  - ❖ Sandals, slippers, or high heels

- Where and how to ride
  - When riding on a sidewalk or bike path, walk the bike across intersections, especially busy ones.
  - Just like the driver of a car, bikers need to learn the rules of the road and respect traffic laws:
    —Ride on the right, the same direction as traffic—not against it.
    —Always stop and look left-right-left when entering the road—especially from a driveway, alley, or curb—or crossing an intersection.
    —Be predictable and communicate your intentions; use hand signals.
    —Obey all traffic signals and signs and pavement markings.
    —Ride in single file.
    —Ride on bike paths and sidewalks instead of in the road. However, sidewalks are not without risks. Teach your child to be cautious when riding past shrubs, fences, and buildings that create blind spots for both bicycles and motorists at driveways and intersections (13.5).
  - Keep watch for obstacles, such as wet leaves, puddles, potholes, ice patches, sand, trash, loose gravel, rocks, and, especially, storm grates, railroad tracks, and opening car doors (13.6).
  - Don't attempt stunts. (If your children do it, at least teach them not to do it near traffic.)
  - Don't ride double, especially not on the handlebars.
  - Children and adults are encouraged to take cycling education classes. (See "For More Information" below.)
  - Parents are children's best role models. Always follow these safety rules yourself.
- When to ride
  - Avoid riding at dawn, dusk, or at night. If any family member has to ride during low light, make sure that the bike is equipped with a headlight, a taillight, and reflectors and the clothing and bicycle have retroreflective materials attached to them.
  - Avoid riding in wet weather.

For More Information About Bicycle Safety

For more information or free pamphlets on bicycle helmets, contact the Bicycle Helmet Safety Institute by writing to 4611 Seventh Street S, Arlington, VA 22204, or by calling (703) 486-0100, or by faxing (703) 486-0576, or by E-mailing info@helmets. org, or by visiting their website: www.helmets.org.

The home pages of the CPSC and the National Highway Traffic Safety Administration (NHTSA) have a kid's site with bicycle safety activities to both teach and entertain your children. Contact either of these agencies for free publications on bicycle safety. Contact the CPSC by calling (800) 638-2772, or by visiting their website: www.cpsc.gov.

Contact the NHTSA by calling (800) 424-9393 or (888) DASH-2-DOT [327-4236], or by visiting their website: www.nhtsa.dot.gov.

To locate a class in your area that will teach how to ride a bicycle safely, contact the League of American Bicyclists by writing to 1612 K Street NW, Suite 401, Washington, DC 20006, or by calling (202) 822-1333, or by E-mailing bikeleague@bikeleague.org, or by visiting their website: www.bikeleague.org.

In-Line Skating

Mother used to say:
"Go outside and play! It isn't good for you to stay in the house."

As every parent well knows, in-line skating has become an extremely popular sport with our children today and it is a great sport. However, it can be hazardous if the skater does not wear appropriate safety gear or fails to learn how to skate and to stop safely. For example, in 1997, nearly 60,000 children ages five to fourteen were treated in hospital rooms for in-line skating–related injuries (13.7). Most injuries to skaters are to wrists, arms, and legs (13.8).

Vigilance Can Prevent Injuries

All beginning skaters should learn how to in-line skate from a teacher certified by the International In-Line Skating Association (IISA). See the "For More Information," section below on how to contact them. The IISA recommends that a smooth surface free from debris and safe from cars is best for in-line skating, since it is designed to be done outdoors. An indoor skating rink is also a great place to take your child skating. That's the place where many younger children and less experienced skaters skate. Wherever your children skate, have them follow these guidelines:

- Wear quality and well-maintained skates.
- Wear a helmet, elbow pads, knee pads, and wrist guards. (See "The Right Helmet," on bike helmets, earlier in this chapter.)
- Note for aggressive in-line skaters (trick or freestyle) and skateboarders: Wear multi-impact helmets sold specifically for these activities and that meet safety standards for these sports. These helmets have more coverage for the back of the head (13.9).

- Take lessons.
- Learn to stop safely by using the brake pads at the heel of the in-line skates. With one foot somewhat in front of the other, raise the toes of the front foot and push down on the heel brake (13.10).
- Skate only on smooth, paved surfaces without any traffic, such as bike paths and sidewalks. Avoid skating on streets and driveways.
- Avoid skating anywhere there is water, oil, or sand.
- Obey all traffic regulations. Skaters are subject to the same obligations as a bicyclist or the driver of an automobile.
- Never skitch! (Holding on to a moving vehicle to hitch a ride while on skates is skitching.) Skitching can kill.
- Avoid skating at night. No one can see you, and you can't see obstacles or other skaters.

For More Information About In-Line Skating

To find an instructor or for more information on in-line skating, contact the International In-Line Skating Association by writing to 105 South Seventh Street, 306, Wilmington, NC 28401, or by calling (910) 762-7004, or by faxing (910) 762-9477, or by E-mailing director@iisa.org, or by visiting their website: www.iisa.org.

Team Sports

Mother used to say:
"Winning isn't everything."

Every day millions of children across the United States participate in sports activities. Baseball, basketball, soccer, football, and hockey are among the most popular sports played by our children today. Playing sports is a positive aspect of our children's lives. It not only improves physical fitness and coordination, but it promotes self-esteem and confidence. Sports can provide children with an excellent opportunity to learn teamwork.

Unfortunately, sports activities can result in injuries. Some, such as bruises, abrasions, strains, and sprains, are minor. Others, such as fractures, concussions, and internal and dental injuries, are major concerns. The most serious of all are blows to the head and chest, the impact of which may cause death. Each year more than 775,000 children ages fourteen and under are treated in hospital emergency rooms for sports-related injuries (13.11).

Preventing Sports Injuries

■ Your child is in good physical condition for the sport she or he has chosen.
  ❖ Before she begins any training program or competition, take her to a doctor for a physical exam and for an assessment of any special injury risks your child may have.
  ❖ If you are not sure whether it is safe for your child to perform a certain technique or move, ask her pediatrician and coach for their assessment.
■ Your child wears all the appropriate protective equipment required for the sport.
■ Such equipment has been properly fitted.
  ❖ Face guards that attach to batting helmets for kids facing pitchers
  ❖ Helmets and body padding for hockey players
  ❖ Shin guards for soccer players
  ❖ Mouth guards for baseball and basketball players
■ The children are always adequately supervised by adults.
■ The coach has appropriate qualifications to supervise the sport.
  ❖ She provides well-maintained safety equipment.
  ❖ He teaches proper training and conditioning for the sport.
■ The coach is certified in CPR and first aid.
■ The children receive the proper training in the sport.
  ❖ They know and abide by all the rules of the sport.
  ❖ They understand how to use the equipment properly and safely.
■ The children are grouped according to their size, ability, and maturity, not just their age or grade.
■ The children are properly hydrated. Have a water bottle on hand and encourage them to drink, even if they aren't thirsty.
■ The children are warmed up before playing the sport.
■ A safe playing environment is provided.
  ❖ The soccer goal posts are securely anchored into the ground. (Movable goals can tip over and seriously injure or kill a child.) Note: "Heading" the soccer ball (striking the ball with the head) is controversial for children because of the risk of head injuries. Consult your pediatrician.
  ❖ There are no potential tripping hazards, such as tree roots or stumps, rocks, or concrete footing.
  ❖ The area is free of litter, such as broken glass, cans, or animal droppings.
■ Your child avoids playing when she feels ill, is very tired, or has an injury or is in pain.

For More Information About Team Sports Safety

For a free "Play It Safe Sports" brochure or for fact sheets on various sports, contact the American Academy of Orthopaedic Surgeons by sending a number ten SASE and writing to Play It Safe Sports, American Academy of Orthopaedic Surgeons, P.O. Box 1998, Des Plaines, IL 60017, or by calling (800) 824-BONES [2663], or by visiting their website: www.aaos.org. For further information you may contact the National Youth Sports Safety Foundation, Inc. (NYSSF), by writing to 333 Longwood Avenue, Suite 202, Boston, MA 02115, or by calling (617) 277-1171, or by E-mailing nyssf@aol.com, or by visiting their website: www.nyssf.org.

For referrals and a wide variety of information on preventive dentistry for infants, children, and adolescents, contact the American Academy of Pediatric Dentistry by writing 211 E. Chicago Avenue, Suite 700, Chicago, IL 60611, or by visiting their website: www.aapd.org.

Hobbies and Crafts: Art Supplies

Mother used to say:
"Don't put anything into your mouth that isn't food.
Don't inhale anything that isn't air.
Don't put anything on your skin that isn't soap or water."

Children enjoy using art supplies and other creative materials. However, some of these supplies can expose your budding artists to hazardous or toxic substances, including lead, cadmium, nickel, and organic solvents.

Relying on Labels and Seals

Look for the Label
- Under the federal Labeling of Hazardous Art Materials Act (LHAMA), art, crafts, and other creative materials must be properly labeled for the consumer.
  - ❖ They must include information about any ingredient that may be hazardous.
  - ❖ They must give warning if special precautions need to be taken when using the product.
  - ❖ They must specify if the product is inappropriate for use by children.
- Read the label when buying any art supplies, such as crayons, paint sets, and modeling clay.
  - ❖ Each product should contain the statement "Conforms to ASTM D-4236," which means that it has been evaluated by a toxicologist to ensure that it is properly labeled.

- ❖ If the product contains no hazardous materials, there will be no warning, but the statement "Conforms to ASTM D-4236" should still be there.
- ■ LHAMA is administered by the CPSC.

Look for the Seal

- ■ Since 1940, the Art and Creative Materials Institute, Inc., (ACMI) has sponsored a certification program for children's art materials, certifying that these products are non-toxic.
- ■ The seals:
  - ❖ CP (Certified Product)
  - ❖ AP (Approved Product)
  - ❖ HL "No Health Labeling Required" (Health Label)
- ■ Products that bear the CP, AP, or HL "No Health Labeling Required" seals are certified to be completely non-toxic whether ingested, inhaled, or absorbed through the skin.

ACMI is now in the process of changing its seals. During a transition period lasting several years, you'll find some products with the old seals and some with the new seals. All of the old seals will be replaced by two new ones: the AP (Approved Product) seal and the CL (Cautionary Labeling) seal. The new AP seal will be used only on non-toxic products and will replace the old AP, CP, and HL "No Health Labeling Required" seals. The new CL seal will only be used on products that must be labeled with ingredient, health, or safe use information and will replace the old HL "Cautions Required" seal.

Avoiding Toxic Materials

Art Supplies

- ■ Children under age twelve should never be allowed to use hazardous art materials.
- ■ Elementary schools are prohibited from purchasing any hazard-labeled art materials for use in prekindergarten through grade 6.

Cleaning Products

Make sure cleaners or solvents are also certified nontoxic. You will find many cleaners (soaps and detergents) that are nontoxic. Very few solvents are certified nontoxic.

Taking Care with Toxins

- ■ Always read and carefully follow warning directions on the product label.
- ■ Use all protective equipment specified on the label.
- ■ Keep your work area well ventilated, using a system that takes out old air and brings in new air.

- Wash hands, and clean the work area and supplies immediately after use.
- Don't sweep the dust; wet mop or sponge the area clean.
- Don't eat, drink, or smoke while using the product.
- Keep younger children away from the area when such products are being used.
- After use, promptly store the materials safely.
- Always keep products in their original container. (See Chapter 8.)
- Do not use a product in any way that is not specified on the label (e.g., using a marker for face painting).

Teaching Art Safety

- Even the youngest child participating in crafts can learn art safety skills.
  - ❖ Do not put art and crafts materials in your mouth.
  - ❖ Do not put your fingers into your mouth or near your eyes while using these products.
  - ❖ Do not inhale the product.
  - ❖ Do not put it on your skin.
  - ❖ Promptly clean up your supplies and work area.
  - ❖ Wash your hands immediately after using the product.
- As soon as the child has the skill, teach her to read the product's label and follow directions for safe use. The foundation for following these directions will have already been laid.
- Don't serve milk and cookies until the work area has been cleaned and everyone has properly washed their hands.

Looking for "Family Friendly" Art Supplies

There is a wide variety of non-toxic alternatives for the entire family to use.

Shopping Tips

- Avoid these products:
  - ❖ Solvents
  - ❖ Aerosol sprays
  - ❖ Dry powders
  - ❖ Epoxy glue
  - ❖ Airplane glue
  - ❖ Rubber cement
  - ❖ Instant bonding adhesives
  - ❖ Instant papier-mâché
  - ❖ Permanent felt-tip markers

- Look for these products:
  - ❖ Talc-free, low-silica clay
  - ❖ Dustless chalk
  - ❖ White glue or paste
  - ❖ Water-based paints
  - ❖ Food and vegetable dyes
  - ❖ Water-based markers

For More Information About Art Supplies

The ACMI has free updated lists of the many products that are authorized to carry one of the three seals discussed earlier in this chapter. This list is updated semiannually. The ACMI also has published a free booklet, *What You Need to Know About the Safety of Art and Craft Materials.* Request it by writing to P.O. Box 479, Hanson, MA 02341, or by calling (781) 293-4100, or by faxing (781) 294-0808 or by visiting their website: www.acminet.org.

For health and safety services to the arts, contact Arts, Crafts and Theater Safety by writing to 181 Thompson Street, 23, New York, NY 10012-2586, or by calling (212) 777-0062, or by visiting their website: www.caseweb.com/acts/.

14

Hazards of the Fall
Kids Don't Come Equipped with Wings

Mother used to say:
"Don't run with a stick in your mouth.
You might fall!"

Of all the childhood injuries, falls are the leading cause of hospitalization and emergency room visits. Each year approximately 130 children ages fourteen and under die from falls; nearly three million are treated in emergency rooms. For infants, the greater risk from falls is associated with furniture, stairs, and baby walkers. The risk for toddlers, on the other hand, is in falls from windows. Older children are more likely to sustain injuries due to falls from playground equipment (14.1).

Preventing Injuries

General Rules of Caution

- Inspect and maintain carpets and throw rugs.
  - ❖ Make sure there are no holes or tears.
  - ❖ Check to ensure there are no turned-up edges.
  - ❖ Put nonskid backing on all throw rugs.
- Invest in furniture padding.
  - ❖ Every small child bumps into household furniture.
  - ❖ Cushion the bump or fall throughout your home by attaching corner and edge protectors to all sharp edges.
    - —Tabletops
    - —Countertops
    - —Chairs
    - —File cabinets

—Ping-pong tables

—Coffee tables (You might consider doing what we did for the first four years of our child's life. We put our coffee table in storage . . . after our son used it as a launching pad.)

- Never leave your family in the dark.
  - ❖ Purchase power-failure night-lights.
    - —They function as regular night-lights but switch to an emergency light automatically when the power fails.
    - —They generally cost about $10 each, but they're well worth it!
  - ❖ Place them in the bedrooms, hallways, stairways, and bathrooms to create a lighted path for your family.
  - ❖ During a recent electrical thunderstorm, the light in my daughter's bedroom served as an immediate comfort to her after a total loss of power. The other lights guided me safely into my children's rooms.
- Important Don'ts
  - ❖ Don't let your child run around the house in socks on polished floors or any slippery surfaces. (By the way, a non-slip floor is recommended.)
  - ❖ Don't let your child play alone on a balcony, fire escape, or high porch.
    - —Make sure spaces between railings and slats are no wider than 3½ inches apart; attach plastic or mesh barriers if spaces are wider.
    - —Don't allow railings or boards to become loose; maintain regularly.
  - ❖ Don't allow railings or boards to become loose; maintain them regularly.
  - ❖ Don't leave spills on the kitchen floor. Wipe up promptly, especially grease spills.
  - ❖ Don't leave your child (even in an infant carrier) alone on a bed, couch, or any furniture where he can roll over and fall off.
  - ❖ Don't leave your baby unattended in a high chair, walker, infant seat, stroller, or swing, and always use restraint belts.
- A safe step for all
  - ❖ Invest in a sturdy step stool.
  - ❖ You and other family members will not need to climb on furniture or use a chair.
  - ❖ Keep this stool inaccessible to younger children. You don't want them climbing up to areas that are off limits to them.

Note: Consider choosing one with a handrail that you can hold on to while standing on the top step.

Dangerous Places

- Stairs
  - ❖ Light them well.
    - —Have a light switch at the bottom and top of the stairs.
    - —Keep power failure night-lights at each end, as well.
  - ❖ Don't wax the stairs or landing area.
  - ❖ Teach and practice with your child again and again the proper way to walk up and down the stairs.
    - —Hold on to the hand railing.
    - —Railings on both sides of the stairs should be sturdy.
  - ❖ Make sure your children understand that stairs are a no-play zone.
- Gates
  - ❖ Making a choice
    - —Hardware mounted (screwed into the wall)
    - —Pressure mounted, easily removable
  - ❖ *What* to install
    - —Choose a gate with a straight top edge and rigid mesh screen.
    - —Avoid older gates with *V*-shaped openings along the top edge and diamond-shaped openings between the slats that may be large enough to entrap a child's head.
    - —Do not use a pressure gate at the top of the stairs; a young child could push on it and, together with the gate, fall down the stairs.
  - ❖ *How* to install
    - —Follow manufacturer's instructions carefully.
    - —Gates with pressure bars should be installed with the bar side away from the baby. (The pressure bar could be used as a toehold and enable your child to climb over.)
    - —At the top of the stairs, the hardware-mounted gate must be securely anchored to a wall.
  - ❖ *When* to install
    - —When your baby begins to crawl, it's time to block stairways and doorways with gates.
    - —This could be as early as six months.
  - ❖ *Where* to install: at both the top and bottom of the stairs.
  - ❖ When to *remove*: When your child is old enough to climb over the gate (about two years), remove the gates.
  - ❖ Remember: gates work for the purpose intended only if they are securely closed, so make sure that you close them every time.

- Windows
    - Install window guards on all windows, even those on the ground floor, except for those designated as emergency fire exits.
    - For fire exit windows
        - Lock them or install window guards that are equipped with a quick-release mechanism.
        - Make sure you can easily operate the mechanism or lock but your child cannot operate it. (Check first with your community fire department regarding local fire codes and window-guard regulations.)
    - If possible, open windows from the top, not the bottom.
    - Avoid a false sense of security.
        - A child can fall from a window that is opened as little as five inches.
        - Screens cannot keep children from falling out. These are no more than flimsy barriers to keep bugs and insects out.
    - Do not keep cribs, chairs, benches, tables, toy boxes, or even a bookcase near the window. These are an open invitation for the child to climb up to it.
- The bath
    - Prevent slips.
        - Apply a rubber suction bath mat or nonskid appliqués.
        - Install grab bars in the bath and shower.
        - Install a liquid-soap dispenser on the wall. Think about it: how many times during a shower do you bend down to retrieve fallen soap?
        - Use a rubber-backed rug on the floor, for stepping out of the tub or shower.
    - A cushion that fits securely over the tub spout is recommended, in case a fall does occur.
    - Remember, never leave your small child alone in the water, not even for a minute. (For information on household drowning, see Chapter 16.)
- Trampolines
    - Trampolines should never be used at home, in routine physical education classes, or on outdoor playgrounds. That's the recommendation of the American Academy of Pediatrics (AAP).
    - Why not?
        - According to the Consumer Product Safety Commission (CPSC) estimates, in 1996 alone there were 83,000 injuries associated with trampolines that required emergency room attention.
        - About 75 percent of the victims were under fifteen years of age, and 10 percent were under five.

❖ Reasons for injuries and deaths
 — Colliding with another child
 — Landing improperly
 — Falling on trampoline springs or frames
 — Falling or jumping off the trampoline
❖ If you choose to allow your child to go on one in spite of these warnings, follow CPSC guidelines:
 — Place the trampoline away from structures and other play areas.
 — Install shock-absorbing pads that completely cover the springs, hooks and frame.
❖ Teach and practice these safety rules (14.2):
 — No more than one person on the trampoline at a time
 — No somersaults
 — No child under six on a full-size trampoline
❖ Uninterrupted adult supervision is absolutely required, no matter what the age of the child.
 — Assist your child in getting off the trampoline.
 — Never let your child jump off the trampoline.

■ Escalators

I remember many years ago my sister Madeleine got her skirt caught in an escalator while exiting. Fortunately, the only injury she received was severe embarrassment, while standing there in just her slip! But injuries do occur, to the tune of about 6,000 hospital emergency room visits yearly, according to the CPSC. That's why safe escalator skills are a must.

❖ Watch out for strings and things.
 — Shoelaces must always be tied to avoid tripping and getting trapped.
 — Items like drawstrings should be removed (see "Strangulation," in Chapter 6).
 — Other items that can also get caught include scarves, mittens, pants, skirts, or other loose clothing.
❖ Safety rules
 — Always hold the hand of a younger child or carry her or him.
 — Always face forward and hold the handrail.
 — Children should hold the handrail or hold an adult's hand.
 — Don't touch the sides.
 — Stand in the center of the escalator step to avoid the edges, where entrapment can occur.

— Do not bring a child onto an escalator in a stroller or cart.

— Don't carry large or heavy packages on the escalator. You could lose your balance. Head for the nearest elevator instead.

— The escalator is a no-play zone, which means absolutely no running, playing, or sitting on the handrails or on the steps.

❖ Show your child how to step on and off carefully.

❖ Just in case, learn where the emergency shutoff switch is. It is usually under the handrail at the top and bottom of the escalator.

Taking Care with Baby Equipment

The first step in preventing injuries with baby equipment is to take care when purchasing. Always look for the Juvenile Products Manufacturer Association (JPMA) certification label.

Baby Walker

More children are injured in wheeled baby walkers than with any other nursery product. In 1997, the CPSC estimated that walkers were involved in 14,300 hospital emergency room–treated injuries to children younger than fifteen months, with most injuries (and the most severe) caused by falling down stairs with the devices. Walkers have been involved in thirty-four deaths since 1973.

Both the National SAFE KIDS Campaign and the AAP recommend that you do not use a wheeled baby walker, for the following reasons:

Your child can

— tip it over,

— fall out of it,

— fall down the stairs in it, or

— reach places where hot foods or heavy objects can be pulled down on himself (14.3).

If you choose to use a wheeled baby walker in spite of this advice, the CPSC strongly recommends that you replace your old walker with a new-generation baby walker. These walkers meet new standards and are certified by the JPMA.

■ Requirements for new certification. It must be

❖ too wide to fit through a standard doorway or

❖ have features, such as a gripping mechanism, to stop the walker at the edge of a step.

- Look for the label that states "Meets New Standards."
- Other tips for the safe use of walkers:
    - Use safety gates or keep doors locked.
    - Carefully supervise your child and always keep him in full view while he uses the walker. (A walker is not meant to be a baby-sitter; one second of being unattended could result in an accident.)
    - Make sure you clear away objects on countertops, tables, or stove tops. (The walker enables your child to reach them.)
    - To avoid burns, keep children away from hot surfaces and containers.
    - Beware of dangling appliance cords.
    - Keep children away from toilets, swimming pools, and other sources of water.
    - Use the walker only on smooth surfaces. (Edges of carpets, throw rugs, or raised thresholds can cause a walker to tip over.)
    - Opt for a play center or stationary walker. These stay in place but still allow children to move their legs.

Changing Table

- Buying it
    - Buy a table with safety straps.
    - Make sure the table is sturdy, stable, and has high sides.
- Using it
    - Always use the safety straps.
    - Never leave your child unattended, not even for a second.
    - Keep diapers and all toiletries out of Baby's reach but easily within yours. That way you won't need to leave the baby.

High Chair

- Buying it
    - Select a high chair with a wide, stable base.
    - For safety, it should be equipped with a waist belt and a crotch strap.
      — Test straps before buying.
      — Choose ones that are sturdy as well as easy to fasten and unfasten. That way you'll be more likely to use them all the time.
- Using it
    - Make sure the tray is locked securely in place.
    - Always use the crotch strap and the belt around the waist.
      — Don't rely on the tray to keep the child from falling out.

— A child can easily slide down beneath the tray and strangle. The CPSC reports deaths occurring when children have done just this.

❖ Make sure the locking device on a folding high chair is locked each time you assemble it.

❖ Place the high chair far away from the table, counter, or wall so baby can't use them to push off.

❖ Never allow your child to stand on the chair.

❖ Stay within a close range of your child while she is in the high chair.

Stroller

■ Buying it

  ❖ Choose a stroller or carriage that has a base wide enough to prevent tipping, even when your baby leans over to one side.

  ❖ Make sure the waist belt is strong and durable and easy to open and close.

  ❖ If the seat adjusts to a reclining position, make sure the stroller won't tip over backward when the child lies down.

  ❖ Look for these qualities in the brakes.

    — Brakes should be convenient to operate.

    — They should actually lock the wheels.

    — Having brakes on two sides provides an extra measure of safety (14.4).

  ❖ A shopping basket for carrying items should be low on the back of the stroller and in front of or directly over the rear wheels.

■ Using it

  ❖ Always secure the restraining belts.

  ❖ Always use the locking device to prevent unintentional folding.

  ❖ Always apply the brakes to limit rotation of the wheels when the stroller is stationary (14.5).

  ❖ Don't hang your handbag, diaper bag, or other items over the handles because this may cause tipping.

  ❖ Close leg openings when using a stroller or carriage. A baby may slip through feet first and become entrapped by his head between the seat and the hand-rest bar. It could result in a strangulation death.

  ❖ When you fold or unfold the stroller or when the seat back is being reclined, keep your child away from pinching areas.

  ❖ Do not allow other children to push it without permission and supervision.

  ❖ Do not allow other children to climb onto it.

  ❖ Check to make sure no surfaces are hot if it was standing out in the sun.

The Older Child's Bed: Reducing Falls from the Top Bunk

- Children under the age of six should never sleep on the top bed.
- There should be guardrails on both sides.
- All spaces between the guardrail and the bed frame and in the head- and footboards should be less than three and one half inches.
- Establish rules that children understand.
  - ❖ Always use the ladder to get on and off the top bunk.
  - ❖ Do not engage in horseplay or jump from the top bunk.

Things That Go Bump Day and Night

Toys and games are not the only things that can fall on someone. Furniture can tip over and tumble down right on top of your child. The CPSC estimates that in the United States alone, 8,000 to 10,000 victims are treated each year in hospital emergency rooms for injuries associated with furniture tipping over. Out of these injuries, there are about six deaths each year. The majority of these deaths and injuries are to children.

Furniture Can Hurt

Look around your home. Items such as bookshelves, cabinets, dressers, hutches, desks, home-entertainment units, television stands, oven ranges—all are possible candidates for causing disaster. And there are a variety of ways furniture can tip. Your child may fall against the furniture and cause it to tip. He may climb up on it, perhaps in an effort to retrieve an item. She may sit on it or try to move it. Or he may simply be trying to open or close a door, drawer, or compartment.

- Avoid buying certain items.
  - ❖ Furniture pieces with wide shelves or footholds would encourage climbing.
  - ❖ Floor lamps, standing coat racks, or other freestanding items can easily topple over on your child.
- Safe placement
  - ❖ Place TVs, VCRs, and stereo systems on lower furniture, as far back as possible.
  - ❖ Use angle braces or anchors to secure furniture to the wall (14.6).
  - ❖ Place table lamps behind or at the back of other furniture. Or use a ceiling light fixture.
- Safe storage
  - ❖ Place heavier items on the lower shelves to keep the center of gravity low.
  - ❖ Place heavy, tippable objects in an inaccessible place.

❖ Knickknacks, breakable items, and heavy, tippable objects should be kept out of the reach of your children.

Look Out for Falling Doors

The garage door is the largest moving object in the home. At least eighty-five children in the United States have had permanent brain damage or have died as a result of injuries involving automatic door openers since 1974 (14.7).

- Safety devices
  - ❖ Auto-reverse features
    - —How it works: This feature, built into garage door operators, senses an obstruction in the motion of the door's down travel and reverses its direction.
    - —What it does: It causes the door to reverse striking an object, moving it back to a fully open position.
  - ❖ Photoelectric sensor
    - —How it works: This "electric eye" projects an invisible light beam across the inside of the garage-door opening.
    - —What it does: If anything interrupts the beam while the door is going down, it will automatically reverse the door before making contact.
  - ❖ Door edge sensor
    - —How it works: It acts much like the sensor on elevator doors.
    - —What it does: It causes the door to stop and reverse when it strikes object. The force is small, approximately fifteen pounds.
- Installation
  - ❖ Federal law (enforced by CPSC) has required that automatic garage-door openers manufactured on or after January 1, 1993, be equipped with an entrapment protection feature, such as the photoelectric sensor or the door edge sensor.
  - ❖ Companies that install garage-door openers can install these safety devices.
- Safety Tips
  - ❖ Refer to the manufacturer's instructions for ongoing maintenance of the garage door and operator, as well as regular testing of the safety reversing features.
  - ❖ Inspect your garage door monthly to see if it is operating properly. If it is not operating properly, disconnect the automatic opener from the door (as specified in the owner's manual) and manually open and close the door until it is repaired.

- ❖ Keep the opener's reversing force set as low as possible.
- ❖ Operate the garage-door opener only when the door is in full view and you are sure that it is free of any children, pets, or any obstructions.
- ❖ Keep children and pets a safe distance away from the door while it is moving.
- ❖ Be vigilant! Watch the door until it has completely opened and has completely closed. Don't pull out of the driveway until the door has completely closed.
- ❖ No one should be allowed to run underneath a moving door. Parents, don't do it. Be a role model.
- ❖ Keep activation buttons at least six feet above the floor to restrict access by children (14.8).
- ❖ Warn your child of the potential dangers of crossing under a moving garage door.
- ❖ Keep remote-control door-operating devices locked in the car and away from children.
- ❖ Do not let a child operate or play with the opener or ride up and down on the door.
- ❖ Store children's toys and other play items away from the garage door and controls.

Hazards of Falling at the Playground

Each year in this country approximately 200,000 children go to hospital emergency rooms with injuries associated with playground equipment, the CPSC reports. Seventeen children die yearly from playground-related injuries (14.9).

At home and at other playgrounds, know the dangers and take appropriate steps.

- ■ Provide a soft landing. According to National Program for Playground Safety, the type of surface on the playground is one of the most important factors in the number and severity of injuries due to falls (14.10).
  - ❖ To provide adequate cushioning, the ground under the playground equipment should be soft.
    - —Acceptable surfaces are hardwood fiber, mulch chips, pea gravel, sand, or shredded rubber, maintained at a depth of twelve inches.
    - —Synthetic or rubber mats are also appropriate for use under play equipment; they require less maintenance, but cost more initially.
  - ❖ Unsafe surfaces
    - —Asphalt, concrete, grass, and soil surfaces are not safe. A fall onto one of these hard surfaces could be life threatening.

—Indoors: Climbing equipment used indoors on hard surfaces can pose a danger. Falls on cement, tile, and other hard surfaces, even if covered with carpet, can result in serious head injuries or death. Use such equipment only outdoors on the shock-absorbing surfaces listed above or on shock-absorbing materials such as mats indoors (14.11).

■ Define fall zones.
  ❖ Protective surfacing material is essential under and around all equipment where your child could fall.
  ❖ The shock-absorbing material should extend a minimum of at least six feet in all directions from stationary pieces of play equipment.
  ❖ In front of and behind swings, the material should extend a distance equal to twice the height of the suspending bar.

■ Provide guardrails.
  ❖ Elevated surfaces, like platforms and ramps, should have guardrails to prevent falls.
  ❖ At twenty inches for preschoolers: Because preschool-age children are more at risk for falls, equipment intended for children in this age group should have guardrails on every elevated surface higher than twenty inches.
  ❖ At thirty inches for school-age children: Equipment intended for school-age children should have a guardrail on every elevated surface higher than thirty inches.

■ Equipment at home
  ❖ Make sure the playground equipment meets the manufacturer's requirements for your child's age and weight.
  ❖ Take care when installing.
    —Carefully read and follow the manufacturer's directions.
    —The area should be level and well drained.
    —Equipment should be anchored firmly to the ground.
    —Install it at least six feet from walls, fences, electrical wires, or other obstacles.
  ❖ Inspect and maintain your equipment and the protective surfacing on a regular basis.

■ Inspect the equipment at home and at the park and playgrounds.
  ❖ Make sure it is anchored safely in the ground.
  ❖ Check for dangerous hardware, such as *S* hooks or protruding bolt ends.
  ❖ Be on the lookout for sharp points or edges.
  ❖ Make sure there are no exposed moving parts.
  ❖ Make sure the equipment and surfacing are in good condition.

- ❖ Check for potential tripping hazards, such as tree roots or stumps, rocks, and concrete footing.
- Patrol the playground for maintenance problems.
  - ❖ It should be free of litter, such as broken glass or cans. Are there animal droppings around? Yuck!
  - ❖ Make sure the playground has a designated official who periodically inspects the play equipment for preventive maintenance.
  - ❖ Promptly report any problems to the designated official or organization responsible.
- Know the importance of spaces.
  - ❖ Make sure openings in guardrails and spaces between platforms and ladder rungs measure less than three and one half inches or greater than nine inches wide.
  - ❖ Because children often enter openings feet first, they can get trapped and strangle if the opening is large enough to fit their bodies through but too small to permit the head to go through.
  - ❖ Equipment play structures should be spaced at least twelve feet apart.
- Appropriate use of the playground
  - ❖ Areas for preschool children (ages two through five) should be separate from those areas intended for school-age children (ages five through twelve).
  - ❖ Make sure your children are using age-appropriate playground equipment.
    — Younger children should not use equipment designed for older children.
    — Older children should not use equipment designed for younger children.
  - ❖ Make sure your children are using playground equipment according to its intended purposes.
  - ❖ Teach your children the correct way to use each piece of equipment.
  - ❖ Explain to them the dangers of using it incorrectly.
- Swing rules
  - ❖ Equipment
    — Swings and other moving equipment should be located in an area away from other structures.
    — The AAP recommends that swing seats should be made of soft materials such as rubber, plastic, or canvas.
    — No more than two swing seats should be suspended in the same section or bay of the support structure.
  - ❖ Appropriate attire
    — Do not allow your child to wear necklaces, scarves, garments with drawstrings, oversized clothing, or any outer attire with emblems or buttons

that could get snagged on equipment. Make sure children remove their bicycle helmets before playing.

—Your child should wear sneakers or other closed-toe shoes. No sandals. Make sure the laces are tied to avoid tripping or getting them caught in equipment.

❖ For safety, teach your child:

—Always walk far behind a swing when someone is on it.

—Never walk or play close to a moving swing.

■ Playground etiquette to teach your child

❖ Always wait your turn.

❖ Don't push, shove, fight, or play roughly.

■ Responsibility of the parent

❖ Adult supervision is always necessary when children play on playgrounds at school, day care, in neighborhood parks, and at home. Equipment will not supervise children.

❖ Why supervise? Forty percent of playground injuries are related to inadequate supervision (14.12).

■ Government regulations

❖ There are no mandatory federal regulations regarding playground safety.

❖ Voluntary playground safety guidelines and standards have been developed by the CPSC, the American Society for Testing and Materials (ASTM), the National Program for Playground Safety, and the Consumer Federation of America.

❖ Five states—California, Michigan, New Jersey, North Carolina, and Texas—have enacted playground safety legislation mandating many of these recommendations (14.13).

For More Information

You can receive a free copy of the JPMA's publication "Safe and Sound for Baby: A Guide to Juvenile Product Safety, Use and Selection" or learn more about selecting JPMA-certified infant products by sending a number ten SASE to JPMA Public Information, 236 Route 38 W, Suite 100, Moorestown, NJ 08057. You may also receive information from JPMA by calling (609) 231-8500, or by faxing (609) 231-4664, or by visiting their website: www. jpma.org.

To receive the free publications "Safe Nursery, the Buyer's Guide: A Booklet to Help Avoid Injuries from Nursery Furniture and Equipment" and "Handbook for Public

Playground Safety" and home playground safety tips, contact the CPSC by writing Washington, DC 20207, or by calling (800) 638-2772, or by visiting their website: www.cpsc.gov.

For a free "Play it Safe Playgrounds" brochure, contact the American Academy of Orthopedic Surgeons by writing P.O. Box 1998, Des Plaines, IL 60017, or by calling (800) 824-BONES [2663], or by visiting their website: www.aaos.org.

For information about building safe playgrounds, contact KABOOM! Let Us Play Campaign by writing to KABOOM! Our Work Is Child's Play, 2213 M Street NW, Suite 200, Washington, DC 20037, or by calling (202) 659-0215, or by visiting their website: www.kaboom.org.

For information about playground safety, contact the National Recreation and Park Association, whose staff persons are available M–F, 9 A.M.–5 P.M. EST, by writing to 22377 Belmont Ridge Road, Ashburn, VA 20148, or by calling (703) 858-0784, or by faxing (703) 858-0794, or by E-mailing info@nrpa.org, or by visiting their website: www.activeparks.org.

Further information may be obtained from the National Program for Playground Safety, which is staffed M–F, 8 A.M.–5 P.M. CST, by writing to University of Northern Iowa, School for Health, Physical Education, and Leisure Services, Cedar Falls, IA 50614-0618, or by calling (800) 554-PLAY [7529], or by E-mailing playground-safety@uni.edu, or by visiting their website: www.uni.edu/playground/.

To order child safety equipment and devices, contact The Right Start by writing to 5388 Sterling Center Drive, Unit C, Westlake Village, CA 91361-4627, or by calling (800) LITTLE-1 [548-8531], or by faxing (800) 762-5501. You may also order from Perfectly Safe, by writing to 7835 Freedom Avenue NW, Suite 3, North Canton, OH 44720-6907, or by calling (800) 837-KIDS [5437], or by faxing (330) 492-8290, or by E-mailing psafe@cannet.com, or by visiting their website: www.4perfectlysafe.com. You may also order from One Step Ahead, by writing to P.O. Box 517, Lake Bluff, IL 60044, or by calling (800) 274-8440, or by visiting their website: www.onestep ahead.com.

15

Stepping Out (Safely)

Mother used to say:
"Stay in the shade. Too much sun will make you sick."

Some Like It Hot

Due in part to the depletion of the ozone layer, children are exposed now more than ever to the sun's harmful, ultraviolet (UV) rays. The increase in exposure also comes from people's behavior, e.g., changing fashions, tanning behaviors, and attitudes. According to the Environmental Protection Agency (EPA), overexposure to UV radiation not only causes painful sunburn, but it can lead to other serious health problems, including melanoma, a life-threatening form of skin cancer. As little as one or two blistering sunburns during childhood may double the risk of melanoma later in life. In addition to melanoma, excessive UV exposure can lead to premature aging of the skin, nonmelanoma skin cancers, and immune system suppression. These effects, however, may not appear until later in life. The majority of sun exposure occurs before the age of eighteen, and studies suggest a link to early exposure and skin cancer as an adult. Follow these simple sun-safety precautions in order to protect your children from overexposure.

Planning Activities by the UV Index

The UV Index was developed by the National Weather Service (NWS) and the EPA. The index is a daily forecast of the expected intensity of the sun in cities across the United States. It provides important information to help you plan your outdoor activities in order to prevent overexposure to the sun.

Although you should always take precautions (see "Use Sun Sense" on the next page) to protect your family against overexposure, special care should be taken when the UV Index predicts exposure levels of moderate or above. Watch the local news, look in your newspaper, or use the site listed in "For More Information About Safety in the Sun," at the end of this section, to find your city's UV Index.

Index Numbers and Exposure Danger

- 0–2: minimal
- 3–4: low
- 5–6: moderate
- 7–9: high
- 10+: very high *Please stay indoors if possible!*

The Shadow Knows

Even if you don't know the UV Index on a particular day, an easy way to tell how much UV exposure you are getting is to play the shadow game. If your shadow is shorter than you are, you are being exposed to high levels of UV. Seek shade (15.1)! Don't be lulled into a false sense of security if your skin is not fair. Even though some skin types do not burn as easily as others, *everyone* is at risk for UV-related health effects.

Use Sun Sense

A child's sensitive skin can burn more easily than an adult's.

- Whenever possible, limit sun exposure during peak hours (10 A.M.–4 P.M.), when rays are the strongest.
- Be aware that water, sand, and snow can reflect harmful rays, even under hats and umbrellas. Uv is a year-round concern!
- Use sunscreen with a Sun Protection Factor (SPF) of at least 15.
  - ❖ Apply it liberally to children's skin all year round, even if they will be going outside only for recess.
    - —Before your child dresses, slather lotion over skin that will be exposed; don't forget the rims of ears, the backs of neck and hands, and even the tops of feet if they will be exposed.
    - —Rub it in until it can no longer be seen.
    - —Apply it at least thirty minutes before going outdoors.
  - ❖ Be sure the sunscreen is broad spectrum, protecting against both UVA and UVB rays.
  - ❖ Use sunscreen even on cloudy or cool days. Uv rays can penetrate the clouds and it is possible for skin to burn even if neither you nor your child feels warm. (Skiers frequently burn!)
  - ❖ Reapply it every two hours and after your child has been swimming or perspiring, even if the product you use is waterproof. Sunscreen can come off when your child towels off. Consult instructions on the bottle.
- Use zinc oxide for areas such as the nose and ears, which are most sensitive to the sun. There are new, cool colors on the market now.

- Use a lip screen with at least an SPF of 15 and UVA and UVB protection.
- Take extra precautions in some situations.
  - Surfaces such as water, sand, concrete, and snow reflect up to 85 percent of the sun's damaging rays.
  - High altitudes also increase the need for protection.
- Have everyone in your family wear UV protective sunglasses.
  - This will reduce the risk of cataracts or other eye damage.
  - Check the label to make sure the glasses provide 99 percent to 100 percent UVA and UVB protection.
  - Wraparound glasses work best because they keep rays from sneaking in from the side or behind.
- Dress to "cover up" while in the sun.
  - A hat with a wide brim offers shade.
  - Lightweight T-shirt—keep it dry; a wet one offers much less UV protection than a dry one.
  - Wear a cover-up over a bathing suit when not in the water.
  - Tightly woven, loose-fitting clothing—UV rays can pass through holes and spaces of loosely knit fabrics.
  - Full-length clothing obviously offers the most protection, so these should be worn when it is possible and practical.
- Seek shade. You can create your own shade in your yard or playground by using tents or canopies.
- Avoid sunlamps and tanning parlors, which can damage the skin and unprotected eyes (15.2).
- Use extra care with babies.
  - Shade the baby from direct sunlight; bonnets and hats are a must.
  - Keep carriages and strollers covered for greater sun protection.
  - Protect the baby by avoiding too much time outdoors. Consult with your pediatrician for appropriate sun safety for infants.

What to Do About Sunburn

Even the most diligent of parents must sometimes deal with a sunburned child. Calm the child with reassuring words and first-aid treatment.

1. Apply a cold compress to the reddened skin in order to cool it down and reduce irritation.
2. If blisters appear, wash the area carefully.
3. Give a nonaspirin pain reliever to reduce pain and inflammation as directed by your child's pediatrician.

4. Keep the child out of the sun until the burn heals; if the child must go outside, make sure the sunburned areas are covered.

5. Contact your pediatrician at once if there is a fever, fluid-filled blisters, or severe pain, or if an infant under the age of one is sunburned.

Watch Out for These Hot-Weather Emergencies

Heat Stroke

Heat stroke is caused by exposure to extreme heat. It is a serious, life-threatening condition that can lead to permanent damage to the body or even death if immediate emergency treatment is not given. Heat stroke occurs when the body's cooling system (the sweat glands) fail to function and the body is unable to sweat to cool itself down.

The CDC lists the following symptoms and recommendations (15.3). Recognize the symptoms. They vary but may include:

- Skin is hot, red, and dry (no sweating).
- The child has an oral temperature of above 103°F.
- The child has a fast pulse.
- The child has nausea.
- The child has a throbbing headache.
- The child collapses, experiences confusion, has seizures, or lapses into unconsciousness.

  Act fast when symptoms appear!

- Have someone else call for immediate medical assistance while you begin cooling the victim.
  - Bring the child to an air-conditioned room or a cool, shady place.
  - Undress the child.
  - Apply cooling methods such as:
    - Cool sponging
    - Wrapping the child in cool, wet towels
    - Cool bath or shower (Hold the child and carefully watch him, for a drowning could occur.)
    - Cold compress on forehead
    - Vigorous fanning

Heat Exhaustion

Heat exhaustion is the body's response to an excessive loss of the water and salt contained in sweat. If heat exhaustion is untreated, it may progress to heat stroke. Warning signs include:

- Heavy sweating
- Weakness or tiredness
- Cool, pale, or clammy skin
- Dizziness or fainting
- Headache
- Muscle cramps
- Nausea or vomiting
- Weak pulse

Immediately take the child inside to an air-conditioned room or to a shady area and help her to cool off with methods such as cool sponging, cool shower, or bath. Give your child sips of water, as directed by your pediatrician. Seek medical attention immediately if symptoms worsen, or if they last longer than an hour.

Preventing Heat Stroke and Heat Exhaustion

- NEVER leave your child unattended in a car (not even for a few minutes)!
- Dress children in light-colored, loose-fitting, and lightweight clothing on hot summer days. Make sure they wear hats or sun visors. Apply sunscreen, as usual. Remember, a sunburn affects your body's ability to cool itself and causes a loss of body fluids.
- Make sure children are properly hydrated. Have a water bottle on hand and encourage them to drink plenty of fluids often, even if they aren't thirsty. Additional water and frequent rest breaks are required for children who are involved in active play or sports.
- Take time out in the shade to prevent prolonged or excessive exposure to the sun.
- Be especially careful with infants. Limit the amount of time your infant spends outdoors.
- Check regularly on those at greatest risk of heat-related illness: children under the age of five, people who are ill or on certain medications, people who are overweight, people who overexert during work or exercise, and people who are sixty-five years old or older.

For More Information About Safety in the Sun

The EPA ozone protection hot line staff can provide you with a series of free fact sheets that will guide you in protecting your child and yourself from overexposure to the sun's UV rays. An information specialist is available M–F, 10 A.M.–4 P.M. EST, to answer your questions. Contact the EPA by writing to Sun Wise School Program, Mail Code 6205J, 401 M Street SW, Washington, DC 20460, or by calling the Stratospheric

Ozone Hot Line (800) 296-1996 or (301) 614-3396, or by visiting their ozone web-site: www.epa.gov/sunwise.

To obtain today's UV index (as an alternative to checking your local newspaper or broadcast news), log onto this EPA website: www.epa.gov/ozone/uvindex.

For additional sun protection information, you may contact the American Academy of Dermatology by writing to 930 N. Meacham Road, P.O. Box 4014, Schaumburg, IL 60173-4965, or by calling (888) 462-DERM [3376], or by visiting their website: www.aad.org.

Information may also be obtained by contacting the Centers for Disease Control and Prevention (CDC) by writing to Division of Cancer Prevention and Control, 4770 Buford Highway, Chamblee, GA 30341, or by calling (770) 488-4751, or by visiting their website: www.cdc.gov/cancer/.

Ticked Off with Ticks

Lyme disease is named after the town of Old Lyme, Connecticut, where the disease was first recognized in 1975. Caused by a type of bacteria called a spirochete, it is an infection which many mistakenly believe to be carried only by ticks that infest deer. While the adults feed mainly on deer, the larvae and nymphs tend to feed on a variety of hosts. Of these, the white-footed mouse is an especially important one. A tick that has Lyme disease may pass it on to any animal or human it bites.

Deer are more visible, but the tiny white-footed mouse is abundant in fields and underbrush. Hundreds of mice are probably present every time you see a deer, and each mouse can actually carry up to 400 ticks, because its habitat is also infested. Making matters worse, an infected mouse can pass the Lyme disease along to a tick that was previously uninfected. Deer do not pass the disease along in that manner.

A walk in the woods should be relaxing and fun, and it can be if you're confident that you can spot a tick before it harms your child. You need to look carefully though, since a nymphal (immature) tick, which may carry Lyme disease, is very small, about the size of a poppy seed. Actually, two kinds of ticks cause Lyme disease: the "deer" (black-legged) tick in the eastern and north-central states and the western black-legged tick, found in the Pacific states.

Ticks crawl; they do not fly or jump. The risk of exposure is greatest in the woods, but ticks may also be carried by animals into lawns and gardens. In fact, the white-footed mouse inhabits dense ground cover in backyards, gardens, and golf courses as much as in the woods. The only way to get Lyme disease is to be bitten by a tick that carries Lyme disease. Lyme disease is not transmitted from person to person. Although household pets do not directly transmit Lyme disease to us, loose, infected ticks on pets can be a hazard for people around them.

Most tick bites occur in the spring and summer months (May through August are the high-risk months), but be aware that whenever the temperature is higher than 40°F, ticks are active and can bite! Symptoms of untreated Lyme disease can occur at any time of the year. Children under the age of ten are at greatest risk of exposure to the disease because they love to play outside in backyards, woodlands, and parks and cannot easily identify these ticks.

Regions of Greater Risk

According to the Centers for Disease Control and Prevention (CDC), there are three regions in the United States where the risk of getting the disease is much greater than other regions.

1. Northeast (Massachusetts to Maryland)
2. North-Central states (especially Wisconsin and Minnesota)
3. West Coast (California and Oregon)

The best way to prevent Lyme disease is to avoid all high-risk areas, especially if you live in the regions mentioned above. Since this is not always possible for your family, the best way to protect them is to be aware of the causes and symptoms and practice proper preventive measures.

Prevention for Every Member of the Family

- Be careful where you walk and play.
  - Stay in the center of trails in parks and woodlands.
  - Keep away from leaf litter.
  - Don't brush up against tall grass, bushes, trees, or shrubs.
  - Avoid areas that deer or field mice frequent, especially around water and woods.
- Stay away from all wild animals.
- Wear proper clothing.
  - Wear long-sleeved shirts and pants. The shirt should be tucked into the pants and the pants tucked into socks.
  - Do not wear sandals or any type of open shoes. Boots or high-top shoes are best.
  - Wear a hat and keep long hair tied back in a ponytail or bun.
  - Light-colored and tightly woven clothing make it easier to spot ticks and prevent them from going through the clothing.
  - Use tick and insect repellent on clothing.

Taking Care with Repellents

- Carefully read and follow manufacturer's directions. Some commonly used repellents containing permethrin are meant to be applied to clothing only, not the skin.
- Do not allow your children to apply the repellents. Apply it to your hands and then put it on the child.
- Use just enough repellent to cover exposed skin and/or clothing.
- Wash skin with soap and water after returning indoors.
- Wash treated clothing before wearing again.
- Do not breathe in or ingest the repellent.
- Do not spray in an enclosed area.
- Absolutely avoid use on
  - eyes, nose, or mouth;
  - hands of small children;
  - cuts, rashes, sunburns, or any other skin condition; and
  - skin underneath clothing.

Repellents should be applied only to *exposed* skin (as directed on the label). To apply to a child's face, spray repellent on your hands and carefully rub onto child's face, avoiding the eyes, nose, and mouth.

DEET (chemical name—N,N-Diethyl-meta-toluamide) is the active ingredient in many insect-repellent products. When using DEET, use extreme caution if you apply it directly on the child's skin. Some children have experienced adverse health effects after application of DEET.

- Use only small amounts, with low concentrations. The American Academy of Pediatrics (AAP) recommends that for use on children, the product should contain no more than 10 percent DEET.
- Avoid repeat applications. If you suspect that your child is reacting to an insect repellent, discontinue use, wash the treated area, and promptly consult your poison-control center or pediatrician. Take the repellent container with you if you must visit the emergency room or doctor's office.
- Check with your pediatrician before using DEET on a child younger than two years old.

Making a Tick Check Part of the Plan

A tick check is the careful inspection of skin and clothing for crawling or embedded ticks. Teach your children that a tick check is part of the routine that goes along with hiking or playing in the woods or other areas where ticks might be found.

- While on an outing, periodically spot check your children and yourself for ticks on clothes. If you find one, there may be others, so be sure to check thoroughly.
- Shower or bathe children after they have played in woods and areas of known tick infestations.
- Perform a head-to-toe inspection. Because ticks often attach to the more hidden, hairy areas, check especially the groin, armpits, and scalp. You may wish to use a magnifying glass.
- After an outing, immediately put clothing in the dryer on a medium or high temperature for twenty minutes to kill any ticks that might be on clothes. Then machine wash and dry as usual.

Remember that careful daily inspection is necessary any time you engage in outdoor activities when the temperature exceeds 40°F. Believe it or not, you can pick up a stray tick just by walking across your lawn (15.4). For information about protecting your pet, contact your veterinarian.

When the Tick Check Exposes a Tick

- Stay calm and don't panic! There is little risk of infection within the first twenty-four hours. The sooner you remove the tick, the better.
- Remove it with tweezers by grasping the tick as close to the skin's surface as possible and pulling upward with steady pressure. Grasp the tick by the head or mouthparts. Do not grasp the tick by the body (15.5).
  - Clean the bite with alcohol.
  - Kill the tick—once it is removed—by dropping it in alcohol. Put the tick in a plastic reclosable bag, and save the tick so it is available as a reference if Lyme disease–like symptoms start.
- Do not jerk the tweezers or pull quickly because you risk leaving the mouth parts of the tick still in the skin. The mouth parts can cause local infection but will not, by themselves, cause Lyme disease.
- Never try to kill the tick while it is on the skin.
  - Don't try to burn it.
  - Don't cover it with nail polish or petroleum jelly in an attempt to smother it.

Symptoms and Signs of Lyme Disease

Your child may play host to the bloodsucking deer tick without anyone knowing it. Therefore, it is very important to be aware of the early stages of the disease. Prompt treatment with oral antibiotics can provide your child with a quick recovery and a complete cure.

Detect the disease quickly to maximize your child's return to good health. The signs and symptoms follow.

- A skin rash called *erythema migrans* is the first sign of Lyme disease in 60 percent to 80 percent of patients.
  - ❖ Is usually reddish
  - ❖ May appear as an expanding bull's eye
  - ❖ Usually not painful and does not itch
  - ❖ May feel warm to touch
  - ❖ Expands outward from where tick bite occurred
  - ❖ Develops usually three days to one month after the bite of an infected tick
  - ❖ Most common shape is flat, roughly circular, and at least two inches in diameter (average diameter is five–six inches)
  - ❖ Other, more scattered rashes may also appear later on other areas of the skin
- Flu-like illness
  - ❖ No cough
  - ❖ Fever, fatigue, malaise, headache, chills, stiff neck, swollen glands, joint and muscle pain

A Food and Drug Administration (FDA)–approved vaccine developed to prevent Lyme disease is presently available to individuals between the ages of fifteen and seventy. Contact your physician concerning the recommendations governing its usage. Vaccine trials are now underway for children younger than fifteen.

Other Tick-Borne Diseases

Lyme disease is now the most common arthropod-borne illness in the United States—more than 100,000 cases have been reported to the CDC since 1982. There are eighty-two species of ticks collectively causing nine major diseases in the United States.

1. Lyme disease
2. Ehrlichiosis, HME form
3. Ehrlichiosis, HGE form
4. Babesiosis
5. Tick Paralysis
6. Tick-Borne Relapsing Fever
7. Tularemia
8. Rocky Mountain Spotted Fever
9. Colorado Tick Fever

For More Information About Tick-Borne Diseases

Contact the CDC by writing to National Center for Infectious Diseases, Atlanta, GA 30333, or by visiting their website: www.cdc.gov.

Contact the American Lyme Disease Foundation (ALDF) to speak with a specialist M–F, 9 A.M.–3 P.M. EST, by calling (914) 277-6970. Order free materials from the ALDF by calling (800) 876-5963, or by visiting their website: www.aldf.com.

Contact your local or state health department for guidelines concerning the risks of any of these diseases for your specific area. For further information about DEET, call the National Pesticide Telecommunications Network: (800) 858-7378.

The Bug Stops Here

Bees

In most cases, when bees are left alone, they will not attack. However, if provoked, these insects will sting in defense of their nests or themselves. Teach your children not to disturb insects' nests and not to wave their arms (swinging or swatting) when bees or other stinging insects approach. When it comes to preventing insect bites and stings, there are a few ways to make yourself less appealing. Even so, stings and bites can happen in spite of precautions. When they occur, they require prompt, careful attention.

Dos and Don'ts

- Wear lightweight clothing that covers legs and arms.
- Wear a hat to keep the head covered.
- Wear white, beige, and khaki-colored clothing.
- Teach your child to move slowly and carefully around insects.
- Shake towels and clothing before drying and dressing. (Bees, bugs, and insects can hide in towels and clothes.)
- Don't use perfumes, cologne, hair sprays, or scented soaps and lotions.
- Avoid bananas and banana-scented toiletries.
- Don't wear bright colors (yellow, red, green), flowered or floral patterns.
- Don't feed children outdoors. (Food aromas attract insects.)
- Don't kick or move logs.
- Don't go barefoot outside.
- Stay away from garbage cans, stagnant water, decaying fruits, picnic areas, and gardens when flowers are in bloom.

When the Bee Stings

- Find the stinger; then promptly and carefully remove it.
  - ❖ Use your fingernail, a piece of cardboard, or a credit card and gently scrape the stinger away.
  - ❖ Do not squeeze it or try to remove it with tweezers, for in doing so you may crush the poison sac attached to the stinger, pumping more poison into the body.
- Wash the affected area with soap and water and apply ice or a cold compress to reduce swelling and itchiness. (Most insect bites and stings are generally not serious.)
- Contact your pediatrician or your nearest poison control center
  - ❖ if redness, swelling, or pain persists or
  - ❖ if you have any questions concerning further treatment.
- Take your child to the pediatrician or to an emergency room for immediate medical attention
  - ❖ if an allergic reaction occurs, the most common symptoms are
    — breathing difficulties, wheezing
    — swelling of the mouth, throat
    — dizziness,
    — loss of consciousness, or
    — hives; or
  - ❖ in the case of multiple insect stings.

A family member who is extemely sensitive (allergic) to stings should wear a medical ID bracelet, and carry an insect sting allergy kit. Either of these items can be obtained from your physician. An allergic person should seek emergency treatment if stung, for reactions can be deadly.

Spiders

There are an estimated 20,000 species of spiders that live in the United States. Although they all are capable of biting, very few can penetrate skin. Bites can be painful and may cause redness, swelling, and infection. Two spiders that are considered harmful to humans are the Black Widow and the Brown Recluse. Immediately contact your poison control center or your doctor if you or your child is bitten by one of these poisonous spiders or by any spider if the bite seems severe. Clean the area with plenty of soap and water and apply a cool compress over the affected area.

For More Information About Bites and Stings by Bees, Spiders, and Other Critters

Contact your local poison control center or your local cooperative extension agent. For more information on safely removing known nests, contact your local cooperative extension agent. You may also consider calling a beekeeper if a problem has developed with bees inside, and you have nests in your walls.

The Rap on Reptiles

Mother used to say:
"Let that snake alone!"
(Maybe Mom was right.)

In recent years, a growing number of parents have bought such reptiles as iguanas, snakes, and turtles as household pets. Unfortunately, these scaly creatures are particularly likely to carry *salmonella* bacteria. It is not recommended to treat healthy reptiles with antibiotics because of the potential for causing antibiotic resistant *salmonella* strains, which might pose a greater health risk to people. Most healthy adults and older children who are infected with salmonella will recover within a week from the diarrhea, fever, and abdominal cramps without any serious side effects. However, infants, young children, and anyone with a suppressed immune system are likely to suffer severe or fatal illness as a result of salmonellosis. These bacteria can be transmitted easily to children from the reptiles' feces, which may stick to its body or cage. If a person does not wash her hands thoroughly with soap and water after handling the reptile or after cleaning its cage, the fecal material can be ingested or can contaminate any items (such as a pacifier). It is best to go outside to clean the reptile, its cage, and its bowl.

The CDC recommends that three categories of people avoid contact with reptiles:

1. Children five years of age and younger and child care centers
2. Immunocompromised persons
3. Entire households inhabited by children under age one and/or immuno-compromised persons

Do not permit unsupervised handling of reptiles by children under age twelve.

Note: *Salmonella* may also be found in the feces of other pets, especially those with diarrhea. Make it a practice to always wash your hands after contact with any animal or animal waste.

Raccoons, Bats, and Rabies

Mother used to say:
"Stay away from that animal! He's acting strange."

The old folks might have said, "Look out! That animal's in a rage." Indeed, the word *rabies* comes from a Latin word that means "to rage." Rabies got its name because animals with rabies sometimes act as if they are angry. In reality, rabies is a very serious viral disease that attacks the brain and other nervous-system tissue. Although it is almost always fatal if left untreated, the good news is that immediate protective treatment (thorough cleaning of the wound and the vaccine regimen) is effective in preventing the disease from developing.

In fact, the CDC reports that tens of thousands of people are successfully treated each year after being bitten by animals that may have rabies. A few people may die of rabies each year, usually because they do not recognize the risk of rabies from the bite of a wild animal and do not seek medical advice (15.6).

Common carriers are wild animals such as skunks, bats, foxes, and raccoons. In fact, rabies in raccoons is epidemic from Florida to Maine, southwest to Alabama, and westward to Ohio. Dogs and cats may also become infected with rabies, too. Rabies is extremely rare in smaller rodents such as mice and rats and those cute little squirrels in the park. That's because they're so small they usually die when involved in an encounter with another animal. However, larger rodents, such as woodchucks (a.k.a. groundhogs), may carry rabies.

Any infected mammal can transmit rabies to humans through a bite or if the animal's saliva or nervous system tissue enters an open wound or mucus membrane (e.g., the eyes, nose, or mouth) of a human.

The CDC recommends that if you or your child has any such contact with an unfamiliar animal, you should wash the wound thoroughly with soap and water for at least five minutes and seek medical attention immediately. Teach your child to notify you immediately if bitten, licked, or scratched by an unfamiliar or wild animal.

The following steps are recommended by the CDC to help protect your family from rabies.

- Avoid contact with wild animals and unfamiliar dogs and cats.
- Do not feed or handle wild animals or strays.
- Enjoy watching wildlife from afar.
- Learn the facts about bats.
  - A bat may not always leave a bite mark.
  - If you see a bat in a room with your child, seek medical attention.

- Vaccinate your dogs, cats, and ferrets against rabies.
- Never leave any young child alone with any pet.
- Look out for strays.
  - ❖ Report them to your local animal control so that the strays can be captured.
  - ❖ Stay away from any stray.
- Although you cannot tell if an animal has rabies just by looking at it, some signs of rabies in animals are:
  - ❖ Nervous or aggressive behavior
  - ❖ Excessive drooling or foaming at the mouth
  - ❖ A wild animal that appears tame
  - ❖ A nocturnal animal seen in the daytime

For More Information About Rabies

Contact your state or local health department or the Division of Viral and Rickettsial Diseases at the National Center for Infectious Diseases of the CDC by writing to Rabies Section MS G-33, 1600 Clifton Road NE, Atlanta, GA 30333, or by calling (404) 639-1050, or by visiting their website: www.cdc.gov/ncidod/dvrd/rabies. The CDC also has a rabies site for kids found at this URL.

16

Getting into the Swim of Things

Mother's rules about swimming
seemed endless when we were young.
Now we know she was right.

Drowning is the second most common cause of unintentional injury or death for children ages fourteen and younger. It isn't just swimming pools that are potentially dangerous. An infant or small child can drown in as little as one inch of water. Buckets and pails, bathtubs, wading pools, and toilets may be as dangerous as the backyard pool or an ocean. It takes only a momentary lapse of adult supervision, four to six minutes—the time it takes to answer the phone or door to go to the bathroom—that can cause tragedy. And because drowning is a silent death, it is unlikely that there will be any splashing or screaming to alert anyone that the child is in trouble.

If you turn around and find that your child is missing, every second counts. Before you look anywhere else, check your pool or spa.

Never Let Down Your Guard

According to The National SAFE KIDS Campaign (16.1), the most likely drowning places change as the child grows older:

- First year—bathtubs, buckets, and toilets
- Ages one to four—swimming pools, hot tubs, and spas
- Ages five to fourteen—swimming pools and open water sites

Never leave your young child alone near any water: bathtubs, toilets, liquid-filled buckets, coolers with melting ice, diaper pails, wading pools, swimming pools, hot tubs, fountains, wells, canals, ponds, lakes, or other bodies of water.

Household Drowning

Keep small children away from any liquid-filled bucket; particularly hazardous are five-gallon buckets. A curious toddler can pull herself up, peer in, and fall inside and drown. Every child who drowns this way was left unsupervised.

- Eliminate the danger of bucket drowning.
  - Immediately empty the bucket after you have finished using it and turn it upside down. It is also especially important for pails and buckets kept outside to be turned upside down, for they can collect rainwater.
  - Store it out of reach of children.
  - If you are temporarily interrupted during use, remove the bucket to a safe place.
  - Keep diaper pails securely closed and out of the reach of a young child.
- The bathroom presents drowning dangers, too.
  - The bathtub
    - Never leave a young child in a tub (or anywhere in the bathroom) without adult supervision, even for a second.
    - Gather all bath items before bath time so that you won't have to leave the bathroom to get them.
    - If the telephone rings, either ignore it or wrap the baby in a towel and carry her with you.
    - Don't use a bathtub supporting device as a substitute for adult supervision.
  - The toilet bowl
    - Keep toilet bowls closed.
    - Install a toilet lid lock on all toilets.
  - Make the bathroom off limits, except for bath or potty time.
    - Keep the bathroom door closed.
    - Attach a doorknob cover or install a door latch out of your child's reach.

Swimming Pool and Spa Safety

- Install safety devices to restrict access to the pool or spa—put as many barriers as possible between your child and the water. When a child is missing, these give the parent additional time to locate the child.
  - The best safety device is a four-sided isolation pool fence.
    - It should be five feet high, with no footholds, around the entire perimeter.
    - Do not use the house as one of the sides.
    - The fence should completely separate the pool from the house and play area of the yard.

- ❖ Use gates and latches.
  - —Gates should open away from the pool.
  - —Use only gates that are self-closing and self-latching. (You'll never have to wonder if you locked the gate.)
  - —Latches should be out of the reach of young children.
  - —Check frequently to see that gates and latches are in good working order.
- ❖ Don't leave furniture nearby that might enable your child to climb over the fence.
- ❖ All doors leading to the pool or spa should have child-resistant locks and be self-closing, if possible.
- ❖ Never prop open the gate to a pool area. (If the service or lawn care company visits your home, emphasize to the manager, as well as the technician, the importance of always securing the pool gate.)
- ❖ Set alarms.
  - —Install audible alarms on all doors and windows leading to the water.
  - —An alarm on the pool fence is also a good idea.
- ❖ Pool covers are useful.
  - —Use in conjunction with a pool fence. A motorized cover operated by a switch must meet the standards of the American Society for Testing and Materials (ASTM)
  - —Follow manufacturer's directions for safe use, installation, and maintenance.
  - —Never leave a pool cover partially in place; a child can be trapped underneath.
  - —Drain any standing water from the surface of your pool cover. An infant or young child can drown in the smallest amount of water.
  - —A locked safety cover should be used for your spa.
- ■ Ensure the safety of all swimmers.
  - ❖ Read and carefully follow all operating and maintenance instructions furnished by the pool manufacturer.
  - ❖ Follow instructions for pool equipment and pool chemicals.
  - ❖ Inspect the pool and equipment regularly.
  - ❖ Have a professional make any necessary repairs.

Supervision

- ■ Keep alert. Constant eye contact and close supervision is required when children are around water.
  - ❖ Never leave them alone, not even for one second.
  - ❖ Use the buddy system, in which each child is paired with another. If one of the buddies gets out of the water, the other must get out, too. They must stay

together throughout the activity for which they have been designated as buddies. This way, each keeps an eye on the other. Even with this system, there is no substitute for constant adult supervision. Children, regardless of their age, must be supervised by an adult (not an older sibling).

❖ Teach your children that even adults must always swim with a buddy. No one should ever swim alone.

■ The adults who watch

❖ The adult must know how to swim and have taken cardiopulmonary resuscitation (CPR) training.

❖ Don't rely on a neighbor who knows CPR. She may not be around in an emergency.

❖ Instruct all caretakers about potential pool hazards and the use of protective devices, such as door alarms and latches and, of course, the need for constant adult supervision.

❖ During social gatherings, designate an adult as a "water watcher" to supervise children in and around water. When parents become preoccupied, children are at risk.

■ Water recreation and chemical substances

❖ Adults should not consume alcoholic beverages or other drugs while supervising children around water, nor while they themselves are in a pool, spa, or hot tub or when boating.

❖ Teach and reinforce in your older children the same precautions. Remember that children learn by example.

■ Have a clear view of the pool from the windows of your home. This may require you to remove trees, bushes, or other obstacles.

■ Don't rely on flotation devices to keep your child afloat. These devices should never be a substitute for adult supervision.

■ Older children should never swim in unsupervised areas such as canals, quarries, or ponds. They may overestimate their swimming ability, putting them at risk for drowning.

Lessons for Life

Enroll your children in a learn to swim program and/or water safety class taught by qualified instructors when the children are ready. Check with your pediatrician first.

■ Water safety includes these safety rules.

❖ Safety near the water

— No running or horseplay

— No jumping

- ❖ Safety in the water
  - —No diving
  - —No pushing others under water
  - —Familiarize children with water depths and safe areas to play.
  - —Install a float line across your pool to indicate where the deep water begins.
  - —Make sure children understand what the float line means.
  - —Teach children never to pretend they are drowning.
- Make sure your child has learned how to roll over onto her back and float.
  - ❖ This life-saving skill can keep a young child breathing if he should fall into the water.
  - ❖ An older child can float on her back when she becomes tired.
- Do not consider young children to be drownproof simply because they have had swimming lessons. All children must be watched closely while swimming.
- Make sure your child takes refresher swimming lessons every year.

Special Rules for Diving

Diving headfirst into shallow water is the leading cause of spinal cord injuries in the water. Diving into any water can be dangerous without proper guidance. The following rules have been gleaned from suggestions by the American Academy of Pediatrics, The American Red Cross, and the National Spa and Pool Institute.

- Special rules for children
  - ❖ Before allowing your child to dive, have him or her take lessons from a qualified instructor.
  - ❖ Do not allow your child to dive without the permission of an adult who knows the depth of the water.
- Rules for all divers
  - ❖ Obey all "No Diving" signs.
  - ❖ Ease or walk into the water first to determine if it is deep enough and if there are any obstacles.
  - ❖ Never dive headfirst into
    - —crashing waves,
    - —cloudy or murky water, or
    - —the shallow end of a pool.
  - ❖ Never allow anyone who has been drinking to dive.
  - ❖ Never allow horseplay or competition dives in a backyard pool.
- Rules about the pool
  - ❖ Do not dive unless the pool meets all current dimensional standards for a diving pool. Have a pool professional measure your pool.

❖ Never dive into an above-ground pool.
❖ Rules about the diving board
  The presence of a diving board doesn't necessarily mean it's safe to dive.
  — Dive off the end of the diving board.
  — Do not run on the board or try to dive far out.
  — Do not bounce on the board more than once.
  — Have only one person on the board at a time.
  — Swim away from the board immediately after diving, before the next person dives.
  — Remove any earplugs when diving. Pressure can build as one goes down under water.

After the Swim

■ Take toys out of the pool area when finished so children won't be enticed to go back in.
■ Keep your children's playthings and tricycles away from the pool area.
■ Make sure the gate and pool cover are locked.
■ Take off your child's swimsuit immediately after swimming. This will signal no more pool time.
■ Empty inflatable and wading pools immediately after each use.
■ Place the tamperproof cover over the pool.
■ Remove the steps to an aboveground pool.

Electrical Hazards

■ Keep electrical appliances, including telephone wire, away from the pool or spa.
■ Keep electrical outlets near the pool or spa covered.
■ Use a ground fault circuit interrupter (GFCI) on any appliance that must be near the pool or spa.
■ When possible, use battery-operated appliances.

Other Hazards Around the Pool and Spa

■ Pool slides. The American Academy of Pediatrics recommends that you avoid them.
■ Thunderstorms. Avoid swimming or using the spa during inclement weather, especially thunderstorms.
■ The drain
  ❖ Routinely inspect drain covers to be sure they are in place and are not cracked or missing. A missing, askew, or broken drain can cause serious

injury to children because of its strong suction action. Dual drains are recommended.

- ❖ Equip the drains with anti-vortex covers. (If your are not sure whether you have this kind, consult with a trained pool or spa professional.)
  - — Some states require them for all commercial pools and spas.
  - — Without such covers, a person can be held down under water when her hair, arm, leg, or part of her torso becomes entrapped in the drain.
  - — Do not allow your child in a wading pool unless it is equipped with a securely attached anti-vortex drain cover.
- ❖ Make sure everyone knows where the cutoff switch for the pump is located.
- ❖ Instruct your children to keep away from the drains.
- ❖ All swimmers with long hair should either wear bathing caps or tie up their hair to prevent it from becoming entangled in drain covers.
- ■ The deck
  - ❖ Do not use breakable objects such as glass around the pool or spa area.
  - ❖ Keep the pool deck clear of any objects that children may trip over.
- ■ Supplies: Store pool and spa chemicals and supplies in a locked cabinet. (See Chapter 8)

Other Spa and Hot Tub Precautions

- ■ Anyone sensitive to high temperatures should consult a physician before using a hot tub or spa. These include
  - ❖ pregnant women,
  - ❖ young children,
  - ❖ diabetics,
  - ❖ heart patients, or
  - ❖ anyone taking prescription medicine.
- ■ Watch the temperature.
  - ❖ 104°F or below is the level recommended for your spa by the Consumer Product Safety Commission (CPSC).
  - ❖ Soaking in high water temperatures can elevate body temperature beyond safe limits.
  - ❖ High temperatures can cause
    - — drowsiness,
    - — unconsciousness,
    - — heat stroke, or
    - — death.
  - ❖ Do not soak for more than fifteen minutes at one sitting in 104° F water.
- ■ Keep your spa in good, safe working order with regular professional maintenance.

Be Prepared for an Emergency

- Keep a portable phone at poolside.
  - ❖ You won't need to go away from the pool to answer a telephone call, or waste precious time in an emergency.
  - ❖ Have emergency numbers affixed to that phone.
- Keep rescue equipment near the pool: a life preserver, a ring buoy with line securely attached, and a long handled hook to assist or retrieve a victim from the water.
- Keep first-aid kits on hand.
- Post CPR and rescue instructions in a visible location near the pool.
- Do not wait for paramedics to arrive to begin CPR. Four to six minutes without oxygen can cause permanent brain damage or death.
- Inspect other pools in the neighborhood, as well as those at the homes of relatives or friends that you frequently visit.
  - ❖ Make sure they are properly fenced off and the gates are kept locked.
  - ❖ Forbid your children to swim anywhere without your permission.
- Have your children always wear a U.S. Coast Guard–approved personal flotation device (PFD) when on a boat or playing near natural bodies of water.

Safety at Public Swimming Areas

- Always heed local health department advisories. Never allow your child to swim in any recreational waters that do not meet health standards.
- Allow your child to swim only if there is a lifeguard on duty. However, do not rely on a life guard to personally supervise your child. They have too many children to watch to be able to give one child individual attention.
- Fecal accidents can result in the spread of infectious diseases. Germs such as Cryptosporidium can survive in chlorinated water and E. Coli 0157:H7 bacteria are killed only if the chlorine is at proper levels. If your child accidentally swallows contaminated pool water, he can become infected. These germs can cause stomachaches and diarrhea; in some cases, this can be deadly. It's best to avoid taking your family to wading pools or water parks, where diaper-aged children frequent. However, since "bathroom accidents" can potentially occur in any pool, follow these Center for Disease Control (CDC) safety guidelines to protect your children and family.
  - ❖ Do not allow your child to swim if she has had diarrhea. (She can contaminate the pool water even without having an accident.)
  - ❖ Take extra care to wipe and wash your child's bottom for several weeks after the diarrhea has stopped. (Germs that caused their illness can remain in their feces for several weeks after the diarrhea ends.)
  - ❖ Make sure you and your children bathe or shower with soap and water thoroughly before entering the water.

- ❖ Teach your children not to drink or swallow water from a pool or any recreational waters.
- ❖ Take your children frequently to the bathroom to lessen the chance of a fecal accident in the water.
- ❖ Make sure you and all family members wash their hands thoroughly with soap and water after using the bathroom.
- ❖ Diaper changing should be performed only in the bathroom, never poolside.
- Check to ensure that grates and drain covers are in good repair and are securely in place.

For More Information

CPR courses are available through a number of organizations, such as the American Red Cross, the American Heart Association, or your local fire department or community hospital. For swimming lessons, call your local chapter of the American Red Cross or the YMCA.

To receive the free guides "Children Aren't Waterproof," "Layers of Protection," and "Pool and Spa Emergency Procedures for Swimming Pools and Spas," contact the National Spa and Pool Institute by writing to 2111 Eisenhower Avenue, Alexandria, VA 22314, or by calling (800) 323-3996, or by visiting their website: www.nspi.org.

For the free booklets "Safety Barrier Guidelines for Home Pools" and "Guidelines for Entrapment Hazards: Making Pools and Spas Safer," contact the CPSC by writing to Washington, DC 20207, or by calling (800) 638-2772, or by visiting their website: www.cpsc.gov.

For more information on boating safety, contact the U.S. Coast Guard Boating Safety Information Line by calling (800) 368-5647, or by E-mailing infoline@navcen.uscg.mil, or by visiting their website: www.uscgboating.org. To locate a boating course in your area, contact the Boat US Foundation, 8 A.M.–6 P.M. EST, by calling (800) 336-2628, or by visiting their website: www.boatus.com/courseline.

17

Rules of the Road

Mother used to say:
"It's better to be safe than sorry."

More children in the United States are killed and injured in motor vehicle crashes than from any other cause of injury, but the practice of car-safe behavior can significantly reduce the number of injuries and fatalities. All it takes is one minute to make a difference and save a life. The life you save may be your child's.

Air Bags

We're not talking about a big, soft, fluffy cushion, here. An air bag, which is designed to protect an adult, is forceful when it deploys, and it has a velocity that can crush ribs. Because an air bag inflates at tremendous speed—100 to 200 mph, a force comparable to a prizefighter's punch—a child sitting too close to its path can sustain serious or fatal injuries. Even a low speed crash, a minor "fender bender," can trigger an air bag's deployment. This is by design; the intent is that the bag inflates in any frontal collision when the speed is more than about twelve mph.

Ensure Your Child's Safety
- Never place a rear-facing child seat in the front seat of a car with an active air bag. The back of the car seat is located very close to the dashboard where the air bag is housed. In the event of a crash, the air bag could strike the back of the infant seat very hard, resulting in serious or fatal injuries to the infant's head and brain.
- All children twelve and under should ride in the back seat of the car, according to the National Highway Traffic Safety Administration (NHTSA).
- No matter what age, children should be properly restrained, either in an appropriate car seat or by a seat belt.

Tips for Adults

Adults should not fear using air bags for their own protection. To date, airbags have saved more than 5,000 lives, according to estimates by the NHTSA. Here are some safety tips for their use by adults:

- Be properly belted.
- Keep at least a ten-inch distance between the air-bag cover and your breastbone (17.1).

Child Restraint Systems

In all fifty states and the District of Columbia, state laws require infants and children to ride buckled up in safety seats or seat belts.

Effective Safety Seat Use

- Select a child safety seat that fits your child, your particular car, and is easy to use.
- Child safety seats that are installed and used correctly will provide very effective crash protection for your child, reducing the risk of death
  - by as much as 71 percent for infants (under age one); and
  - by as much as 54 percent for toddlers (ages one to four) (17.2).
- Use it correctly and use it every time you travel, even to drive one block. Most car crashes happen close to home.
- Purchase an infant safety seat (or a convertible car seat) even before the baby is born. You will need to put the baby in the car seat when you drive her home from the hospital.
  - Use an infant seat that is designed for motor vehicles. On any car safety seat you buy look for the DOT label—FMVSS213 (Federal Motor Vehicle Safety Standard 213).
  - Before purchasing, you may have to try several child safety seats to find the one that is most compatible with your car. If you choose a convertible seat, try it facing both rearward and forward.
  - Fill out and mail in the car seat registration form. In case of a safety recall, the manufacturer can contact you.
  - Do not use a household infant carrier as a car seat.
- Buy new.
  - It is highly recommended that you purchase a new child safety seat for your child. If this is not possible, make sure you know the history of the used car

seat. Do not purchase it if it has been in a crash, has been subject to a recall, or is missing parts or the manufacturer's instructions.

❖ Be sure it has no missing parts.

❖ Insist on having the manufacturer's instructions.

❖ Do not use a child safety seat past the wear date set by the manufacturer or if it is more than ten years old.

■ Never hold your child in your arms while traveling in a car. Although a baby doesn't weigh much, a crash impact can pull an infant from a parent's arms with a force of 300 pounds or more (17.3).

■ One person, one safety belt

Using Appropriate Restraints

Age and weight determine whether the child's car seat should face backward or forward. Although age, height, and weight limits on specific products may vary—so that one should always read and follow manufacturer's and vehicle instructions—the general guidelines are as follows:

■ From birth to one year and twenty pounds—use an infant car seat or convertible car seat that *faces the rear*. In this position, the safety seat cushions the infant's large head to reduce the risk of head and cervical spinal cord injuries during a crash or sudden stop. Choose a seat that meets the higher rear-facing weight limit for heavier babies not yet one year of age.

■ Ages one to four years, twenty to forty pounds—use a forward-facing convertible car seat.

■ Ages four to eight years, forty to eighty pounds—use a booster seat, a transition from the forward facing car seat to the adult seat belt.

■ When the child is big enough to fit correctly in the rear lap and shoulder belt alone, he may move from the booster seat. Follow these guidelines to assess proper fit:

❖ The shoulder belt rests snugly across the child's chest and shoulder and does not cross in front of the face or neck. Never allow the child to put the shoulder belt behind her back or under her arm.

❖ The lap belt stays low on the child's upper thighs and doesn't ride up across the abdomen. A belt across the abdomen in a crash can apply a force that could cause serious or fatal injuries.

❖ The child's legs are bent over the edge of the vehicle seat with his feet on the floor (to prevent the child from slouching).

Proper Installation

Eighty percent of children are improperly restrained.

- Check your child's safety seat instruction manual and your vehicle owner's manual for correct installation information. Some vehicles may require supplemental hardware, such as a locking slip or an accessory belt.
- Most newer forward-facing car seats are equipped with a tether strap, an attachment that anchors the top of a car seat to a vehicle to keep it more secure.
- Good news: By September 1, 2002, all new vehicles will be equipped with a universal anchorage system called LATCH (lower anchors and tethers for children).
- To correctly install a child safety seat, the NHTSA recommends these steps:
  - ❖ Place your knee into the seat and lean into it while tightening the belt.
  - ❖ Test to see if the restraint is secure. A child restraint that is not properly secured does not protect your child as well as it could.
  - ❖ Check by firmly pulling the base of the seat (at the belt path) from side to side and forward. The seat should not move more than an inch in any direction (17.4).
- Fasten the child safety seat harness snugly over the child's shoulders. No more than one finger should fit between the harness and the child's body at the collarbone.
- If you need assistance in properly installing your child's safety seat, call the NHTSA's toll-free hot line or your state highway safety office, in the state government listing of your phone book.

Additional Safety Tips

Beware of Flying Objects

Remove all loose objects (boxes on ledges, pencils, books) from inside the car. They could strike you or your child in the event of a sudden stop, swerve, or crash.

Use Headlights All the Time

Other drivers can see your vehicle more quickly when you use your headlights, even in the daytime. In inclement weather, low beam headlights also help you see better. Keep your headlamps and windshield clean.

Learn How to Correctly Use the Antilock Braking System (ABS)

The antilock braking system (ABS) is found in newer vehicles. It works with the regular brakes on your vehicle, automatically controlling braking pressure to prevent wheels from locking during braking. This is important, for when wheels lock, the car will skid. The ABS is activated only when an electronic sensor detects that your wheels are about to lock, such as when the driver slams on the brakes.

- When the ABS activates, there may be a grinding noise, and the brake pedal may pulsate; don't panic when it happens.
- Don't pump the brake pedal.
- Hold your foot firmly on the brake pedal, allowing the system to automatically pump the brakes.
- Steer your vehicle to a safe stop.

Because ABS may be different from the system you are used to, you should receive proper training from your car dealer and practice using ABS in an empty parking lot (17.5).

Regularly Maintain Your Car

- Have your car inspected for safety at least once a year.
- Practice periodic maintenance.

Keep Your Car Doors Locked

- Make sure doors are properly locked before driving. If your car is equipped with safety locks, use them.
  - ❖ Children can easily open the doors and fall out.
  - ❖ Intruders might enter when you slow down or stop your car.
  - ❖ Locked doors are less likely to spring open in a crash.
- When you leave the car, always lock up, even when you have parked in your own driveway.
  - ❖ Children could wander in and get trapped inside. (See Chapter 6 for safety guidelines.)
  - ❖ An intruder might enter and wait for you to return.

Teach Children Not to Lean or Put Hands Out the Window

To ensure that a young child does not lean or put hands out the window—and for security reasons—it's a good idea to keep windows either closed or rolled down only a few inches.

Stay Sober

- Don't drink or take drugs when driving.
- If you take any medication (including over the counter), check with your physician and read the product label and packaging about its potential effects on your driving ability.

Drive Safely

- Stay alert to avoid accidents.
- Drive carefully and defensively.

Don't Talk on the Phone While Driving

Avoid cellular phone conversations while driving. For safety's sake, pull over to the side when using the phone. A recent report on the use of cellular phones while driving reveals a hazardous connection: a four-fold increased risk of having a crash (17.6).

Never Leave Children Alone in a Car

Don't ever leave your children (or pets) alone in a car, even for a minute. Here's why:

- *Heat.* The temperature in the interior of the car quickly soars up to extreme levels, which can cause tragedy.
- *Chance.* Leaving the engine running so that the air conditioner can remain engaged is not safe, either. The child might inadvertently move the car or get burned by the cigarette lighter.
- *Security.* Someone might enter the car and harm the child.

Have the Child Enter and Exit the Car on the Sidewalk Side

Try to keep your children away from the traffic side of the car. When closing the door, make sure precious fingers are not in the way.

Look Behind Your Car Before Backing Up

A small child may be playing behind your car, and you may not be able to see him in your rearview window.

Read Your Entire Car Manual

When you purchase a new car, spend some time reading the car manual. Your car may have safety features of which you are unaware or for which you will need advice on proper operation.

Be a Role Model

Use your safety belt all the time, and practice safe driving. The best way to teach your child is by example. Your child will one day be a teenage driver!

Don't Treat Your Children Like Cargo

More than 200 people die each year as a result of riding in the cargo area of pick-up trucks, and more than half of those who die are children and teenagers. In addition to the obvious hazard of being thrown from the truck—even a child under a truck canopy can be thrown out—there is also the danger of carbon monoxide poisoning from exhaust fumes. The cargo area of a station wagon or a van is also dangerous.

A Busy Child = Calm Parents

During trips in the car, especially on long journeys with your family, it is best for everyone in the car if you can keep the children happily engaged in some fun activities. Bring along coloring books, reading material, soft toys, and games to help keep them amused. Soft foods are helpful too, but avoid foods that cause choking. It is a good idea to stop every hour or so for a stretch break.

Lifesaving Devices to Have in Your Car

- First-aid kit. Keep a fully supplied kit on hand.
- Flashlight equipped with new batteries. Keep it in your glove compartment, not your trunk, so that it is readily available.
- Cellular phone. In an emergency, you can call for help immediately and without ever having to leave the car. There are many affordable phone plans available, as well as corporate plans through your place of employment. Remember to keep the battery charged.
- During colder weather, keep on hand blankets, snowbrush with ice scraper, and nonperishable snacks.
- Jack and inflated spare tire. Check it periodically to make sure it isn't flat. Carry a tire inflater, a device that can be plugged into your car's cigarette lighter to automatically pump air into your tire.
- Jumper cables
- Flares or reflectors
- Spare change
- Can of motor oil
- Basic tool kit
- Center punch. This is a tool that can be used to shatter a car window. Ideally you should open a window as soon as you recognize that your car is heading for water. If your car is submerged in water and you are unable to open the car door or the electric windows, you place the point of the center punch firmly against the car door window and push.
- A twenty-four-hour car emergency service. Keep the card handy in your wallet. Just in case, always let someone know your exact route and anticipated arrival time.

For More Information

For answers about air bags, child safety seats, child safety seat recalls, and a list by zip code of certified passenger safety technicians, contact the NHTSA by calling (800) 424-9393 or (888) DASH-2-DOT [327-4236], or by visiting their website: www.nhtsa.dot.gov.

The American Academy of Pediatrics provides a free shopping guide for child safety seats. You can receive it by writing 141 Northwest Pointe Boulevard, P.O. Box 927, Elk Grove Village, IL 60009-0927 or by visiting their website: www.aap.org.

Contact the National SAFE KIDS Campaign to receive free "SAFE KIDS Buckle Up" materials by calling (800) 441-1888. To attend a General Motors (GM) supported SAFE KIDS child safety seat check up event in your area, at which you can have your car seats checked for correct installation and usage by a child passenger safety specialist, visit their website: www.safekids.org.

Shorter drivers can obtain information about pedal extensions and receive the names of dealers within their geographical area that do conversions. Contact the National Mobility Equipment Dealers Association by writing to 909 E. Skagway Avenue, Tampa, FL 33604, or by calling (813) 932-8566.

Many communities have child safety seat programs. Call your public health department or your local hospital. Your child's pediatrician can provide car safety information as well.

For more information about **drinking and driving,** contact Mothers Against Drunk Driving (MADD), whose personnel are available M–F, 8 A.M.–5 P.M. CST, by writing to P.O. Box 541688, Dallas, TX 75354-1688, or by calling (214) 744-MADD [6233] or (800) 438-6238, or by faxing (792) 869-2206, or by visiting their website: www.madd.org. You may also wish to contact Students Against Destructive Decisions (SADD), which is staffed M–F, 8 A.M.–4 P.M. EST, by writing to P.O. Box 800, Marlboro, MA 01752, or by calling (508) 481-3568 or (toll-free) (877) SADDINC [723-3462], or by visiting their website: www.saddonline.com.

For additional information on **car safety and teen driver safety,** contact your local automobile club affiliated with the American Automobile Association (AAA) Public Relations Department. You may also contact the AAA Foundation for Traffic Safety by writing, 1440 New York Avenue NW, Suite 201, Washington, DC 20005; by calling (202) 638-5944; by faxing (202) 638-5943; or by visiting their website: www.aaafts.org.

18

Hazards in the Community

Mother used to say:
"Cross at the green . . . not in between."

Walking Safely

Children under ten years of age should not cross the street alone. As a general rule, they lack the cognitive skills and judgment that are essential for such an important task.

According to the National SAFE KIDS Campaign, few young children can judge how fast traffic is moving for three basic reasons: (1) their field of vision is one-third that of adults; (2) they cannot tell where sounds come from; and (3) they think cars can stop instantly. Young children don't recognize danger, and, therefore, do not react to it (18.1).

Children are not young adults. They have never driven a motor vehicle and they cannot understand the complexity of streets and roadways (18.2). To add to the danger, the smaller the pedestrians, the less likely it is that drivers can see them. Younger children should be closely supervised at all times. Hold onto your child's hand and teach her never to cross a street without an adult.

Remember that children learn best by example. Teach your child to be street savvy by demonstrating, as well as explaining, the rules of walking safely.

Don't Dart

- Always stop at the curb or the edge of the street and look left, then right, and then left again before crossing.
- Never dart into the street.
- According to the National Highway Traffic Safety Administration (NHTSA), midblock dart-outs are more likely to involve children age nine and under.

Don't Run. Walk Quickly Across the Street, but Do Not Run.

- A child who runs not only risks falling, but also may be more careless—resulting in disobeying safety rules.
- When a child stops first before crossing, the driver has a chance to see him and the child has enough time to look properly for oncoming vehicles.

Cross Only at the Corner or at a Crosswalk. Don't Cross in the Middle of the Block if There is a Designated Crosswalk.

- Wait on the sidewalk or grass until you are ready to cross and look both ways before you take your first step.
- A parent with a stroller must remember to compensate for its length. Because it extends a few feet, one must be extra careful to keep it from sticking out in the path of traffic.

Look in All Directions

- Always look left, right, and left again before crossing any street.
  - ❖ Cross when it is clear.
  - ❖ It's safe to cross when no vehicles are coming in either direction.
- While crossing the street,
  - ❖ continue to look and listen for any approaching vehicles; and
  - ❖ at an intersection, be aware of turning vehicles by checking over your left and right shoulders, as you cross.

Wait till the Traffic Passes

- If a car is coming, wait until it passes.
- Then look left, right, and left again before crossing.

Learn and Follow the Rules

- Understand the meaning of traffic signals, traffic signs, and pavement markings.
- Always obey these important road rules, for they apply to pedestrians as well as motorists.

Always Look!

- It is safest to cross when the "Walk" sign or a green light is illuminated.
- Teach your children that the signal does not mean to automatically cross the street without looking, it is only giving permission to look left, right, and left for any oncoming vehicles.

- The same rules apply to crosswalks with crossing guards. Even then, always look left, right, left, before crossing.
- Never start to cross on a yellow light or flashing "Don't Walk" sign. However, if you have already started to cross when it begins to flash, promptly finish crossing.

Walk on Sidewalks Whenever Possible

- If sidewalks are not available and there is no alternative route, walk facing traffic, but try to stay off the road as much as possible.
- Walk single file.
- Note: Bicycle rules are the opposite. You always ride in the same direction as traffic.

Don't Enter the Street Between Obstacles

- Do not enter the street from between parked cars.
- Do not enter the street from behind any other obstacle, such as bushes or shrubs, without making sure no traffic is approaching.
- Always choose the safest route to walk and the safest place to cross, even if it means going a little out of the way.
- Children, as well as adults, can benefit from a little more exercise.

If a Car Is Parked Where You Are Crossing

- Make sure there is no driver in the car.
- Proceed to the edge of the car and look left, right, left, to see that no cars are coming before crossing (18.3).

Expect the Unexpected

- Don't assume the driver can see you or that she will stop.
- Don't assume that a driver will stop at a crosswalk or when he has a red light.
- Before crossing in front of any vehicle, cross only if you are certain that the driver has actually seen you and only after the vehicle has stopped. NHTSA recommends that you try to make eye contact with the driver.

Weather Alert

- Remember to be extra careful and attentive during bad weather.
- Visibility may be impaired for both the pedestrian and the driver.
- It also may be more difficult for drivers to stop their vehicles in bad weather.

Watch Out for Emergency Vehicles

- When racing to save a life, emergency vehicles such as fire trucks, ambulances, and police cars may need to
  - ❖ drive at high speeds,
  - ❖ go through red lights, or
  - ❖ ignore "the rules of the road."
- Extra care must be taken around these vehicles.
  - ❖ Do not enter the road when you hear a siren.
  - ❖ Do not enter the road if you see an emergency vehicle.
  - ❖ If you are crossing a street and hear a siren, or see an emergency vehicle, move quickly to get out of the way.

Dress to Be Seen

- Children should be dressed in bright or fluorescent colors during the day to make it easier for drivers to see them.
- If a child must be out at night, dress him or her with care.
  - ❖ Attach retroreflective tape to your child's shoes, jacket, backpack, hat, or elsewhere to reflect headlights of cars coming toward him.
  - ❖ Have her carry a flashlight.
  - ❖ Make sure he knows to walk facing traffic.

Practice Makes Perfect

Crossing the street is a learned behavior that takes many years of practice. Children age ten and under should always be supervised when playing outdoors or crossing the street.

When to Trust Your Child to Cross Alone

- The child understands the correct way to cross.
- The child understands the risks.
- The child has repeatedly demonstrated to you that she can safely do so.

Even after you are convinced that all these conditions have been met, set strict guidelines about what streets your child can or cannot cross alone. Teach him not to take risks.

Walking to School or Bus Stop

Should you allow your older child to walk to school or the bus stop without an adult? The answer depends on a variety of factors.

- How far will your child have to walk?
- Is there a safe route available?
- Does she have a buddy who will always accompany her?
- Are there dangerous intersections?
  - ❖ Are there crossing guards present?
  - ❖ Call your school or local police to find out where the crossing guards are stationed and learn the preferred walk route.
- At what hour will he have to leave the house?
- At what time will she be returning from school?
  - ❖ After daylight savings time, it is still very dark in the mornings.
  - ❖ It becomes dark in the late winter afternoons.

If you feel comfortable with allowing your children to walk, take these precautions.

- Accompany them the first several times, both in the morning and the evening.
- So that no child ever walks alone, each child must name a *walking buddy*, a friend who is always with her to and from school or the bus stop.
- Purchase a backpack or schoolbag for school items so that the children's things won't fall out while they walk, especially while crossing a street. Be sure to put retroreflective tape on it to increase your child's visibility.
- Teach your child to be most alert on bad weather days. Make sure she is dressed in clothing that makes her visible to motorists.
- Always accompany your child on those days when his walking buddy can't go.
- Plan safe walk routes to all the places your child will be walking. Remember, however, that a route is only as safe as the person using it.
- Instruct him to always walk on the main sidewalks and not take shortcuts through woods or empty lots.
- Provide her with a whistle to blow if she is in danger.
- Always call the school if your child will be absent, and make sure the school knows how to contact you if he does not show up.

When Playing Outdoors

Make sure your child learns these rules:

- Never play in the street, in driveways, or in parking lots. There are many other fun areas to play, such as your fenced-in backyard, the playground, and the park.
- Never run out into the street chasing a pet, an ice cream truck, or a rolling ball. Even if it is an emergency, you must always look left, right, left, before crossing. Younger children must get an adult to help them cross.

- Do not play behind or between parked cars.
- Know the dangers of strangers. (For more on this subject, see Chapter 19.)
- Invest in a "Children at Play" sign to alert motorists to drive slowly.

For More Information About Walking Safely

Contact the NHTSA by writing to NTS-15, 400 Seventh Street SW, Washington, DC 20590, or by calling (800) 424-9393 or call (888) DASH-2-DOT [327-4236].

For free pedestrian safety pamphlets, contact your local Automobile Club affiliated with the American Automobile Association (AAA) Public Relations Department. You may also contact the public safety department in your area.

Contact the AAA Foundation for Traffic Safety by writing to 1440 New York Avenue NW, Suite 201, Washington, DC 20005 or by visiting their website: www.aaafts.org.

School Bus Safety

Mother used to say:
"It's better to be early than late."

Right again, Mom, especially when it comes to catching the school bus. Here are some guidelines for you and your child, so that the school bus is a convenience, not a tragedy.

At School Bus Stops, There's No Such Thing as "Fashionably Late"

It's always best to arrive a few minutes early (about five minutes) so that your child is not rushed. But don't allow your child to arrive too much earlier, especially if you are not going to wait there with her. Children with extra time on their hands are more likely to engage in horseplay, inviting mishaps. The best procedure is having the parent or other responsible adult wait with the child at the bus stop until the child is safely seated on the bus, especially when the child is under the age of ten. The greatest danger to a child is not in *riding* a school bus but in *approaching* and *leaving* the bus.

The Pupil Transportation Safety Institute reports: "Four out of five children who have been killed in school bus accidents were killed as they were boarding onto or exiting off the bus" (18.4). Since 1987, half of all school-age pedestrians killed in school bus–related crashes were between the ages of five and seven (18.5).

While Waiting

- Everyone should be lined up away from the street as the bus approaches.
- Stand a minimum of at least ten feet (or five giant steps) away from the road.
- Do not run or engage in any horseplay.
- Stay out of the street.

Your child's school district can obtain a stencil of a yellow school bus (or it can be as simple as a painted large rectangle) to be placed at the bus stop where the child should wait. The painted area serves two purposes: (1) in the morning, it shows students exactly where they need to stand to wait for the bus; and (2) in the afternoon, it shows students where to go to wait until the bus drives away.

In addition, your child should be instructed to wait before stepping into the street until the bus has stopped, the red light is flashing, and the driver has signaled for him to enter.

Getting Loaded and Safely Seated

- Always use the bus handrails when entering and exiting.
- Enter and exit by walking in a single file.
- Be polite to the bus driver and other passengers.
  - ❖ Follow the driver's directions.
  - ❖ Use appropriate bus behavior.
    - No screaming
    - No yelling
    - No fighting
    - No throwing things
    - Keep the aisles clear.
- If the bus has seat belts, use them. (If you do not know the proper way to wear them correctly, ask your parent to show you how.)
- Remain seated correctly throughout the entire bus ride.
  - ❖ Keep hands, arms, legs, and head inside the bus.
  - ❖ Don't stick or throw objects out the window.
- Know where emergency exits are located and how to use them correctly.

Exit (Look) Stage Right

- Stay in your seat until bus comes to a complete stop.
- Develop the habit of looking to the right before stepping off the school bus. Sometimes car drivers ignore safety rules and try to slip by the bus on the right.
- Exit from the bus only after it comes to a complete stop.

- Always exercise extreme caution.
- Walk five giant steps away from the bus immediately after getting off.

Don't Get Snagged

Drawstrings, straps, and other parts of clothing can snag or get caught on school bus handles or in the door. Follow these guidelines from the Consumer Product Safety Commission (CPSC) and the NHTSA:

- Remove drawstrings from hoods and necks of children's jackets and sweatshirts.
- Make sure waist or bottom drawstrings measure no more that three inches from where the strings extend out of the garment.
- Recognize that scarves, oversized clothing, or dangling key chains can also be dangerous.
- Be careful that book bags and backpacks don't get caught.

According to the NHTSA, school bus manufacturers have taken steps to remove snagging hazards associated with school bus handrails. Parents should check with the school principal or the local school bus transportation director to see if their children's school bus has been recalled for a handrail problem and if so, whether it has been repaired (18.6).

Be There to Greet Them

A parent or other responsible adult should be at the bus stop in the afternoon before the bus arrives. Wait for the child on the same side of the street as the bus stops. According to "Traffic Safety Facts," there are "[m]ore school-age pedestrians . . . killed in the afternoon than in the morning, with 43 percent of the fatalities occurring in crashes between 3:00 and 4:00 P.M." (18.7). No matter who meets the bus, it is important never to distract the child—with shouted instructions, for example. It is critical that your child personally knows and follows all safety rules.

Stay out of the "Zones"

Children should be taught to stay out of the school bus danger zones. Have your child draw a picture of a bus the way a flying bird would see it. Then draw the danger zones: ten feet (five giant steps) on each side and at the front and back of the bus. Any blind spot that obstructs the bus driver's view should be included in the drawing. Your child should be taught never to walk behind a school bus. The driver will not be able to see her.

Meeting of the Eyes

- If a child must cross the street in front of the bus teach her or him how.
  - ❖ Do so only after the bus has come to a complete stop and its red lights are flashing.

❖ Walk on the sidewalk or along the side of the road to a point at least five giant steps (ten feet) ahead of the bus before crossing.

■ For an extra measure of safety, the Pupil Transportation Safety Institute recommends these tips:

❖ "Teach them to go out far enough in front to see the driver's face and shoulders."

❖ "Eye contact between driver and student is critical during the crossing procedure."

❖ "Children should be taught: I see the Driver, the Driver sees me."

❖ The child should then cross when the driver has signaled that it's safe to cross.

❖ Even then, teach your children to pause at the second headlight before going on to cross the street. They should always remember to stop and look left, right, left, as well as to listen for approaching vehicles before entering the unprotected lanes of the street (18.8).

Some states now require that their new school buses be equipped with a crossing control arm mounted on the front bumper. The arm swings out when children are to cross. Students are required to cross in front of the arm. The edicts "I see the driver and the driver sees me" and "Proceed with caution" apply here, as well.

If It Drops, Leave It There

Teach your child that if she drops something near the bus, she should not pick it up. The driver may not see her. Tell her to tell the bus driver and then follow his instructions. The child should never get the object without the driver's knowledge. Even if the bus runs it over, your children must understand that you can always replace a lunch box, pencil case, or any other item but you can't replace them! If your child can't get the driver's attention, tell her to get a teacher or a parent. It's a good idea to put all your child's things into a backpack or schoolbag. That way he won't be dropping things along the way.

Stay Put

Children who don't have to cross the street after exiting the school bus should be taught not to play or run but to stay put on the sidewalk until the bus has driven away.

Don't Dress in Yellow

Especially during inclement weather when visibility is impaired, it is best to dress your child in bright colors, but not yellow. It will blend in with the school bus.

For More Information About School Bus Safety

Contact your local school district or state director of pupil transportation. Or contact the NHTSA by calling their auto safety hot line at (800) 424-9393, or (888) DASH-2-DOT [327-4236] or by visiting their website: www.nhtsa.dot.gov. Visit the NHTSA "Safety City" site with your children for fun learning activities on pedestrian and school bus safety.

To order a bus stencil or other school bus safety materials, contact the Pupil Transportation Safety Institute by writing to 443 W. Warren Street, Syracuse, NY 13202, or by calling (800) 836-2210, or by visiting their website: www.ptsi.org.

Shopping-Cart Safety

Most parents conveniently use shopping carts to wheel their young children around the supermarket or department store. What you may not realize is that this practice can have serious consequences. According to the CPSC, falls from shopping carts are among the leading causes of head injuries to young children treated in hospital emergency rooms. Every year in this country, an average of 21,600 children ages five and under are treated in emergency rooms for shopping-cart injuries. The serious types of injuries that can result are concussions, fractures, contusions, lacerations, and internal injuries.

Most injuries to children result from them standing up, climbing, and falling out of shopping carts. Moreover, a cart has a relatively narrow wheelbase compared to its height. This factor increases the risk of it's tipping over. To make matters worse, when the child does fall, it is onto a cold, hard floor.

To ensure your child's safety and prevent falls from shopping carts, follow these safety tips.

- Inspect the cart for any defects before using it.
- Use a safety belt to keep your child restrained. If none are available at the store, purchase your own and bring it with you.
- Stay in control of the cart at all times.
  - Never leave the cart.
  - Watch your child closely. A child can find a way out of the cart in a matter of seconds.
  - Do not allow another child to push or steer the cart.
  - Watch what the child touches in the cart.
    — Juices from raw meats or poultry may have leaked onto the cart before you entered the store. (See Chapter 3 under "The Good Guy: Vigilance with Groceries.")
    — Clean the handles before you put your child into the cart.

- Teach your child not to stand up in the cart. Explain to the child how easily the cart can tip over.
  - ❖ Do not allow the child to climb into or out of the cart.
  - ❖ Do not allow a child to ride on the outside of the cart.
- Avoid using an infant carrier seat that is attached to the top of the shopping cart. According to an article in *Pediatrics* (18.9), "The weight of the child and carrier seat contribute to a high center of gravity and exacerbate the tip-over potential of the cart. . . ."

For More Information on Shopping Carts

Contact the CPSC by writing to Washington, DC 20207, or by calling (800) 638-2772, or by visiting their website: www.cpsc.gov.

19

The Street-Smart Kid

Mother used to say:
"Never talk to strangers . . . even if he offers
to take you to Palisades Park!"

When I was growing up, Palisades Amusement Park was the best place in the world for fun. So I knew Mom was serious about not talking to strangers! By the time I was three, Mom had begun to teach me what a stranger was. Here's the way she explained it:

A stranger is a person we don't know very well. He or she doesn't have to look scary or be mean. In fact, some strangers are very good looking and nice. They deliver mail to our home, work in the bank, and live down the street.

A stranger is different from a friend. We know friends very well and we trust them. When we don't know people well, we call them strangers. Most of them won't try to harm us, but we can't always tell the bad guys from the good guys. We just can't tell by looking. That's why, to protect yourself, you must stay away from anyone who is not a trusted friend.

Knowing that a definition alone may not be useful to a child, my mom gave me some guidelines:

- Never talk to a stranger.
- Never approach a stranger's car or drive with a stranger in her car.
- Always walk on the sidewalk in the direction facing traffic so that a vehicle can't approach undetected from behind.
- Never take anything from a stranger without permission.
  - Money
  - Candy
  - Gifts
  - Nothing!

These days, it's not that simple. Our children need to know more about protecting themselves, especially because most abductors are known as friends to the child. There are other skills that the street smart child should know.

- Identification
  - ❖ The goal is to memorize.
    - —First and last name
    - —Complete address, including city and state
    - —Phone number, including area code
  - ❖ For younger children, start with simpler information.
    - —At least the first digits of your address
    - —Street name
    - —Color of your house
- Telephone—demonstrate and practice with your child these concepts:
  - ❖ Know what constitutes an emergency.
  - ❖ Know how to use the phone.
    - —Know how to dial local and long-distance calls.
    - —Know how to dial 911 or 0 for emergencies.
    - —Know how to make a collect call.
  - ❖ Know that no money is needed for these calls:
    - —911 calls
    - —Collect calls
- Have a password.
  - ❖ Don't go anywhere with anyone without your parents' permission, unless the person coming for you knows the family password.
    - —Even if someone tells the child she must come along because her parent is in the hospital, she should ask for the family password.
    - —If the person doesn't know the password, the child should *not* go with him!
  - ❖ Practice the password.
    - —Periodically review the family password.
    - —Make sure the child has not told anyone your password.
    - —Practice situations so that the child understands the kinds of circumstances in which a stranger who doesn't know the password might be persuasive.
- Have an authorized pickup list.
  - ❖ Give your child's school a list of people who are authorized to pick him up from school.
  - ❖ Tell your child who those people are.
  - ❖ Make sure the school checks driver's licenses before releasing your child.

- Don't advertise your child's name to strangers.
  - ❖ Don't put your child's name on the outside of his clothing.
  - ❖ Don't put your child's name on the outside of her possessions.
- Teach your child the tricks abductors may use.
  - ❖ Some lines an abductor might use.
    - — "I'm lost. Can you tell me how to get to . . . ?"
    - — "I have a neat game over here. Would you like to play?"
    - — "I'd like to take your picture. All you have to do is smile."
    - — "I'd like to take a video of you. Just act natural."
    - — "I've lost my puppy. Will you help me find him?"
    - — "Are you having a problem? Here, let me help you."
    - — "Would you like some candy?"
    - — "I have this toy that I'll bet is just right for you. Would you like to have it?"
  - ❖ What the child should do.
    - — Get the parent or another trusted adult if any of these things happen.
    - — Never get close to the stranger or her car.
- Teach your child when to scream and make a scene.
  - ❖ If someone tries to pull a child into a car or building for example, that's when he should scream and make a scene.
  - ❖ In this situation, it's OK to get assistance from a stranger who can help the child get out of danger.
- In public places, stay with trusted faces.
  - ❖ Never let a small child out of your sight.
  - ❖ Teach children not to run, walk, or even hide from their parents in public places.
  - ❖ Because children don't always follow instructions, prepare in advance.
    - — Point out and identify specific people the child can ask for help.
      - • In a grocery store, the person wearing the store uniform (point out the color)
      - • In the mall, a police officer or security officer
    - — Teach the child to stay put if lost from you.
      - • Wait for you.
      - • Don't come looking for you, because you are on the way to get him.
      - • If someone offers to help, your child should ask the person to call or get the police or security officer (19.1).
- Establish a central meeting place for older children.
  - ❖ If you get separated from each other, both of you know to go there.
  - ❖ Examples: a specific information desk in the mall; a store manager's office.

- Use the buddy system: there's safety in numbers.
  - ❖ Your child should always play, walk, and travel with a buddy.
  - ❖ Especially do not allow your child to go alone to video arcades, public rest rooms, parks, malls, or movie theaters.
- Go door to door together.
  - ❖ Accompany your child going door to door to sell items or collect money— even in your own neighborhood, where you think you know everyone.
    — Paper route
    — Fund-raising campaign for school or for a religious organization
  - ❖ Halloween is no exception.
    — Accompany your young child to the door of every house she visits. (Anyway, you don't want to miss seeing the look of enjoyment on her face!)
    — Set these limits for older children (in their teens).
      - Go trick or treating in a group.
      - Stop only at familiar homes.
      - Go only to homes with an outside light on.
      - Never go inside any home.
    — All children should wait to eat candy until a parent has inspected it.
      - Allow them to eat only treats that are unopened, in original wrappers.
      - Throw out all homemade treats.
    — Follow these general safety tips.
      - Wear nontoxic makeup instead of a mask, which can obstruct vision or restrict breathing.
      - Put retroreflective tape on costumes or on bags.
      - Wear wigs, beards, and costumes that are flame resistant. Do not allow children to wear loose-fitting, 100 percent cotton homemade costumes.
      - Wear a costume short enough that it won't cause one to trip.
      - Wear well-fitted, sturdy shoes.
      - Stay on well-lighted streets.
      - Carry a flashlight.
- Teach children to trust their instincts.
  - ❖ Teach your child that if something or someone doesn't look or seem quite right, it's always best to avoid that situation or person. Walk away.
  - ❖ Never berate your child in public when he avoids someone he "feels bad" about. (Explore the subject with him quietly, later.)
- Know where your child is. Know when he will return.
- Get to know the parents of all your children's friends and have their phone numbers and addresses on hand.

- Teach children to ask permission.
  - ❖ A child must learn to always ask permission before going anywhere with anyone (friends and relatives included).
    - —Ask even if it is to run next door for just a second to see the new puppy.
    - —Ask even if the plans change only slightly.
  - ❖ Always check first with a parent; that's the rule!
- Children should know what is private.
  - ❖ Teach your child what parts of the body are private—those covered by the bathing suit.
    - —Except for the pediatrician, with a parent in the room, or a parent or caregiver washing them in the bath or wiping them on the potty, no one should touch them in those areas.
    - —They should not touch another person in those areas, either.
  - ❖ Teach your child to tell a trusted adult immediately if anyone, even a teacher or close relative, touches her in a way that makes her feel uncomfortable.
  - ❖ No secrets—teach your child to tell a parent if any adult asks her to keep a secret (19.2).
- Have important information on hand.
  - ❖ Carry a current photograph.
    - —This is the single most important tool for recovering a missing child (19.3).
    - —The National Center for Missing and Exploited Children recommends taking a color photo every six months.
  - ❖ Have other important data ready and available.
    - —Up-to-date dental and medical records
    - —Videotape of the child
    - —Complete description of the child
    - —Fingerprints
    - —DNA kit

The Baby-Sitter

- Choose a baby-sitter carefully.
  - ❖ Get recommendations from friends, relatives, clerics, doctors, and neighbors.
  - ❖ Interview potential sitters.
    - —Make sure the sitter is at least thirteen years old.
    - —Make sure the sitter is mature enough to handle common emergencies.
    - —Be certain the sitter has had first-aid training and knows cardiopulmonary resusitation (CPR).

—If you like a potential sitter who has not had such training, recommend that he take a baby-sitter training course at a local hospital or safety organization (such as the Red Cross).

❖ Check references thoroughly.

■ Instruct the baby-sitter.

❖ Give the sitter a tour of your home.

—Point out and demonstrate how to use all safety devices you have installed (gates, latches, locks).

—Show the sitter where you store supplies, such as a flashlight, first-aid kit, fire extinguisher.

—Identify those areas of your home that are off limits to your children (and the sitter).

❖ Give the sitter this book to read.

❖ Instruct the sitter to put the baby on his back to sleep.

❖ Make sure the sitter knows that she should never shake an infant or child.

❖ Give specific guidelines (discuss and *write them down*).

—Discuss any special medical needs or medicine the child needs to take.

• Explain dosage.

• The sitter should never give the child any medicine without your permission and instructions.

—Specify foods the child eats or shouldn't eat.

—Explain any allergies the child has.

—Set the child's bedtime or nap time.

—Discuss any bedtime rituals.

—Point out TV/video/books the child may watch or read.

—Introduce favorite toys.

❖ Spell out guidelines you have for the sitter herself.

—No friends are allowed.

—No smoking is allowed in the house.

—The sitter should spend limited time on the phone.

—No cooking

—No one is allowed to use the pool or spa.

—Never leave the child alone—not even for a second.

—I always made sure my sitters understood that they should never hesitate to call or beep me for any questions they had—even if it was minor or appeared silly; I encouraged and welcomed it.

■ Check up.

❖ While away, check in to see how everything is going.

- ❖ At home, observe how the baby-sitter interacts with your children.
- ❖ After the sitter has gone home, ask the children how they feel about the sitter.
- ▪ Give these parting instructions to older children staying alone (and to baby-sitters).
  - ❖ Keep the doors and windows locked.
  - ❖ Never tell a caller you are at home alone.
  - ❖ Never open the door to let anyone (even a friend) into the house unless you have permission first.
  - ❖ (Even when I'm at home, no one opens the door to let anyone in unless I say so.)
  - ❖ Know the emergency plan.
    — Go to the designated neighbor if there is a problem.
    - Someone who is trusted by the family
    - Someone who is almost always at home (such as a new mom or an elderly person)
    — Never enter your home if, upon arrival, a door or window is open or there are any signs that the house has been disturbed.
    - Go to the trusted neighbor's home.
    - Call the police.
  - ❖ Be aware of the emergency information posted by the telephone. (See Appendix A for emergency numbers that should be posted.)

Let's Talk

Every night at bedtime, I spend several moments with each of my children, talking with them about things that happened at school that day or anything else they want to chat about. I have taught them that even if they feel embarrassed, ashamed, or afraid about something—anything—they need to tell me or Dad. We have emphasized that no matter what, we will always love them and will help them get through any problem or situation.

Keep the communication lines open with your child, and be there to really listen to them . . . throughout their lives.

For More Information

For information about crime prevention or to receive a variety of educational materials featuring McGruff the Crime Dog, contact the National Crime Prevention Council by writing to 1000 Connecticut Avenue NW, Second Floor, Washington, DC 20036, or by calling (202) 466-6272, or by visiting their website: www.ncpc.org. Parents and children can visit McGruff's website: www.mcgruff.org. If you want McGruff to visit your child's school, contact your local police precinct.

Publications addressing various aspects of the missing and exploited child issue are available free of charge in single copies from the National Center for Missing and Exploited Children. Their hot line for receiving information on missing and exploited children is open twenty-four hours per day. Contact them by writing to Charles B. Wang International Children's Building, 699 Prince Street, Alexandria, VA 22314-3175, or by calling: (800) THE-LOST [843-5678] or (703) 274-3900, or by faxing (703) 274-2222, or by visiting their website: www.missingkids.com.

For information on the Kidguard Safety Program and where you can get free photo ID cards, fingerprinting, and safety rules, contact Child Watch of North America. This organization maintains a twenty-four-hour toll-free line for information on missing children and inquiries from searching parents. Child Watch also actively searches for missing children with licensed investigators, free of charge. Contact them by writing to 7380 Sand Lake Road, Suite 500, Orlando, FL 32819, or by calling (407) 290-5100 or hot line (888) CHILDWATCH [244-5392], or by faxing (407) 290-1613, or by visiting their website: www.childwatch.org.

Child Find of America can help when children are missing or have been abducted by a parent. Call (800) 426-5678 (M–F, 9 A.M.–4 P.M. EST) to locate missing children or (800) 292-9688 (M–F, 9 A.M.–4 P.M. EST) for parental abduction mediation.

For a free copy of the brochure *A Parent's Guide to the Internet*, which will inform you about ensuring your child's safety on the Internet, call the U.S. Department of Education at (800) USA-LEARN [872-5327]. It is also available on their website: www.ed/gov/pubs/parent/internet/.

For a free copy of the brochures "Teen Safety on the Information Highway" and "Child Safety on the Information Highway," call the National Center for Missing and Exploited Children at (800) 843-5678.

Free baby-sitter pamphlets are also available. "The Super Sitter" is provided by the U.S. Consumer Product Safety Commission (CPSC). "Just in Case: Parental Guidelines in Case You Need a Baby-Sitter" is provided by the National Center for Missing and Exploited Children.

For information about child care and help in locating child-care resource and referral agencies closest to your home, contact Child Care Aware. Contact them by writing to 1319 F Street, Suite 810, Washington, DC 20004, or by calling (800) 424-2246, or by visiting their website: www.naccrra.net.

For information about baby-sitter training, contact your local Red Cross chapter by visiting their website: www.redcross.org.

Appendix A
Form for Emergency Numbers

Use this form to collect all emergency numbers for use in your home. In a crisis, it should be handy for you or anyone staying in your home to use. Post it near your telephone.

Emergency	911 or 0
Police	_____
Fire Department	_____
Ambulance	_____
Pediatrician	_____
Family doctor	_____
Poison Control Center	_____
Pharmacy	_____
Dentist	_____

Information to Give in an Emergency

Child's name: _____

Date of birth: _____

Weight: _____

Allergies: _____

Current medications: _____

Medical conditions: _____

Home address (include all cross-streets so that directions can be given)

_____

_____

Home phone number _____

How to Reach Family Members

Work numbers for Mom _____ Work numbers for Dad _____

_____ _____

(include beeper numbers and cellular phone numbers)

Nearest relative or neighbor _____

Appendix B
Federal Agencies
for Panic-Proof Help

CDC–Centers for Disease Control and Prevention

Contact the CDC by writing—1600 Clifton Road, Atlanta, GA 30333—or by visiting their website at www.cdc.gov. Hot lines and addresses vary with topic. For general information call (800) 311-3435. Operators are on duty M–F 8 A.M.–4:30 P.M. EST.

CPSC–Consumer Product Safety Commission

The CPSC protects the public from unreasonable risk of injury or death from 15,000 types of consumer products under the agency's jurisdiction. To report a dangerous product, a product-related injury, to obtain product safety information, and for information on CPSC's fax-on-demand service, call CPSC's hot line at (800) 638-2772 or CPSC's teletypewriter at (800) 638-8270. To order a press release through fax-on-demand, call (301) 504-0051 from the handset of your fax machine and enter the release number. You can visit CPSC's website: www.cpsc.gov. You can report product hazards to info@cpsc.gov. CPSC operators are on duty M–F 8:30 A.M.–5 P.M. EST.

EPA–Environmental Protection Agency

Contact the EPA by writing—401 M Street SW, Washington, DC 20460. For EPA directory assistance, call (202) 260-2090. Operators are on duty M–F 8 A.M.–6 P.M. EST.

Specific EPA hot lines and addresses vary with topic. You may order EPA publications by writing—U.S. EPA/NSCEP, P.O. Box 42419, Cincinnati, OH 45242-2419—or by calling (800) 490-9198. The international number is (513) 489-8190. You may also send a fax to (513) 489-8695 or E-mail to ncepi.mail@epamail.epa.gov. The website is www.epa.gov. To order online: www.epa.gov/ncepihom/.

FEMA is an independent federal agency that works to reduce risks from disasters and helps victims recover. To order FEMA publications, call (800) 480-2520; operators are available M–F 8 A.M.–5 P.M. EST. For more information about FEMA, visit their website: www.fema.gov.

FDA—Food and Drug Administration

You may contact the FDA's Food Information Line by writing—FDA's Center for Food Safety and Applied Nutrition Outreach and Information Center, Consumer Education Staff (HFS-555), 200 C Street SW, Room 5809, Washington, DC 20204—or by calling (888) SAFEFOOD [332-4010] or (202) 205-4314 for twenty-four-hour recorded information. The line is staffed M–F 12 noon–4 P.M. EST. The FDA website is www.cfsan.fda.gov. To request further information from the FDA on other topics, contact the FDA by writing—FDA (HFE-88), 5600 Fishers Lane, Rockville, MD 20857—or by calling (888) INFO-FDA [463-6332].

NHTSA—National Highway Traffic Safety Administration

You may write to NHTSA, 400 Seventh Street SW, Washington, DC 20590. The NHTSA auto safety hot line is (800) 424-9393 or (888) DASH-2-DOT [327-4236]. The line is staffed M–F 8 A.M.–10 P.M. EST. Their E-mail address is webmaster@nhtsa.dot.gov; their website is www.nhtsa.dot.gov.

USDA—U.S. Department of Agriculture

Contact the USDA by writing—Food Safety Education Staff, Room 2932, South Building, 1400 Independence Avenue SW, Washington, DC 20250—or by calling the Meat and Poultry Hot Line: (800) 535-4555 or (202) 720-3333 for recorded information twenty-four hours a day, every day. The line is staffed M–F 10 A.M.–4 P.M. EST. The USDA website is www.usda.gov/fsis; the E-mail address for Food Safety and Inspection Services (FSIS) is mphotline.fsis@usda.gov. Fax is (212) 720-1843. For general information, write—U.S. Department of Agriculture, Fourteenth and Independence Avenue SW, Washington, DC 20250—or call (202) 720-2791 M–F 8:30 A.M.–5 P.M. EST, or visit their website, www.usda.gov.

Appendix C
Common Poisonous Plants

Do not assume that if a particular plant does not appear on this list that it is safe. This is not an all-inclusive list. Call your local poison control center to be sure. Personnel there can provide you with a list of common poisonous plants in your area.

Angel's Trumpet (*Datura meteloides*)
Autumn Crocus (*Colchicum autumnale*)
Azalea (*Rhododendron*)
Black Locust (*Robinia pseudoacacia*)
Caladium (*Caladium*)
Castor Bean (*Ricinus communis*)
Choke Cherry (*Prunus virginiana*)
Climbing Nightshade (*Solanum dulcamara*)
Daffodil (*Narcissus*)
Daphne (*Daphne mezereum*)
Deadly Nightshade (*Atropa belladonna*)
Deadly Nightshade (*Solanum dulcamara*)
Dumbcane (*Dieffenbachia*)
Elephant Ear (*Colocasia esculenta*)
English Ivy (*Hedera helix*)
Foxglove (*Digitalis purpurea*)
Hyacinth (*Hyacinthus orientalis*)
Hydrangea (*Hydrangea macrophylla*)
Iris (*Iris*)
Jack-in-the-Pulpit (*Arisaema triphyllum*)
Jimson Weed (*Datura stramonium*)

Lantana (*Lantana camara*)
Larkspur (*Delphinium*)
Lily-of-the-Valley (*Convallaria majalis*)
Mayapple (*Podophyllum peltatum*)
Monkshood (*Aconitum napellus*)
Morning Glory (*Ipomoea*)
Mountain Laurel (*Kalmia latifolia*)
Oleander (*Nerium oleander*)
Philodendron (*Philodendron*)
Poison Hemlock (*Conium maculatum*)
Pokeweed (*Phytolacca americana*)
Privet (*Ligustrum vulgare*)
Rhododendron (*Rhododendron*)
Rosary Pea (*Abrus precatorius*)
Sweet Pea (*Lathyrus odoratus*)
Virginia Creeper (*Parthenocissus quinquefolia*)
Water Hemlock (*Cicuta maculata*)—most toxic U.S. plant
Wisteria (*Wisteria*)
Yew (*Taxus*)

Holiday Plants

Christmas Rose (*Helleborus niger*)
Holly (*Ilex*)
Jerusalem Cherry (*Solanum pseudocapsicum*)
Mistletoe (*Phoradendron flavescens*)
Mistletoe (*Viscum album*)

Vegetable Garden Plants

Potato sprouts (*Solanum tuberosum*)
Rhubarb leaves (*Rheum rhaponticum*)
Tomato leaves (*Lycopersicon esculentum*)

Appendix D
Baby Food Basics

Checking Out the Packaging

- At the store before purchasing and again before using at home, check the "use by" date for cans and jars of infant formula and food.
- Do not use a commercial baby food product if the jar lid doesn't "pop" when opened, or when it is not sealed safely.
- Discard jars with chipped glass or rusty lids.
- Wash the lids of formula, juices, and foods before opening.

Feeding Your Baby

- Solid food may be introduced to babies after four to six months of age, but a baby should drink breast milk or formula, not cow's milk, for the first full year of life.
- Neither skim milk nor low-fat milk is recommended in the first two years of life.
- Discuss with your pediatrician specific feeding guidelines. Wash your hands thoroughly before beginning formula or food preparation.
- Discuss with your pediatrician the need to use bottled water or to sterilize water when mixing formula. (See Chapter 4.)
- Carefully follow the manufacturer's recommendations precisely when mixing water and formula.
- To warm a bottle from the refrigerator, heat bottles in a pan of hot, not boiling, water for a few minutes. Do not use the microwave. A bottle warmed in the microwave oven heats unevenly, and even after shaking, it may have hot spots that can burn your child's mouth.
- If you choose to use the microwave, use extreme caution when warming up bottles, beverages, and food for your child. (Carefully follow the steps outlined in Chapter 7 under "Microwave Safety.") Do not use the microwave to heat bottles with disposable inserts, meats, meat sticks, eggs, or jars of food.

■ After heating, but before feeding the baby, always shake the bottle and test the temperature on your inner wrist; stir and taste test the food to see if it's lukewarm. Don't use the same spoon to test the food that will be used to feed your baby. Even your saliva contains bacteria and viruses.

■ Avoid feeding directly from a jar unless you will be finishing all of it right then. Put a small amount in a clean bowl and feed your child from the bowl.

■ After feeding, discard any uneaten food in a dish, and any liquid left over in a bottle. Bacteria from the baby's saliva can contaminate the remaining food or liquid, allowing it to grow and multiply even after refrigeration and reheating.

■ Prior to first use, sterilize new bottles, nipples, and rings.

■ After each use, clean reusable bottles, bottle caps, bottle nipples, and other utensils by washing in a dishwasher or by washing in hot tap water with dishwashing detergent and rinsing in hot water. If the water is from a well and/or nonchlorinated, utensils should be sterilized before use. (See Chapter 4 and consult your pediatrician.)

Safe Storage of Baby Food

■ Store unopened baby food and formula in a dry, cool area.

■ Refrigerate or freeze leftovers. Do not leave baby food solids or liquids out at room temperature for more than one hour. (The guideline for food safety is usually two hours, but with infant's food, one hour is recommended by many experts for safety's sake.)

  ❖ Affix a label with a date on the baby's food so that you can keep track of the original opening date.

  ❖ Follow manufacturer's recommendations for storing, listed on the products' labels.

Liquids

  ❖ Formula
- Refrigerate for two days (keep covered).
- Freezing is not recommended.

  ❖ Whole Milk
- Refrigerate for five days.
- Freeze for three months.

Solids—Opened or Freshly Made

■ Store unused baby food in the original jar with a tightly closed lid.

■ Check with the product's manufacturer to find out whether freezing their particular product is recommended.

- Follow these general guidelines.
  - Strained fruits and vegetables
    - Refrigerate for two to three days.
    - Freeze for six to eight months.
  - Strained meats and eggs
    - Refrigerate for one day.
    - Freeze for one to two months.
  - Meat/vegetable combinations
    - Refrigerate for one to two days.
    - Freeze for one to two months.
  - Homemade baby foods
    - Refrigerate for one to two days.
    - Freeze for three to four months.

The following information on storing human milk comes from La Leche League.

Storing Human Milk

The milk you express from your breasts for your baby is a precious fluid. It combines the best possible nutrition with antibodies, live cells, and other substances that protect babies from infection and help them grow and develop. When you make the effort to provide expressed milk for your baby for the times you can't be there for breast-feedings, you ensure that your baby continues to receive ideal nourishment and protection against allergies and disease.

You'll want to take good care of the milk you pump or hand-express. Think of it as a fresh, living substance—not just a food. How you store it will affect how well its nutritional and anti-infective qualities are preserved.

Human milk's anti-bacterial properties actually help it stay fresh longer. The live cells and antibodies in the milk that discourage the growth of bacteria in your baby's intestines also guard against bacterial growth when the milk is stored in a container.

The guidelines that follow apply to milk that will be given to full-term healthy babies.

Containers for Storage

You can use either hard-sided containers for storing milk or plastic bags. Hard-sided containers, either glass or plastic, do the best job of protecting the milk. Plastic milk storage bags, designed for freezing human milk, offer convenience and take up less room in the freezer.

The glass or plastic container should have a top that fits well. Containers should be washed in hot, soapy water, rinsed well, and allowed to air-dry before use. Don't fill them right up to the top—leave an inch of space to allow the milk to expand as it freezes.

Milk storage bags can be attached directly to a breast pump, so that mothers can collect and store milk in the same container. Some mothers use the disposable plastic nurser bags designed for bottle-feeding to store their milk. These are less durable and are not designed for long-term storage. They may burst or tear, but double-bagging can help prevent accidents. With either kind of bag, squeeze out the air at the top before sealing, and allow about an inch for the milk to expand when frozen. Stand the bags in another container on the refrigerator shelf or in the freezer.

Put only two to four ounces of milk in each container, the amount your baby is likely to take in a single feeding. This avoids waste. Small quantities are also easier to thaw. You can add fresh milk to a container of frozen milk as long as there is less fresh milk than frozen. Cool the fresh milk for 30 minutes in the refrigerator before pouring it on top of the frozen milk in the freezer.

Be sure to label every container of milk with the date it was expressed. If the milk will be given to your baby in a day-care setting, also put your baby's name on the label.

How Long to Store Human Milk

Whenever possible, babies should get milk that has been refrigerated, not frozen. Some of the anti-infective properties are lost when the milk is frozen—though frozen milk still helps protect babies from disease and allergies and is much better for your baby than artificial formula.

How long you can store milk depends on the temperature. Follow the guidelines in this table.

Where	Temperature	Time
At room temperature	66–72°F (19–22°C)	10 hours
In a refrigerator	32–39°F (0–4°C)	8 days
In a freezer compartment inside a refrigerator	Temperature varies	2 weeks
In a freezer compartment with a separate door	Temperature varies	3–4 months
In a separate deep freeze	0°F (–19°C)	6 months or longer

Previously frozen milk that has been thawed can be kept in the refrigerator for up to twenty-four hours. Thawed milk should not be refrozen. It is not known whether human milk left in the bottle after a feeding can be safely kept until the next feeding or if it should be discarded, as is the case with infant formula. Recent studies have shown that human milk actually retards the growth of bacteria, so it may be safe to refrigerate unused milk for later use.

Expressed human milk can be kept in a common refrigerator at the workplace or at a day care center. Both the U.S. Centers for Disease Control and the U.S. Occupational Safety and Health Administration agree that human milk is not among the body fluids that require special handling or storage in a separate refrigerator.

To keep expressed milk cool when a refrigerator is not available, place it in an insulated container with an ice pack. It's a good idea to use ice and an insulated container when transporting milk home from the workplace or to the baby-sitter's, especially on warm days.

Using Stored Milk

- Human milk may separate into a milk layer and a cream layer when it is stored. This is normal. Shake it gently before giving it to the baby to redistribute the cream.
- Human milk should be thawed and heated with care. Just as freezing destroys some of the immune properties of the milk, high temperatures can also affect many of the beneficial properties of the milk.
- Frozen milk: Containers should be thawed under cool running water. Gradually increase the temperature of the water to heat the milk to feeding temperature. Or immerse the container in a pan of water that has been heated on the stove. Take the milk out and rewarm the water if necessary. The milk itself should not be heated directly on the stove.
- Refrigerated milk: Warm the milk under warm running water for several minutes. Or immerse the container in a pan of water that has been heated on the stove. Do not heat the milk directly on the stove.
- Do not use a microwave oven to heat human milk. If the milk gets too hot, many of its beneficial properties will be lost. In general, milk for babies should not be heated in the microwave. Because microwaves do not heat liquids evenly, there may be hot spots in the container of milk, and this can be dangerous for infants.

For more information on breast-feeding or to find a breast-feeding support group near you, contact La Leche League International, which has personnel on duty M–F, 8 A.M.–5 P.M. EST, by writing to 1400 North Meacham Road, Schaumburg, IL 60173-4840, or by calling (800) LA-LECHE [525-3243], or by visiting their website: www.lalecheleague.org.

Appendix E
Shopper's Guide to Essential Safety Devices and Gear

These items can be purchased at hardware stores, baby equipment stores, and supermarkets and can be ordered from mail-order companies. Make sure all these items are properly and carefully installed and are well maintained. Please check them frequently. Remember, use of a child safety device does not mean that the item is completely childproof. Proper supervision is always required.

Food Safety

- Vegetable scrub brush
- Food thermometer
  - Large dial (for testing whole poultry and roasts during cooking)
  - Digital instant read (for use toward end of cooking time for beef patties)
- Appliance thermometers for refrigerator and freezer (Set your refrigerator temperature at 40°F or below and the freezer at 0°F.)

Preventing Choking, Suffocation, and Strangulation

- Small parts tester
- Safety tassels or tie-down devices for drapery or window blind cords
- Cord shorteners to eliminate excess electrical cords

Fire Safety

- Smoke detectors (for installation on every level of the home, in every sleeping area, and in the furnace room)
- Flame-resistant sleepwear for your children (check label)
- Multipurpose fire extinguishers (for kitchen, basement, and workshop area)
- Noncombustible escape ladder (Make sure it supports the heaviest person in the home.)

Preventing Electrocution

- Ground-fault circuit interrupters (GFCIs)
- Outlet covers and plates (for installation throughout the home)
- Cover for computer's surge protector
- Hair dryers with built-in shock protection

Preventing Burns

- Antiscald devices (Also, set water heater at 120°F or below.)
- Guards on stove knobs
- Appliance lock for microwave
- Oven-door lock
- Spill-resistant mug for hot beverages

Preventing Falls and Cushioning Them

- Window guards (For fire exits, install guards equipped with a quick-release mechanism.) Check local fire codes.
- Safety gates (for top and bottom of stairs)
- Power-failure night-lights (for installation in bedroom, hallways, stairways, and bathrooms)
- Corner and edge bumpers (for installation on all sharp edges)
- Nonskid backing on all rugs
- Rubber suction bath mat
- Grab bars for bath and shower
- Angle braces or anchors to secure furniture to wall
- Cushioned spout cover for bathtub
- Automatic garage-door openers
    - ❖ Autoreverse feature
    - ❖ Photoelectric sensor or door edge sensor
- Cushioning for under playground equipment
    - ❖ Hardwood fiber, mulch, pea gravel, or sand (enough for depth of twelve inches)
    - ❖ Synthetic or rubber mats

Keeping Your Child Off Limits

- Doorknob covers
- Door locks
- VCR lock

Keeping Your Child from Injuring Himself

- Decals on glass doors
- Door stops and door holders (to prevent precious fingers from being crushed)

Preventing Poisoning

- Safety latches and locks for drawers and cabinets (Remember, they are not child-proof.)
- Child-resistant packaging for medicine and household products
- Carbon monoxide alarms (for installation in every sleeping area and on the ceiling at least fifteen feet from fuel-burning appliances)
- Appliance lock for refrigerator.

Preventing Harm from Any Firearm in the Home

- Gun locks
- Gun cabinet, vault, or safe (Firearms should be stored unloaded and locked away. Ammunition should be locked away in a separate location.)

Preventing Drowning

- Pool fence (five feet high, surrounding all four sides, with self-closing, self-latching gates)
- Toilet bowl safety lock
- Locked safety cover for spa
- U.S. Coast Guard–approved life preserver, life jackets, and ring buoy with line securely attached and/or a long-handled hook to assist or retrieve a victim from the water

Keeping a Constant Eye on Your Children

- Cordless phone
- Baby monitor (Invest in a portable unit so you can carry it from room to room.)

Being Prepared for Emergencies

- Ipecac syrup (Use only upon advice of poison control center or doctor.)
- Activated charcoal (Use only upon advice of poison control center or doctor.)
- Fully stocked first-aid kit
- Prepared list of emergency numbers (see Appendix A) prominently posted near every telephone
- In case of natural disaster, such as hurricane, tornado or earthquake, keep in stock a supply of nonperishable foods, flashlights, batteries, and water.

Preventing Harm on the Go

- Retroreflective tape (Attach to children's outerwear whenever they are outdoors at dawn, dusk, or night.)
- Bike helmet (It must be properly fitted and meet current national standards.) (See Chapter 13 for guidelines.)
- Car seat that fits your child's age and size and is compatible with your particular car. (Proper installation is essential. Place it in the backseat of your car.) (See Chapter 17 for guidelines.)
  - ❖ Infant seat
  - ❖ Convertible car seat
  - ❖ Booster seat

Appendix F
Room-by-Room Checklist

Check for hazards in your home, at the homes where your child visits, and at your child's daycare or school.

- Look at your home from your child's perspective. Get down on your hands and knees and crawl around in each room. You will be quite surprised at what you find.
- As your child enters a new stage of development, begin preparing for the next, even if it means going out and buying new items. (For example, you should have gates ready for installation before your child becomes mobile.)

General Recommendations

- Install smoke detectors on every level of the home and in every sleep area. (It is also advised to include the furnace room.)
  - Change batteries twice per year.
  - Test them monthly.
  - Replace the units every ten years.
- Install a multipurpose fire extinguisher in the kitchen, where most fires are likely to occur.
  - It is also advised to put a fire extinguisher in the basement and workshop.
  - Learn how to use them.
- Plan escape routes and conduct fire drills with the entire family.
- Dress children in flame-resistant pajamas.
- Keep matches and cigarette lighters out of reach of children.
- Install a carbon monoxide detector in every sleeping area and at least fifteen feet from fuel-burning appliances.
- Make sure all fuel-burning appliances are properly vented and inspected annually.

■ Install ground-fault circuit interrupters (GFCIs) if you do not already have them.

■ Place safety covers over all electrical outlets.

■ Use angle braces or anchors to secure larger furniture—which presents a tipping hazard—to the wall.

■ Cut the loops of window cords. Use safety tassels or tie-down devices.

■ Use door stops and door holders to prevent injuries to precious fingers.

■ Keep children away from exercise equipment. Store and lock it away after use.

■ Install window guards on all windows from the ground floor up (unless they are designated as emergency exits). (Check local fire codes.)

■ If your home was built before 1978, have it tested for lead-based paint. (Call 888-LEADLIST [532-3547] for certified inspectors.) Ask your pediatrician or health department if your child should be tested for lead.

■ Test your home for radon. (Call 800-557-2366 for more information.)

■ Enforce a no-smoking policy in your home.

■ To help prevent asthma attacks, eliminate sources of mold, dust, and insects such as cockroaches. Keep pets and their bedding clean and off the furniture, if possible.

■ Prominently post emergency telephone numbers near every phone in the house.

■ Enroll in a cardiopulmonary resuscitation (CPR) and first-aid course.

■ Check your entire home and your children's day care or school to make sure that no recalled products are being used. Make sure you are kept up to date about future recalls and corrective actions. Parents, schools, and day care providers can receive recall information free by fax, E-mail, or regular mail. Call the CPSC hot line (800) 638-2772, or visit their website: www.cpsc.gov. To check on car seat recalls contact the National Highway and Transportation Safety Administration (800) 424-9393 or (888) DASH-2-DOT or visit their website: www.nhtsa.gov. For food and medicines, contact the Food and Drug Administration (888) SAFEFOOD or visit their website: www.fda.gov. For recalls of meat, poultry, and egg products, contact the USDA (800) 535-4555 or visit their website: www.fsis.usda.gov.

Kitchen

■ Use back burners and keep pot handles turned to the back of the stove.

■ Install guards on stove knobs.

■ Lock it up
  • Keep your oven door locked.
  • Install an appliance lock on the refrigerator. (Raw meats, poultry products, and seafood, as well as medications, such as antibiotics, are stored there.)
  • Install an appliance lock on the microwave oven.

■ Don't use tablecloths or place mats. (They enable younger children to pull hot foods down onto themselves.)

- Keep mugs of hot coffee and other hot foods away from the edge of counters or tables.
- Use a spill-resistant mug for hot beverages.
- Do not hold or carry your child while holding hot foods or beverages.
- Keep children off of the floor in the kitchen while anyone is cooking. Put them in their crib, playpen, or high chair in the kitchen, but safely away from the cooking area and any wall or counter from which they can push off.
- Do not let your child use the microwave.
- Keep round, hard food from children under age six.
- Store all household products, pet supplies, medicine, vitamins, and alcohol in their original containers, locked out of sight and reach of children.
- Tie up in knots and discard plastic wraps and bags promptly or store them locked away from children.
- Store knives and other sharp utensils in drawers or cabinets secured with safety latches.
- Make sure the floor is nonslip and free of grease. Promptly clean up any spills.
- Never leave a filled or partially filled bucket unattended.
- Keep the garbage can covered and out of reach of children.

Bathroom

- Never leave children unattended in the bathroom, even for a few seconds.
- Keep all medicine, vitamins, cosmetics, grooming products, and sharp objects locked out of reach and sight of children.
- Set the water thermostat to 120°F or less.
- Install antiscald devices to the shower and tub.
- Always test the water before you or your children get into the bathtub or shower.
- Place safety locks on all toilet lids.
- Apply a rubber suction bath mat or nonskid appliqués to the tub and shower.
- Install grab bars in the bath and shower.
- Attach a securely fitting cushion over the tub spout.
- Use a rubber-backed rug on the floor for stepping out of the tub or shower.
- Keep electrical appliances away from the water and out of reach of children.

Nursery

- Buy a new crib that meets current safety standards. Look for the Juvenile Products Manufacturers Association (JPMA) certification.
  - ❖ A new crib is much safer to use than a secondhand crib.
  - ❖ In any case, do not use a crib built before 1991.
- Make sure the crib is sturdy, with no loose, broken, or missing hardware.

- Remove all crib toys that are strung across the crib when your child is five months old or as soon as he can push up on his hands and knees (whichever comes first).
- Remove all toys, pillows, and plastic materials from the crib.
- Never hang anything on or above a crib with a string or ribbon longer than seven inches.
- Avoid strings on infant products, including pacifiers and rattles.
- Remove bumper pads and hanging mobiles from the crib when infants are able to pull themselves up and stand.
- Make sure the crib sheet fits properly. (It can pull up and become a strangulation hazard.)
- Put the baby to sleep on her back, on a firm, flat mattress with no soft bedding underneath her.
- Do not place the crib or any other furniture near a window, blind, or drapery cords.
- Do not sleep with your baby or put the baby down to sleep in an adult bed. (This puts her at risk of suffocation and strangulation.)

Living Room and Family Area

- Use safety gates at the top and bottom of stairs (if there are infants and toddlers in the home).
- Keep stairs well lit and clear of clutter. (Have light switches at both the bottom and the top.)
- Avoid the use of scatter rugs. If used, provide skidproof rugs or runners. Tack down loose carpet edges with carpet tape or tacks.
- Do not keep furniture (chairs, benches, tables, toy boxes, or a bookcase) near windows or draperies.
- Remove or keep poisonous plants out of reach of children.
- Keep all small objects, such as knickknacks, small toys, and balloons, out of reach of young children. Buy age-appropriate toys for each child.
- Keep TVs and other entertainment equipment as far back as possible on furniture so it can't be pulled over by your child.
- Use corner and edge bumpers on furniture and fireplace hearths.

Garage

- Keep all tools out of children's reach.
- Store all buckets upside down.
- Store and lock poisonous and flammable materials out of children's reach.

- Never store flammable materials near a heat source.
- Install an autoreverse feature and a photoelectric sensor or door edge sensor to the automatic garage-door opener.

Backyard

- Enclose the backyard.
- Remove or fence in all toxic plants.
- Pull up mushrooms regularly (especially after rainy weather).
- Keep steps and paved areas clean and well maintained.
- Promptly clean up animal droppings.
- Provide cushioning under playground equipment.
  - ❖ Hardwood fiber, mulch chips, pea gravel, or sand at a depth of twelve inches
  - ❖ Synthetic or rubber mats
- Place a cover over the sandbox when children are not using it. (You don't want animals to use it as a litter box!)
- Securely store lawn equipment and garden tools when they are not in use.
- Keep children indoors and supervised at all times when any outdoor power equipment is being used.
- Never take a child for a ride on a garden tractor or riding mower.

Pool

- Install a four-sided fence at least five feet high, equipped with a self-closing, self-latching gate.
- Equip all doors leading to the pool with child resistant locks that are self-closing.
- Enroll children in a learn to swim class and/or water safety class taught by qualified instructors.
- Make sure all children have constant adult supervision when swimming. No child is drownproof.
- Inspect pool and equipment regularly.
- Store pool supplies and chemicals locked out of reach of children.
- Keep rescue equipment, emergency numbers, and a cordless phone poolside.

Endnotes

1. Starting at the Beginning: Guarding the Fetus

1. Williams, Rebecca. "Decreasing the Chance of Birth Defects." *FDA Consumer Magazine* (November 1996), Food and Drug Administration, www.fda.gov (September 1997).
2. "CDC Urges Better Education Efforts from Health Care Providers and Others to Encourage Women to Take Folic Acid Every Day." Centers for Disease Control and Prevention, www.cdc.gov (August 29, 1999).
3. "Current Trends Rubella Vaccination during Pregnancy—United States, 1971–1988." MMWR Weekly, 38, no. 17 (May 5, 1989): 289–293, Centers for Disease Control and Prevention, www.cdc.gov (September 1999).
4. Table on Chicken Pox Vaccine: Indications, Contraindications, Primary Schedule, and Comments. Centers for Disease Control and Prevention, www.cdc.gov (September 1999).
5. Williams, *op cit.*
6. "Toxoplasmosis (TOX-o-plaz-MO-sis)." Division of Parasitic Diseases/National Center for Infectious Diseases, Centers for Disease Control and Prevention, www.cdc.gov (May 1998).

2. Aspirin: A Good Medicine That Should Sometimes Be Avoided

1. "Reye's Syndrome: Because You Need to Know." Pamphlet. Bryan OH: National Reye's Syndrome Foundation (1998).

3. Making Sure Our Food Is Safe

1. Altekruse, S. F., M. L. Cohen and D. L. Swerdlow. "Emerging Foodborne Diseases." *Emerging Infectious Diseases* 3, no. 3 (July–September 1997).

2. "Unwelcome Dinner Guest, The: Preventing Food-Borne Illness." *FDA Consumer* (January–February 1991), Food and Drug Administration, www.cfsan.fda.gov (December 1997).

3. "Bacteria That Cause Foodborne Illness." Fact Sheet. Washington DC: U.S. Department of Agriculture (October 1997) and "Foodborne Illness: What Consumers Need to Know." Food and Drug Administration Center for Food Safety and Applied Nutrition and USDA Food Safety and Inspection Service (September 1999).

4. "Bacteria That Cause Foodborne Illness," *op cit.* and "Organisms That Can Bug You." *FDA Consumer* (1991), Food and Drug Administration, www.cfsan.fda.gov (April 2, 1998).

5. "Botulism (*Clostridium botulinum*): Frequently Asked Questions." Centers for Disease Control and Prevention, www.cdc.gov (August 29, 1999).

6. "Focus on: Holiday or Party Buffets." Food Safety and Inspection Service, U.S. Department of Agriculture, www.fsis.usda.gov (April 11, 1999).

7. Kurtzweil, Paula. "Critical Steps Toward Safer Seafood." *FDA Consumer* (November–December 1997), Food and Drug Administration, www.cfsan.fda.gov (March 1998).

8. "Ounce of Prevention, An: Wash Your Hands Often." Centers for Disease Control and Prevention, www.cdc.gov (July 24, 1999).

9. "Grilling and Smoking Food Safely." Food Safety and Inspection Service, U.S. Department of Agriculture, www.fsis.usda.gov (September 1998).

10. Zuger, Abigail. "Physician's Perspective: For Safety's Sake: Scrub Your Produce." *HealthNews* (June 24, 1997): 3.

11. "Bacteria That Cause Foodborne Illness," *op cit.* and "Unwelcome Dinner Guest, The: Preventing Food-Borne Illness," *op cit.*

12. "Time to Take a Food Safety Inventory for Back-to-School Lunches." Food Safety and Inspection Service, www.fsis.usda.gov (August 1998).

13. "Seasonal Poisoning Hazards." Pamphlet. Miami: Florida Poison Information Center.

4. Knowing What's in Your Tap

1. "Providing Safe Drinking Water in America: 1996 National Public Water System Annual Compliance Report and Update on Implementation of the 1996 Safe Drinking Water Act Amendments." Document. Washington DC: Environmental Protection Agency.

2. "Guidance for People with Severely Weakened Immune Systems." Environmental Protection Agency, www.epa.gov (July 1997).

3. "How Safe Is My Drinking Water?" Environmental Protection Agency, www.epa.gov (September 1997).

4. "Health Effects of Drinking Water Contaminants." North Carolina State University Cooperative Extension Service (September 1996).

5. Waller, K. et al. "Trihalomethanes in Drinking Water and Spontaneous Abortion." *Epidemiology* 9, no. 2 (March 1998): 134–140.

6. "Tap Water and Miscarriage Risks." *HealthNews* (March 10, 1998): 7.

7. "Drinking Water Contamination." Chapter 7 in *Our Children At Risk: The 5 Worst Environmental Threats To Their Health*. Washington DC: Natural Resources Defense Council, Inc., www.nrdc.org (December 1997).

8. "Drinking Water Treatment Units Certified by NSF *International*." Booklet. Ann Arbor MI: National Sanitation Foundation (June 12, 1996).

9. "Frequently Asked Questions." Environmental Protection Agency, Office of Water, www.epa.gov (April 1998).

10. "Bottled Water FAQ." National Resources Defense Council, www.nrdc.org (September 1999).

11. "What Can I Do If There Is a Problem with My Drinking Water?" Environmental Protection Agency, www.epa.gov (September 3, 1997).

5. Taking Care with Pesticides

1. "EPA Children's Environmental Health Yearbook." Booklet (EPA 100-98-100). Washington DC: Environmental Protection Agency (June 1998).

2. Huebner, Albert. "Pesticides: Protecting Your Child." *American Baby* (December 1995): 34–38.

3. "Common Sense Pest Control." Pamphlet. Fort Lauderdale FL: Broward County Department of Natural Resource Protection.

4. "Cast a Vote for a Healthy Planet . . . Buy Organic." Pamphlet. Greenfield MA: Organic Trade Association.

5. Makower, Joel, with John Elkington and Julia Hailes. *The Green Consumer*. New York: Tilden Books/Penguin, 1990.

6. "Greener Greens." *Consumer Reports* (January 1998): 13–17.

7. "For Earth's Sake, for Your Health, *EN* says Choose Organic." *Environmental Nutrition*, 21, no. 4 (April 1998).

8. "Citizen's Guide to Pest Control and Pesticide Safety." Document (EPA 730-K-95-001). Washington DC: Environmental Protection Agency (September 1995).

9. "Seasonal Poisoning Hazards." Pamphlet. Miami: Florida Poison Information Center (no date).

10. Leiss, Jack K. and David A. Savitz. "Home Pesticide Use and Childhood Cancer: A Case-Control Study." *American Journal of Public Health* 85, no. 2 (February 1995): 249–252.

11. "Citizen's Guide to Pest Control and Pesticide Safety," *op cit.*

12. Goo, Robert. "Dos and Don'ts Around the Home." *EPA Journal* (Nov/Dec 1991), reprinted as pamphlet EPA-22K-1005 (no date).

13. "Lawn and Garden Care." Natural Resources Conservation Service, www.usda.gov (August 1997).

6. Making Good Luck Happen: Perils to Avoid

1. Rauchschwalbe, Renae and N. Clay Mann. "Pediatric Window-Cord Strangulations in the United States, 1981–1995." *Journal of the American Medical Association* 277, no. 21 (June 4, 1997): 1696–1698.

2. "Safe & Sound for Baby: A Guide to Juvenile Product Safety, Use and Selection." Pamphlet. 4th ed. Moorestown NJ: Juvenile Products Manufacturers Association (1997).

3. "Airway Obstruction Injury." Fact Sheet. Washington DC: National SAFE KIDS Campaign (September 1997).

4. *Ibid.*

5. "Are You Buying the Right Toy for the Right Age Child?" Consumer Product Safety Commission, www.cpsc.gov (January 12, 1998).

6. "Airway Obstruction Injury," *op cit.* and "CPSC Votes to Implement Child Safety Protection Act." Consumer Product Safety Commission, www.cpsc.gov (September 1999).

7. "Incidence of SIDS Increases During Cold Weather: A Winter Alert to All Caregivers of Infants." National Institute of Child Health and Human Development, www.nichd.nih.gov (September 1999).

8. "Recommendations Revised to Prevent Infant Deaths from Soft Bedding." Fact Sheet (Release 99-091). Washington DC: Consumer Product Safety Commission, www.cpsc.gov (April 1999) and "SIDS and Pacifier Use." Media Advisory, May 10, 1999. SIDS Alliance, www.sidsalliance.org (June 1999).

9. "Statement of the SIDS Alliance: In Response to the Release of Scientific Findings on the Prevalence of Sudden Infant Death Syndrome in Day Care Settings." Media Advisory, March 19, 1999. SIDS Alliance, www.sidsalliance.org (June 1999).

10. "Tipper Gore Alerts Parents About Increased SIDS Incidence During Cold Winter Weather." National Institute of Child Health and Human Development, www.nichd.nih.gov (April 13, 1998).

11. "What Every New Parent Should Know: Facts About Sudden Infant Death Syndrome and Reducing the Risks for SIDS." Pamphlet. Baltimore: SIDS Alliance (1996).

12. "Back-Sleeping Best for Babies." *HealthNews* (December 10, 1996): 6.

13. "Physical Consequences of Shaking an Infant or Toddler." Fact Sheet. Ogden UT. The Child Abuse Prevention Center.

7. Preventing Burns

1. "Feeding Babies and Young Children: A Teen Sitter's Guide to Food Safety." *Food News for Consumers* (Summer 1992), reprinted by U.S. Department of Agriculture Food Safety and Inspection Service (no date) and Williamson, CiCi and Grace Cataldo. "Microwave-Safe for Baby." *Food News for Consumer* (Winter 1992), reprinted by the U.S. Department of Agriculture.

2. Williamson, *op cit.*

3. *Ibid.*

4. "Feeding Babies and Young Children: A Teen Sitter's Guide to Food Safety," *op cit.*

5. "Plastics and Microwaves Aren't Always a Good Combination." *Environmental Nutrition* 21, no. 8 (August 1998): 7.

6. "GFCIs, The. GFCIs [Ground Fault Circuit Interrupters] Fact Sheet. Consumer Product Safety Commission, pub 99 (1996).

7. "Fireworks Safety Tips." Fact Sheet. Washington DC: National SAFE KIDS Campaign and "CPSC Holds Fireworks Safety Press Conference in Mall in Washington." Consumer Product Safety Commission (release 97–150), www.cpsc.gov (July 1997).

8. Watching Out for Poisons

1. "Source Reduction Alternatives Around the Home." Environmental Protection Agency, www.epa.gov (April 21, 1998).

2. "Reducing Hazardous Products in Your Home." North Carolina Cooperative Extension Service (HE-368-2), www.ces.ncsu.edu (August 1997).

3. "Clean and Safe: The Facts About Using Household Cleaning Products Effectively and Safely." Booklet. New York: The Soap and Detergent Association (1993).

4. "Worker's Home Contamination Study." *Report to Congress Conducted Under the Workers' Family Protection Act, 29 U.S.C. 671a.* Washington DC: Department of Health and Human Services (September 1995): vii–x.

9. Staying Ahead of Lead

1. "Lead in Your Home: A Parent's Reference Guide." Booklet (EPA 747-B-98-002). Washington DC: Environmental Protection Agency (June 1998), 5.

2. "Inside Story, The: A Guide to Indoor Air Quality." Fact Sheet (EPA 402-K-93-007). Washington DC: Environmental Protection Agency (April 1995).

3. "Lead in Your Home: A Parent's Reference Guide," *op cit.*, 2.

4. *Ibid.*, 10.

5. *Ibid.*, 9.

6. "Inside Story, The: A Guide to Indoor Air Quality," *op cit.*

7. "Preventing Lead Poisoning in Young Children: A Statement by the Centers for Disease Control." Document. Atlanta: Centers for Disease Control and Prevention (October 1991), 9.

10. Exercising Prudence with EMFs

1. "Growing Pains." *Environmental Health Perspectives* 104, no. 2 (February 1996): 148–149.

2. Williams, Rebecca. "Decreasing the Chance of Birth Defects." *Consumer Magazine* (November 1996): 148–149, www.fda.gov (September 1997).

3. "Workplace VDT Use Not a Risk Factor for Reduced Birth Weight, Premature Birth, NIOSH Finds." Centers for Disease Control, www.cdc.gov (September 1999).

11. Making Sure Our Air Is Safe

1. "Indoor Air Pollution: An Introduction for Health Professionals." Booklet (6607J). Washington DC: Environmental Protection Agency, 9.

2. "Health Effects of Exposure to Radon (BEIR VI)." Document. National Research Council (February 1998).

3. "Every School Should Take This Simple Test." Document (EPA 402-F-94-009). Washington DC: Environmental Protection Agency (October 1994).

4. Lafavore, Michael. *Radon: The Invisible Threat: What It Is, Where It Is, How To Keep Your House Safe.* Emmaus PA: Rodale, 1987, 13.

5. "Citizen's Guide to Radon, A: The Guide to Protecting Yourself and Your Family from Radon." Booklet (402-K-92-001). Washington DC: Environmental Protection Agency (September 1994), 4.

6. "Inside Story, The: A Guide to Indoor Air Quality." Booklet (EPA 402-K-93-007). Washington DC: Environmental Protection Agency (April 1995), 11.

7. "Every School Should Take This Simple Test," *op cit.*

8. "Citizen's Guide to Radon, A: The Guide to Protecting Yourself and Your Family from Radon," *op cit.*, 7.

9. "Buying a New Home? How to Protect Your Family From Radon." Environmental Protection Agency (EPA 402F-98-008), www.epa.gov (April 1998).

10. "Cpsc Urges Seasonal Furnace Inspection, Replacement of Recalled Vent Pipes to Prevent Co Poisonings." Document (Release 98-170). Washington DC: Consumer Product Safety Commission, www.cpsc.gov (September 1998).

11. "Protect Your Family and Yourself from Carbon Monoxide Poisoning." Document (EPA-402-F-96-005). Washington DC: Indoor Environments Division, Office of Air and Radiation (October 1996).

12. "Carbon Monoxide Poisonings Associated With Snow-Obstructed Vehicle Exhaust Systems—Philadelphia and New York City, January 1996." *Journal of the American Medical Association*, 275, no. 6 (February 14, 1996): 426–427.

13. "Cpsc Urges Seasonal Furnace Inspection, Replacement of Recalled Vent Pipes to Prevent Co Poisonings," *op cit.*

14. "Poisoning." Fact Sheet. Washington DC: National SAFE KIDS Campaign (December 1998).

15. "Respiratory Health Effects of Passive Smoking." Document (RD-689/6203J). Washington DC: Environmental Protection Agency (January 1993).

16. "Secondhand Smoke: What You Can Do About Secondhand Smoke as Parents, Decision Makers, and Building Occupants." Flyer (EPA 402-F-93-004). Washington DC: Environmental Protection Agency (July 1993).

17. "Protecting Yourself and Your Family From Secondhand Smoke." Pamphlet. Tallahassee FL: American Lung Association (1994) and "Setting the Record Straight: Secondhand Smoke Is a Preventable Health Risk." Document (EPA 402-F-94-005). Washington DC: Environmental Protection Agency (June 1994).

18. "Smoking and Pregnancy." Centers for Disease Control and Prevention, www.cdc.gov (April 1999).

19. "Asbestos: Try Not to Panic." *Consumer Reports* (July 1995): 468–469.

20. "Facts About Asbestos in Buildings." Pamphlet. Washington DC: Environmental Protection Agency (March 6, 1991).

21. "Asbestos in Your Home." Pamphlet (EPA 400-K-90-100). Washington DC: Environmental Protection Agency (September 1990).

22. "ABCs of Asbestos in Schools, The." Booklet (TS-799). Washington DC: Environmental Protection Agency (June 1989).

12. Taking Steps to Fend Off Danger

1. "Cpsc and Gas-Fired Water Heaters." Consumer Product Safety Commission, www.cpsc.gov (April 1999).

2. "Fireproofing Your Dryer." *Good Housekeeping* (June 1997): 56.

3. "Cpsc Warns About Flammable Loose-Fitting Garments Used as Children's Sleepwear." Fact Sheet (Release 99-025). Washington DC: Consumer Product Safety Commission, www.cpsc.gov (March 1999).

4. "Your Home Fire Safety Checklist." Booklet (380-569/20079). Washington DC: Consumer Product Safety Commission (1994), 8.

5. "1997 Firearms Deaths." Table from the Vital Statistics System (September 1999).

6. "10 Years—Safety for Your Child" *The Injury Prevention Program (TIPP)*. Fact Sheet. Elk Grove Village IL: American Academy of Pediatrics (1994).

7. "Unintentional Firearm Injury." Fact Sheet. Washington DC: National SAFE KIDS Campaign (September 1997).

8. "Word About . . . Guns and Other Weapons, A." *Helping Kids Protect Themselves: A Booklet for Children and Adults*. Booklet. Washington DC: National Crime Prevention Council (no date).

9. Kellermann, Arthur L., et al. "Injuries and Deaths Due to Firearms in the Home." *The Journal of Trauma, Injury, Infection and Critical Care*, 45, no. 2 (December 2, 1998): 263–267.

10. ———. "Gun Ownership as a Risk Factor for Homicide in the Home." *New England Journal of Medicine*, 329 (1993): 1084–1091.

11. ———. "Suicide in the Home in Relation to Gun Ownership." *New England Journal of Medicine*, 327 (1992): 467–472.

12. "Unintentional Firearm Injury," *op cit.*

13. Playing It Safe

1. "Cpsc Issues New Safety Standard for Bike Helmets." Fact Sheet (release 98-062). Washington DC: Consumer Product Safety Commission (February 5, 1998).

2. *Ibid.* and "Your Bicycle Helmet: 'A Correct Fit'." Pamphlet (DOT HS 808 421). Washington DC: National Highway Traffic Safety Administration (September 1996).

3. "What's New About Bicycle Helmets: New Safety Standards for Better Protection." Pamphlet (DOT HS 808-747). Washington DC: Consumer Product Safety Commission, (August 1998).

4. "Cpsc Releases Bicycle Safety Tips." Fact Sheet (release 97-138). Washington DC: Consumer Product Safety Commission (June 5, 1997).

5. "Bicycle Suitability Map: Hints for Parents." Pamphlet. Ft. Lauderdale FL: Broward County (1998).

6. "Danger Zone." National Highway Traffic Safety Administration, nhtsa.dot.gov (April 1999).

7. "Sports and Recreational Activity Injury." Fact Sheet. Washington DC: National SAFE KIDS Campaign (December 1998).

8. "Skate, But Skate Safely—Always Wear Safety Gear." Fact Sheet. Washington DC: Consumer Product Safety Commission (November 1996).

9. "What's New About Bicycle Helmets: New Safety Standards for Better Protection," *op cit.*
10. "Skate, But Skate Safely—Always Wear Safety Gear," *op cit.*
11. "Sports and Recreational Activity Injury," *op cit.*

14. Hazards of the Fall:
Kids Don't Come Equipped with Wings

1. "Falls." Fact Sheet. Washington DC: National SAFE KIDS Campaign (September 1997).
2. "Trampoline Safety Alert." Consumer Product Safety Commission (51160), www.cpsc.gov (April 1999).
3. "Six to 12 Months: Safety for Your Child." *The Injury Prevention Program (TIPP).* Fact Sheet. Elk Grove Village IL: American Academy of Pediatrics (no date).
4. "Safe and Sound for Baby: A Guide to Juvenile Product Safety, Use and Selection." 4th ed. Booklet. Moorestown NJ: Juvenile Products Manufacturers Association (1997).
5. *Ibid.*
6. "Hidden Hazards in the Home: Furniture Can Tip Over on Children." Fax. Washington DC: Consumer Product Safety Commission (January 1998).
7. Kriel, Robert L., et al. "Automatic Garage Door Openers: Hazard for Children." *Pediatrics*, 98, no. 4 (October 1996): 770-773.
8. *Ibid.*
9. "Handbook for Public Playground Safety." Booklet. Washington DC: Consumer Product Safety Commission (no date).
10. Thompson D. and S. Hudson. "National Action Plan for the Prevention of Playground Injuries." Document. Cedar Falls IA: National Program for Playground Safety (1996).
11. "Safe Nursery, the (Buyer's Guide): A Booklet to Help Avoid Injuries from Nursery Furniture and Equipment." Booklet (305-009/90330). Washington DC: Consumer Product Safety Commission (1993).
12. Thompson, *op cit.*
13. "State Requirements for Public Playground Equipment." National Program for Playground Safety, www.uni.edu/playground/ (June 22, 1999).

15. Stepping Out (Safely)

1. "Stay Healthy in the Sun: Information About Uv Radiation for Meteorologists." Environmental Protection Agency (EPA 430-K-98-004), www.epa.gov (April 1999).

2. "Action Steps for Sun Protection." Environmental Protection's SunWise School Program, Environmental Protection Agency, www.epa.gov (April 19, 1999).

3. "Extreme Heat: A Prevention Guide to Promote Your Personal Health and Safety." Booklet. Washington DC: Centers for Disease Control and Prevention (June 1, 1996).

4. "American Lyme Disease Foundation Spring 1998 Highlights." *Ticktalk*. White Plains NY: American Lyme Disease Foundation, Inc. (Summer 1998).

5. "Lyme Disease." Booklet. Washington DC: Centers for Disease Control and Prevention (no date).

6. "Bats & Rabies." Centers for Disease Control and Prevention, www.cdc.gov (April 20, 1999).

16. Getting into the Swim of Things

1. "Drowning." Fact Sheet. National SAFE KIDS Campaign (September 1996).

17. Rules of the Road

1. "Safety Fact Sheet." Fact Sheet. Washington DC: National Highway Traffic Safety Administration (September 1, 1998).

2. "Traffic Safety Facts 1998: Occupant Protection." National Highway Traffic Safety Administration, www.nhtsa.dot.gov (September 1999).

3. "Transporting Your Children Safely: Traffic Safety Tips." *NHTSA Facts* (Summer 1996).

4. "Child Safety Seat Compatibility." Washington DC: National Highway Traffic Safety Administration, www.nhtsa.dot.gov (February 1999).

5. "Brakes: Traffic Safety Tips." *AutoFacts* NHTSA (Winter 1994) and "Questions & Answers Regarding Antilock Brake Systems (ABS)." Fax (US DOT/NHTSA ODI). Washington DC: National Highway Traffic Safety Administration (August 1995).

6. "Cellular Phones and Car Accidents." *HealthNews* (March 4, 1997): 6.

18. Hazards in the Community

1. "SAFE KIDS Are No Accident! How to Protect Your Child From Injury." Booklet. Washington DC: National SAFE KIDS Campaign (1996): 4–5.

2. "Florida School Zone." Pamphlet. Heathrow FL: AAA Clubs of Florida, Traffic Safety Departments (no date).

3. "Pedestrian Safety." National Highway Traffic Safety Administration, www.nhtsa.dot.gov (April 1999).

4. "Moment of Truth, The: School Bus Loading and Unloading Safety: Procedures, Tips and Cautions for and from School Bus Drivers." Booklet. Syracuse NY: Pupil Transportation Safety Institute (1997).

5. "Traffic Safety Facts 1997: School Buses." Document. Washington DC: National Center for Statistics and Analysis, Research and Development (no date).

6. "This Could Save Your Child's Life: A School Bus Handrail Handbook." Booklet (DOT HS 808-451). Washington DC: National Highway Traffic Safety Administration (September 1996).

7. "Traffic Safety Facts 1997: School Buses," *op cit.*

8. "Moment of Truth, The: School Bus Loading and Unloading Safety: Procedures, Tips and Cautions for and from School Bus Drivers," *op cit.*

9. Smith, Gary A., et al. "Injuries to Children Related to Shopping Carts." *Pediatrics* 97, no. 2 (February 1996): 161–165, 161.

19. The Street-Smart Kid

1. "Kidguard Safety Program." Fact Sheet. Orlando FL: ChildWatch of North America (no date).

2. "Safety Tips." Fact Sheet. Lake Park FL: Florida Branch of National Center for Missing and Exploited Children (formerly known as Adam Walsh Center) (no date).

3. "Kidguard Safety Program," *op cit.*

Other Sources

1. Starting at the Beginning: Guarding the Fetus

"Be Good to Your Baby Before It is Born." Pamphlet. Wilkes-Barre PA: March of Dimes (July 1998).

"Childhood Illnesses in Pregnancy: Chickenpox and Fifth Disease." *Public Education*. March of Dimes, www.modimes.org (May 1998).

"Deliver the Best." *Having a Healthy Baby*. March of Dimes, www.modimes.org (April 1998).

"Expectant Mothers and Foodborne Illness." Pamphlet. Washington DC: Food Safety and Inspection Service, U.S. Department of Agriculture (May 1999).

"Facts About Fetal Alcohol Syndrome." Centers for Disease Control and Prevention, www.cdc.gov (April 25, 1997).

"Food-Borne Risks in Pregnancy." March of Dimes, www.modimes.org (November 23, 1999).

"Frequently Asked Questions on Hiv Aids." Centers for Disease Control and Prevention, www.cdc.gov (August 1999).

"Health Topics: Mercury." National Toxicology Program (NTP), Center for the Evaluation of Risks to Human Reproduction (CERHR), http://cerhr.niehs.nih.gov/ (February 9, 2000).

"Making the Right Choices: The Facts About Alcohol and Pregnancy." Pamphlet. Wilkes-Barre PA: March of Dimes Resource Center (October 1997).

"Making the Right Choices: The Facts About Drugs and Pregnancy." Pamphlet. Wilkes-Barre PA: March of Dimes Resource Center (May 1997).

Milunsky, Aubrey, et al. "Maternal Heat Exposure and Neural Tube Defects." *Journal of the American Medical Association*, 268, no. 7 (August 19, 1992): 882–885.

"Pre-Pregnancy Planning." *Public Education*. March of Dimes, www.modimes.org (May 1998).

"Preventing Foodborne Illness: Listeriosis." Division of Bacterial and Mycotic Diseases/National Center for Infectious Diseases, Centers for Disease Control and Prevention, www.cdc.gov (August 9, 1996).

"Status of Perinatal HIV Prevention: U.S. Declines Continue." Centers for Disease Control and Prevention, www.cdc.gov (August 1999).

Swartz, Harold M. and Barbara A. Reichling. "Hazards of Radiation Exposure for Pregnant Women." *Journal of the American Medical Association*, 239, no. 18 (May 5, 1978): 1907–1908.

"Think Ahead." *Having a Healthy Baby*. March of Dimes, www.modimes.org (June 1998).

Toppenberg, K. S., D. A. Hill, and D. P. Miller. "Safety of Radiographic Imaging During Pregnancy." *American Family Physician* 59, no. 7 (April 1, 1999): 1813–8, 1820.

"Toxoplasmosis." National Institute of Allergy and Infectious Diseases, National Institute of Health, www.cdc.gov (November 1994).

"Viral Hepatitis B—Frequently Asked Questions." Centers for Disease Control and Prevention, www.cdc.gov (September 3, 1999).

Williams, Rebecca D. "Healthy Pregnancy, Healthy Baby." *FDA Consumer* (March–April 1999).

"Your Source of Information on Pregnancy and Birth Defects." Flyer. Wilkes-Barre PA: March of Dimes Resource Center (1996).

2. Aspirin: A Good Medicine
That Should Sometimes Be Avoided

"CDC Study Shows Sharp Decline in Reye's Syndrome Among U.S. Children." Centers for Disease Control and Prevention, www.cdc.gov (August 29, 1999).

"Medications Containing Aspirin (Acetylsalicylate) and Aspirin-Like Products." Fact Sheet. Bryan OH: National Reye's Syndrome Foundation (1998).

"Reye's Syndrome." Pamphlet. Bethesda MD: National Institute of Neurological Disorders and Stroke (June 1996).

Williams, Rebecca D. "How to Give Medicine to Children." *FDA Consumer* (January–February 1996): 5, Food and Drug Administration, www.fda.gov (April 15, 1999).

3. Making Sure Our Food Is Safe

"ABC's of Safe and Healthy Child Care." Centers for Disease Control and Prevention, www.cdc.gov (August 3, 1999).

"About Aflatoxin: From the Makers of Jif Peanut Butter." Fact Sheet (PNB4). Procter and Gamble (no date).

"Aflatoxins." Fact Sheet (CAS No. 1402-68-2). Washington DC: NIEHS Annual Report on Carcinogens (no date).

"Are Molds Merely Pests or a Serious Problem?" *Environmental Nutrition* 17, no. 1 (January 1994): 1.

"Basics for Handling Food Safely." Fact Sheet. Washington DC: U.S. Department of Agriculture (September 1997).

"E. Coli . . . Salmonella . . . Listeria . . . Bacteria Become Unwelcome House Guests." *Environmental Nutrition* 20, no. 10 (October 1997): 1, 6.

"FDA Information on Aflatoxins." Fact Sheet. Washington DC: Food and Drug Administration (February 1993).

"Focus on: Food Product Dating." Food Safety and Inspection Service, U.S. Department of Agriculture, www.fsis.usda.gov (April 1999).

"'Grill' the USDA Hotline Experts About Safe Summer Cooking." U.S. Department of Agriculture, www.fsis.usda.gov (January 30, 1998).

"Hand Washing." Utah Department of Health, Bureau of Epidemiology, www.health.state.ut.us (August 3, 1999).

"Handling Eggs Safely at Home." Food and Drug Administration, www.fda.gov (August 1998).

Kurtzweil, Paula. "Fruits & Vegetables: Eating Your Way to 5 a Day." *FDA Consumer* (March 1997), reprinted as FDA 98-2310 (December 1997).

"'Lettuce' Learn How to Wash Salad Greens." *Environmental Nutrition* 21, no. 6 (June 1998): 8.

"Preventing Foodborne Illness: A Guide to Safe Food Handling." U.S. Department of Agriculture, www.fsis.usda.gov (September 1990).

Schardt, David and Leila Corcoran. "Safe Cooking: Beat the Heat." *Nutrition Action Health Letter* (June 1998): 4.

"Thermometer Use for Cooking Ground Beef Patties." U.S. Department of Agriculture, www.fsis.usda.gov (August 3, 1998).

"Unpasteurized Cider and Juice Can Contain Bacteria That Make Children and Some Other People Sick." Food and Drug Administration, www.cfsan.fda.gov (August 27, 1997).

"Use a Meat Thermometer and Take the Guess Work Out of Cooking." Fax. Washington DC: U.S. Department of Agriculture, www.fsis.usda.gov (September 11, 1997).

"When to Insert Meat Thermometer." U.S. Department of Agriculture, www.fsis.usda.gov (September 11, 1997).

4. Knowing What's in Your Tap

"Common Water Quality Problems." *The Informed Consumer*. Water Quality Association, WQA Home Page (April 9, 1998).

"Environmental Health Threats to Children." National Agenda to Protect Children's Health from Environmental Threats, Environmental Protection Agency, www.epa.gov (November 1997).

"EPA Releases Overview of America's Drinking Water." Environmental Protection Agency, www.epa.gov (September 1998).

"Home Water Testing." Fact Sheet (EPA 570/9-91-500). Washington DC: Environmental Protection Agency, Office of Water (June 1991).

"Is Your Drinking Water Safe?" Booklet (EPA 810/F-94-002). Washington DC: Environmental Protection Agency, Office of Water (May 1994).

McGowan, Bill. "Drinking Water Well Management in Home*A*Syst: An Environmental Risk–Assessment Guide for the Home." Ithaca, NY: NRAES.

"Unfiltered Truth About Home Water-Treatment Devices, The." *Environmental Nutrition* 21, no. 2 (February 1998): 2.

"What Do I Need to Know to Protect My Private Drinking Water Supply?" Environmental Protection Agency, www.epa.gov (September 1997).

5. Taking Care with Pesticides

In Our Food

"Consumers Win New Pesticide Regulations." *Environmental Nutrition* 19, no. 9 (September 1996): 1.

"Environmental Health Threats to Children." Document (EPA 175-F-96-001). Washington DC: Environmental Protection Agency (September 1996).

"EPA Children's Environmental Health Yearbook." Booklet (EPA 100-98-100). Washington DC: Environmental Protection Agency (June 1998).

"Extra Caution Urged for Common Pesticides." *HealthNews* (March 10, 1998): 7.

Foulke, Judith E. "FDA Reports on Pesticides in Foods." *FDA Consumer Magazine* (November 1993), FDA reprint 94-2270.

"Healthy, Sensible Food Practices." Environmental Protection Agency, www.epa.gov (August 1999).

"Home Pest Services." *Consumer Reports* (June 1997).

Ikramuddin, Aisha. "School Days, Sick Days: Lessons in Pesticides and Classrooms." *Green Guide*, no. 44 (September 14, 1997): 1–2.

"Inside Story, The: A Guide to Indoor Air Quality." Document (EPA 402-K-93-007). Washington DC: Environmental Protection Agency (April 1995).

"Nation's New Pesticide Law, The." Environmental Working Group, www.ewg.org (January 15, 1998).

"Pesticides and Your Fruits and Vegetables." Pamphlet. Washington DC: National Coalition Against the Misuse of Pesticides (no date).

"Pesticides in Produce Pose Minimal Risk." *Environmental Nutrition* (December 1997): 1.

"Produce and Pesticides: A Consumer Guide to Food Quality and Safe Handling." Pamphlet. Washington DC: Food Marketing Institute (1989).

"Riskiest Pesticides Will Be Assessed First Under New Food Safety Act." Environmental Protection Agency, www.epa.gov (August 4, 1997).

In the Yard and Garden

"Common Sense Pest Control." Booklet. Fort Lauderdale FL: Broward County Department of Natural Resource Protection (no date).

"Environmental Health Threats to Children." Document (EPA 175-F-96-001). Washington DC: Environmental Protection Agency (September 1996).

"Frequently Asked Questions." Environmental Protection Agency, Pesticides and Toxics Branch, www.epa.gov (November 17, 1997).

"Healthy Lawn, Healthy Environment: Caring for Your Lawn in an Environmentally Friendly Way." Document (700-K-92-005). Washington DC: Environmental Protection Agency (June 1992).

"Reregistration of the Insect Repellent DEET." Environmental Protection Agency, www.epa.gov (April 3, 1999).

"Safe Storage and Disposal of Pesticides." *INFOletter: Environmental and Occupational Health Briefs*, 6, no. 3 (1992): 7.

"Think Before You Spray: Alternatives to Lawn and Garden Pesticides." *INFOletter: Environmental and Occupational Health Briefs*, 6, no. 3 (1992): 1–4.

"Tips for Safer Roach Control." Pamphlet 904-F-97-902. Washington DC: Environmental Protection Agency (October 1997).

"Tracking Toxins Indoors." *HealthNews* (November 19, 1996).

"Using Insect Repellents Safely." Environmental Protection Agency, www.epa.gov (April 3, 1999).

"Your Child and the Environment: Guidelines for Parents." American Academy of Pediatrics, www.aap.org (November 1997).

6. Making Good Luck Happen: Perils to Avoid

"Abdominal Thrust—Self Administered." Pamphlet. Falls Church VA: American Red Cross (1992).

"Babies Break: So Never, Ever, Ever, Shake Your Baby." Pamphlet (150-285:6-97). Tallahassee: Florida Department of Health (June 1997).

"Children Can Strangle in Window Covering Cords." Consumer Product Safety Commission (document 5114), www.cpsc.gov (June 1999).

"Cpsc Warns About Child Entrapment in Household Appliances and Picnic Coolers: Safety Alert." Consumer Product Safety Commission (document 5073), www.cpsc.gov (January 1999).

"Fatal Car Trunk Entrapment Involving Children—United States, 1987–1998." Centers for Disease Control and Prevention, www.cdc.gov (August 1999).

"For Kids' Sake: Think Toy Safety." Pamphlet. Washington DC: U.S. Consumer Product Safety Commission (no date).

"Guidelines for Drawstrings on Children's Outerwear." Pamphlet. Washington DC: Consumer Product Safety Commission (February 1996).

Heimlich, Henry J. Letter to the Editor. *The New England Journal of Medicine,* 381, no. 11 (March, 17, 1988).

"Know the Facts About Shaken Baby Syndrome." Fact Sheet. Hollywood FL: Joe DiMaggio Children's Hospital (no date).

"Make Window Coverings Safer for Your Kids." Pamphlet. Washington DC: Consumer Product Safety Commission and Window Covering Safety Council (no date).

"New Data Highlights U.S. Sids Decrease." Document. Elk Grove Village IL: American Academy of Pediatrics (October 29, 1996).

"Number of Children Who Strangle in Window Cords Has Been Under-Reported According to a New Study in Jama, The." Consumer Product Safety Commission (Document 97136), www.cpsc.gov (June 1997).

Poussaint, Alvin F. and Susan Linn. "Fragile: Handle with Care." *Newsweek* (Special Issue, no date): 33.

"Questions and Answers for Professionals on Infant Sleeping Position and Sids." American Academy of Pediatrics, www.aap.org (November 1997).

"Safe kids Gear Up! Guide: The Things You Need to Know and the Gear You Need to Use." Preface by C. Everett Koop. Booklet. Washington DC: National safe kids Campaign.

"Safe Nursery, the (Buyer's Guide): A Booklet to Help Avoid Injuries from Nursery Furniture and Equipment." Booklet (305-009/90330). Washington DC: Consumer Product Safety Commission (1993).

"Shaken Baby Is a Shattered Life, A." Pamphlet. Hollywood FL: Project of the Junior League of Greater Fort Lauderdale (no date).

"Shaken Baby Syndrome." Pamphlet. Pueblo CO: Parents Anonymous (no date).

"Shaken Baby Syndrome." *Periodical Abstracts* (1991).

Srinivasan, Kalpana. "Beware Dangerous Toys, Consumer Study Warns." Associated Press (no date).

"Strings, Cords, and Necklaces Can Strangle Infants." Fact Sheet. Washington DC: Consumer Product Safety Commission (July 1990).

"Sudden Infant Death Syndrome." National Institute of Child Health and Human Development, www.nichd.nih.gov (April 1997).

"Tips for Your Baby's Safety." Pamphlet. Washington DC: Consumer Product Safety Commission (no date).

"Toy Boxes and Toy Chests." Document (74). Washington DC: Consumer Product Safety Commission (no date).

"Toy Injury." Fact Sheet. Washington DC: National SAFE KIDS Campaign (September 1997).

"Trunks Are for Elephants. . . Not for Kids." Pamphlet. Washington DC: National SAFE KIDS Campaign and General Motors (no date).

"Ways to Reduce the Risks of SIDS." SIDS Alliance, www.sidsalliance.org (June 1999).

"Which Toy for Which Child: A Consumer's Guide to Selecting Suitable Toys." Booklet (285). Washington DC: Consumer Product Safety Commission (no date).

Young, Carol. "Buying Second-Hand Baby Equipment? Think First About Safety!" *Today's Parent* (July 1998).

"Your Used Crib Could Be Deadly: Safety Alert." Document (5020). Washington DC: Consumer Product Safety Commission (no date).

7. Preventing Burns

"Burn Injuries Don't Take a Summer Vacation." Fact Sheet. Allentown PA: Burn Prevention Foundation (1999).

"Burn Injury." Fact Sheet. Washington DC: National SAFE KIDS Campaign (September 1997).

Burn Prevention Tips. Booklet. Tampa FL: Shriners Hospitals for Children November 1999.

"Cord Safety." *HealthNews* (August 26, 1997): 8.

"CPSC and Gas-Fired Water Heaters." Consumer Product Safety Commission, www.cpsc.gov (November 1998).

"CPSC Issues Warning on Tubular Halogen Bulbs." Consumer Product Safety Commission (release 96-174), www.cpsc.gov (July 1996).

"Electrical Spaceheater." Fact Sheet (98). Washington DC: Consumer Product Safety Commission (no date).

"Fire Stops with You." U.S. Fire Administration, www.usfa.fema.gov (November 14, 1998).

"GFCIS, The." Fact Sheet (99). Washington DC: Consumer Product Safety Commission (1996).

"Hot Liquids Burn Like Fire." *Safe Kids Are No Accident: How to Protect Your Child from Injury.* Washington DC: National SAFE KIDS Campaign (September 1996).

"Hot Tap Water and Scald Burns." Burn Prevention Foundation, www.burnprevention.org.

"Hot Water Safety for Families With Small Kids." Pamphlet. Washington DC: National SAFE KIDS Campaign (no date).

"New Hair Dryers Prevent Electrocutions." Fact Sheet. Washington DC: Consumer Product Safety Commission (no date).

"Safe Kids Gear Up! Guide. The Things You Need to Know and the Gear You Need to Use." Booklet. Washington DC: National SAFE KIDS Campaign (no date): 2–6.

Wald, Matthew L. "Anti-Scalding Device That Is Easy to Install." *The New York Times* (May 2, 1996).

"Young Children and Teens Burned by Curling Irons." Fact Sheet. Consumer Product Safety Commission (no date).

8. Watching Out for Poisons

"Beautiful But Dangerous: Common Poisonous Plants of Florida." Flyer. Miami: Florida Poison Information Center (no date).

"Clean and Safe: The Facts About Using Household Cleaning Products Effectively and Safely." Booklet. New York: The Soap and Detergent Association (1993).

"Cleaning Blues, The." *The Green Guide*, no. 53 (April 14, 1998).

"Consumer's Guide to Environmental Claims in the Marketplace, A." Fact Sheet. Oakland CA: Scientific Certification Systems (no date).

Dickey, Philip. "Safer Cleaning Products." *Alternatives.* Fact Sheet. Washington DC: Washington Toxics Coalition (May 1998).

"Do's & Don'ts Around the Home." Pamphlet. Fort Lauderdale FL: Broward County Department of Natural Resource Protection (no date).

"First Aid For Poisoning." Pamphlet. Tampa: Florida Poison Information Center at Tampa General Hospital (no date).

"First Aid Tips For Poisoning." Fact Sheet. Miami: University of Miami, Department of Pediatrics: Florida Poison Information Center (no date).

"Frequently Asked Questions: Which Household Plants Are Poisonous?" National SAFE KIDS Campaign, www.safekids.org (November 1998).

Hammett, Wilma. "Hazardous Household Products: The Healthy House." Document (HE-368-1/WQWM-61). Raleigh: North Carolina Cooperative Extension Service (January 1993).

Hingley, Audrey T. "Preventing Childhood Poisoning." *FDA Consumer Magazine* 30, no. 2 (March 1996): 7–11.

"Household Hazardous Waste: Steps to Safe Management." Pamphlet (EPA/530-F-92-031). Washington DC: Environmental Protection Agency (April 1993).

"Inside Story, The: A Guide to Indoor Air Quality." Document (EPA 402-K-93-007). Washington DC: Environmental Protection Agency (April 29, 1995).

"Is Your Home Poison Proof?" Pamphlet. Miami: Florida Poison Information Center (no date).

"Locked Up Poisons Prevent Tragedy." Pamphlet. Washington DC: Poison Prevention Week Council/Consumer Product Safety Commission (1995).

"Look-Alikes: Don't Be Fooled." Flyer. Miami: Florida Information Center (no date).

"Material Safety Data Sheet." Fact Sheet. Cincinnati OH: Proctor and Gamble (no date).

"Poison Lookout Checklist." Fact Sheet. Miami: Florida Poison Information Center (no date).

"Poison Prevention Guide." Pamphlet. Tampa: Florida Poison Information Center at Tampa General Hospital.

"Poison Prevention Tips to Keep Our Children Safe." American Association of Poison Control Centers, www.aapcc.org (April 9, 1999).

"Prevent Home Poisonings." Fact Sheet. Miami: Florida Poison Information Center at the University of Miami, Jackson Memorial Hospital (no date).

"Prevent Poisoning and Death with Iron-Containing Medicine." Fact Sheet. Washington DC: Consumer Product Safety Commission (no date).

"Seasonal Poisoning Hazards." Pamphlet. Miami: Florida Poison Information Center (no date).

9. Staying Ahead of Lead

Blumenthal, Dale. "An Unwanted Souvenir: Lead in Ceramic Ware." *FDA Consumer Magazine* (December 1989/January 1990), reprinted by the Department of Health and Human Services, Inc., document 90-1157 (no date).

"CPSC Finds Lead Poisoning Hazard for Young Children in Imported Vinyl Miniblinds." Consumer Product Safety Commission (96-150), www.cpsc.gov (April 13, 1998).

"CPSC Staff Recommendations for Identifying and Controlling Lead Paint on Public Playground Equipment." Fax (6005). Washington DC: Consumer Product Safety Commission (October 1996).

Foulke, Judith E. "Lead Threat Lessens, But Mugs Pose Problem." *FDA Consumer Magazine* (April 1993), as reprinted by the Food and Drug Administration, doc. 93-1209 (August 1993).

"Get the Lead Out!" Fact Sheet. Miami: Dade and Broward Counties labs and testing services (no date).

"Important Facts About Childhood Lead Poisoning Prevention." Pamphlet. Atlanta: Centers for Disease Control and Prevention (no date).

"Lead Poisoning and Your Children." Pamphlet (EPA 800-B-92-002). Washington DC: Environmental Protection Agency (February 1995).

"Lead in Your Drinking Water." Document (EPA 810F-93-001). Washington DC: Environmental Protection Agency (June 1993).

"Protect Your Family from Lead in Your Home." Booklet (EPA 747-K-94-001). Washington DC: Environmental Protection Agency (May 1995).

"Testing for Lead Poisoning." Document (706). Washington DC: National Lead Information Center (August 1998).

"Testing Your Home for Lead." Fact Sheet. Champaign IL: U.S. Army Construction Engineering Research Laboratories (June 1993). Distributed by the National Lead Information Center.

10. Staying Out of Dangerous Fields

"Fields from Electric Power." Summary Document. Pittsburgh PA: Department of Engineering and Public Policy, Carnegie Mellon University (1995).

"High Tension Wire." Fact Sheet. Washington DC: Environmental Health Clearinghouse (April 1998).

"Magnetic Field Exposure and Cancer Studies at the NCI." National Cancer Institute, www.nci.nih.gov (July 6, 1998).

"Mobile Phone—Brain Tumor Risk in the Limelight Again." *Microwave News*, XIX, no. 3 (May/June 1999): 1, 6-7.

"Power Lines Project." Booklet. Albany: New York Sate Department of Health (October 1993).

"Questions and Answers About Electric and Magnetic Fields (EMFs)." Booklet (EPA 402-R-92-009). Washington DC: Environmental Protection Agency (December 1992).

"Questions and Answers About EMF: Electric and Magnetic Fields Associated with the Use of Electric Power." Booklet (DOE/EE-0040). Washington DC: National

Institute of Environmental Health Sciences and Department of Energy (January 1995).

"Workplace VDT Use Not a Risk Factor for Reduced Birth Weight, Premature Birth, NIOSH Finds." National Institute for Occupational Safety and Health, www.cdc.gov (September 14, 1999).

"Your Child and the Environment." Document. Elk Grove Village IL: American Academy of Pediatrics (1997).

11. Making Sure Our Air Is Safe

"Asbestos in the Home." Booklet. Tallahassee: Florida Department of Environmental Protection (no date).

"Asbestos Informer, The." Booklet (EPA 340/1-90-020). Washington DC: Environmental Protection Agency (December 1990).

"Building a New Home: Have You Considered Radon?" Environmental Protection Agency (EPA/402F-98-001), www.epa.gov (April 23, 1999).

"Cancer Facts." Pamphlet. Washington DC: National Cancer Institute, National Institute of Health (April 25, 1996).

"Cancer Facts: Questions and Answers About Asbestos Exposure." Document. Washington DC: National Cancer Institute, National Institutes of Health (February 27, 1996).

"Carbon Monoxide." Fact Sheet (466). Washington DC: Consumer Product Safety Commission (no date).

"Carbon Monoxide Detectors." *Guide to Implementing a Fire Prevention Week Campaign in Your Community!* Booklet. Quincy MA: National Fire Protection Association (October 1996).

"Consumer's Guide to Radon Reduction: How to Reduce Radon Levels in Your Home." Booklet (402-K-92-003). Washington DC: Environmental Protection Agency (August 1992).

"CPSC Warns About Asbestos in Consumer Products." Fax (5080). Washington DC: Consumer Product Safety Commission (February 7, 1998).

"Environmental Tobacco Smoke: A Danger to Children." *Indoor Air Pollution: An Introduction for Health Professionals.* Pamphlet (HE0168). Elk Grove Village IL: American Academy of Pediatrics (1994).

"Facts About Asbestos: Lung Hazards on the Job." Pamphlet. Tallahassee FL: American Lung Association (June 1990).

"Help Protect Your Family from Carbon Monoxide." Booklet (CM886). Washington DC: National SAFE KIDS Campaign (1995).

"Home Buyer's and Seller's Guide to Radon." Pamphlet (402-R-93-003). Washington DC: Environmental Protection Agency (March 1993).

"Indoor Air Facts: No. 5, Environmental Tobacco Smoke." Document (EPA 402-R-94-007). Washington DC: Environmental Protection Agency (June 1989).

"Indoor Air Pollutants and Their Sources: Carbon Monoxide." Environmental Protection Agency, www.epa.gov (September 13, 1996).

"Radon: A Physician's Guide." Document (402-K-93-008). Washington DC: Environmental Protection Agency (September 1993).

"Reducing Radon Risks." Document (EPA 520/1-89-027). Washington DC: Environmental Protection Agency (September 1992).

"Senseless Killer, The." Pamphlet (GPO 1993 0-356-764). Washington DC: Consumer Product Safety Commission (1993).

"Smoking Prevalence and Exposure to Tobacco Smoke Among Children." Centers for Disease Control and Prevention, www.cdc.gov (April 1999).

"Sources of Information on Indoor Air Quality." Environmental Protection Agency, www.epa.gov (April 1999).

"What You Should Know About Combustion Appliances and Indoor Air Pollution." Pamphlet (GPO 1994 0-152-176). Washington DC: Environmental Protection Agency (1994).

12. Taking Steps to Fend Off Danger

Fire Safety

"Curious Kids Set Fires: A Fact Sheet for Teaching Children Fire Safety." U.S. Fire Administration, www.usfa.fema.gov (September 1998).

"Fireproof Your Home: Because No Child Should Die in a Fire." Pamphlet. Washington DC: National SAFE KIDS Campaign (no date).

"Get Out Safely: A Fact Sheet on Fire Escape Planning." U.S. Fire Administration, www.usfa.fema.gov (September 8, 1998).

"National Fire Protection Association Community Awareness Kit: Hot Tips to Send to the Media." Document. Quincy MA: National Fire Protection Association (1996).

"Residential Fire Injury." Fact Sheet. Washington DC: National SAFE KIDS Campaign (September 1996).

Gun Safety

"Child Access Prevention Laws." Fact Sheet. Washington DC: National SAFE KIDS Campaign (August 1996).

"Child Access Prevention Laws: Questions & Answers." Document. Washington DC: Handgun Control, Inc. (November 5, 1997).

"Child Safety Lock Legislation." Document. Washington DC: Handgun Control, Inc. (October 1997).

"Children & Guns." Fact Sheet. Washington DC: Center to Prevent Handgun Violence (June 18, 1997).

"Firearm Facts." Fact Sheet. Washington DC: Center to Prevent Handgun Violence (October 21, 1997).

"Parents' Guide to Gun Safety." Document (ES 12850). Fairfax VA: National Rifle Association (May 1996).

13. Playing It Safe

Bicycles, In-Line Skating, and Team Sports

"AAP Recommends Measures to Cut In-Line Skating Risk." Press Release. Atlanta: American Academy of Pediatrics (April 7, 1999).

"Bicycle Injury." Fact Sheet. Washington DC: National SAFE KIDS Campaign (December 1998).

"Bicycle Safety Message to Parents, Teachers and Motorists." Fact Sheet. Washington DC: Department of Transportation/National Highway Traffic Safety (January 1991).

"Bicycles." Flyer (346). Washington DC: Consumer Product Safety Commission (no date).

"Choosing the Right Size Bicycle for Your Child." The Injury Prevention Program (TIPP), www.aap.org.

"CPSC Releases Study of Protective Equipment for Baseball." Fact Sheet (release 96-140). Washington DC: Consumer Product Safety Commission (June 4, 1996).

"CPSC Warns Consumers: Anchor Soccer Goals to Prevent Tipover." Fact Sheet (release 96-192). Washington DC: Consumer Product Safety Commission (September 25, 1996).

"Play It Safe." American Academy of Orthopaedic Surgeons, www.aaos.org (April 17, 1999).

"Play It Safe Sports: A Guide to Safety for Young Athletes." American Academy of Orthopaedic Surgeons, www.aaos.org (April 7, 1999).

Safe Kids Are No Accident: A Traffic Safety Magazine for Kids. Washington DC: National SAFE KIDS Campaign (September 1996).

"Safe Kids Gear Up! Guide. The Things You Need to Know and the Gear You Need to Use." Booklet. Washington DC: National SAFE KIDS Campaign.

"Safety Commission Warns About Hazards with In-Line Roller Skates: Safety Alert." Consumer Product Safety Commission (Document 5050), www.cpsc.gov (April 7, 1999).

"Traffic Safety Outlook: Bicycle Safety." Pamphlet. Washington DC: Department of Transportation/National Highway Traffic Safety Campaign Safe and Sober (1996).

Hobbies and Crafts: Art Supplies

Babin, Angela, Perri A. Peltz and Monona Rossol. "Children's Art Supplies Can Be Toxic." New York: Center for Safety in the Arts (1992).

"CPSC Promotes Safety Labeling for Art and Craft Materials." Fact Sheet (GPO 1990-272-729/10162). Washington DC: Consumer Product Safety Commission (July 1990).

"Law Requires Review and Labeling of Art Materials Including Children's Art and Drawing Products." Fact Sheet (5016). Washington DC: Consumer Product Safety Commission (no date).

Rossol, Monona. "Selecting Children's Art Materials." Document. New York: Arts, Crafts & Theater Safety, Inc. (April 22, 1998).

"Safe and Successful Use of Art Materials, The." Booklet. Boston: Art and Creative Materials Institute, Inc. (no date).

"What You Need to Know About the Safety of Art and Craft Materials." Booklet. Boston: Art and Creative Materials Institute, Inc. (June 1995).

"Whenever You Buy Art and Craft Materials . . . Look for These Seals." Pamphlet. Boston: Art and Creative Materials Institute, Inc. (no date).

14. Hazards of the Fall: Kids Don't Come Equipped with Wings

"CPSC Gets New, Safer Baby Walkers on the Market." Fact Sheet (release 98-142). Washington DC: Consumer Product Safety Commission (July 15, 1998).

"CPSC, Manufacturers, Importers Announce Recall of Wooden and Metal Bunk Beds." Consumer Product Safety Commission, www.cpsc.gov (July 1999).

"Dirty Dozen, The: Are They Hiding in Your Child's Playground?" Document. Ashburn VA: National Playground Safety Institute/National Recreation and Park Association (no date).

"Escalator Safety." Document (5111). Washington DC: Consumer Product Safety Commission (no date).

"For Kids' Sake: Think Toy Safety . . . By Knowing the Nine Toy Dangers." Pamphlet. Washington DC: Consumer Product Safety Commission (no date).

"Home Playground Safety Tips." Fact Sheet (323). Washington DC: U.S. Consumer Product Safety Commission (no date).

"Non-Reversing Garage Door Openers a Hazard." Fact Sheet (009112). Washington DC: Consumer Product Safety Commission (no date).

"Number of Trampoline Related Injuries Doubled Over Six-Year Period." Press Release. Elk Grove Village IL: American Academy of Pediatrics (March 2, 1998).

"Play It Safe! A Guide to Playground Safety." Pamphlet. Rosemont IL: American Academy of Orthopaedic Surgeons (1991).

"Playground Injury Fact Sheet." Fact Sheet. Washington DC: National SAFE KIDS Campaign (April, 1998).

"Playground Safety: Guidelines for Parents." Pamphlet. Elk Grove Village IL: American Academy of Pediatrics (March 1994).

"Public Playground Safety Checklist." Fact Sheet. Washington DC: Consumer Product Safety Commission (no date).

"Safe Kids Are No Accident! How to Protect Your Child from Injury." Booklet. Washington DC: National SAFE KIDS Campaign (September 1996).

"Safe Kids Gear Up! Guide. The Things You Need to Know and the Gear You Need to Use." Booklet. Washington DC: National SAFE KIDS Campaign.

"Safe T Rider." Teacher's Guide. Target audience, second graders. Booklet. Mobile AL: Elevator Escalator Safety Foundation (no date).

"Safety Commission Publishes Final Rules for Automatic Garage Door Openers." Consumer Product Safety Commission (release 93-024), www.cpsc.gov (May 1999).

"Safety on Escalators." *Weekly Reader*, Edition 3, 60, no. 16 (January 25, 1991).

"Safety Rules and Rationale." Mobile AL: Elevator Escalator Safety Foundation (September 15, 1996).

"Safety Tips for Home Playground Equipment." *The Injury Prevention Program (TIPP)*. Booklet. Elk Grove Village IL: American Academy of Pediatrics (1994).

"Ten Steps Toward a Safer Playground." Fact Sheet (327). Washington DC: Consumer Product Safety Commission (no date).

"Tips for Public Playground Safety." Fact Sheet (324). Washington DC: Consumer Product Safety Commission (May 1995).

"Tips for Your Baby's Safety." Pamphlet. Washington DC: Consumer Product Safety Commission (no date).

"To Prevent Falls At Home . . . At Play." Pamphlet. Washington DC: National SAFE KIDS Campaign (no date).

"Toy Boxes and Toy Chests." Fact Sheet (74). Washington DC: Consumer Product Safety Commission (October 1995).

"Toy Injury." Fact Sheet. Washington DC: National SAFE KIDS Campaign (November 1997).

"Which Toy for Which Child: A Consumer's Guide for Selecting Suitable Toys (Age Birth Through Five)." Booklet (283). Washington DC: Consumer Product Safety Commission (1995).

15. Stepping Out (Safely)

"Always Use Sunscreen When Outside on a Sunny Day." EPA's Stratospheric Protection Division, www.epa.gov (May 2, 1998).

"Bambi, Take Heart; Mickey, Run for Cover." *Newsweek* (July 28, 1997): 77.

"Be Wary of Bats." *HealthNews* (February 17, 1998): 6.

"Bites and Stings." West Virginia University, www.hsc.wvu.edu (June 28, 1999).

"Facts About Rabies." Centers for Disease Control and Prevention, www.cdc.gov (April 20, 1999).

"FEMA Advises Caution in Extreme Heat." Federal Emergency Management Agency, www.fema.gov (August 1999).

"Florida Critters." Pamphlet. Miami: Florida Poison Information Center (no date).

"General Facts About Lyme Disease and Its Transmission." Fax (351701). Washington DC: Centers for Disease Control and Prevention (September 18, 1996).

"Health Effects of Overexposure to the Sun: Uv Index." Fact Sheet (EPA 430-F-95-003). Washington DC: Stratospheric Protection Division in Collaboration with the National Weather Service and the Centers for Disease Control and Prevention (April 1995).

Lewis, Carol. "The Fright of the Iguana." *FDA Consumer* (November–December 1997), Food and Drug Administration, www.fda.gov (November 1, 1998).

"Lyme Disease." American Lyme Disease Foundation, Inc., www.aldf.com (September 6, 1999).

"Lyme Disease." Fact Sheet. White Plains NY: American Lyme Disease Foundation, Inc. (no date).

"Lyme Disease: A 'New' Illness Worries Americans." *INFOletter: Environmental and Occupational Health Briefs* 5, no. 2 (1991).

"Media Advisory: Tips on Managing Heat." Centers for Disease Control and Prevention, www.cdc.gov (August 1999).

"News Bites: On the Horizon." *HealthNews* (July 15, 1997).

"Ozone Depletion: Uv Index." Fact Sheet (EPA 430-F-95-001). Washington DC: Stratospheric Protection Division, in collaboration with the National Weather Service and the Centers for Disease Control and Prevention (April 1995).

"Practice Safe Sun." Bookmark (EPA 545-002) . Washington DC: Environmental Protection Agency (1991).

"Prevention & Control: Rabies." Centers for Disease Control and Prevention, www.cdc.gov (April 21, 1999).

"Quick Guide to Lyme Disease, A: How to Protect Yourself and Your Family from Serious Infection." Booklet (MKT3269). White Plains NY: American Lyme Disease Foundation (no date).

"Rabies: General Information." Centers for Disease Control and Prevention, Division of Viral and Rickettsial Diseases, National Center for Infectious Diseases, www.cdc.gov (January 1999).

"Rabies Virus, The." Centers for Disease Control and Prevention, www.cdc.gov (April 1999).

"Salmonella Infections from Reptiles." Fact Sheet. Atlanta: Centers for Disease Control (May 1995).

"Sun Protection for Children: Uv Index." Fact Sheet (EPA 430-F-95-0004). Washington DC: Stratospheric Protection Division, in collaboration with the National Weather Service and the Centers for Disease Control and Prevention (January 1995).

"Symptoms of Acute Lyme Disease." Fax (351702). Washington DC: Centers for Disease Control and Prevention (September 19, 1996).

"Tick and Insect Repellents." Fact Sheet. New York: New York State Department of Health (January 1996).

"Treatment of Lyme Disease." Fax (351703). Washington DC: Centers for Disease Control and Prevention (September 19, 1996).

"Using Insect Repellents Safely." Fact Sheet. Washington DC: Environmental Protection Agency, Office of Pesticide Programs. (June 1999).

"Uv Index: Sun Protection for Children." Environmental Protection Agency, www.epa.gov (June 1999).

"Uv Radiation: Uv Index." Fact Sheet (EPA 430-F-95-006). Washington DC: Stratospheric Protection Division, in collaboration with the National Weather Service and the Centers for Disease Control and Prevention (April 1995).

16. Getting into the Swim of Things

"Children Aren't Waterproof." Pamphlet. Alexandria VA: National Spa and Pool Institute (April 1989).

Committee on Injury and Poison Prevention. "Drowning in Infants, Children and Adolescents." *Pediatrics* 92, no. 2 (August 1993): 292–294.

"Community Water Safety." Booklet. St. Louis: Mosby Lifeline, for the American Red Cross (1995).

"*Cryptosporidium* and Cryptosporidiosis: Information for Recreational Water Patrons." Centers for Disease Control and Prevention, www.cdc.gov (June 1999).

"Drowning #1 Threat to Our Children in Florida." Pamphlet. Ft. Lauderdale: Parents of Near Drownings (June 1992).

"Guide to Water Safety." Booklet. Upper Marlboro MD: The American Trauma Society (no date).

"Home Water Hazards for Young Children." *The Injury Prevention Program (TIPP).* Fact Sheet. Elk Grove Village IL: American Academy of Pediatrics (1994).

"How to Plan for the Unexpected: Preventing Child Drownings." Document (359). Washington DC: Consumer Product Safety Commission (1994).

"Invisible Pool Guests Can Cause Kids to Get Sick." Centers for Disease Control and Prevention, www.cdc.gov (September 2, 1999).

"Layers of Protection: To Enhance the Enjoyment of Your Pool or Spa." Pamphlet (50M-1/96). Alexandria VA: National Spa and Pool Institute (January 1996).

O'Flaherty, Jennifer E. and Phyllis L. Pirie. "Prevention of Pediatric Drowning and Near Drownings: A Survey of Members of the American Academy of Pediatrics." *Pediatrics* 99, no. 2 (February 1997): 169–174.

"Parent's Guide to Water Safety, A." Pamphlet (HEO198). Elk Grove IL: American Academy of Pediatrics (1996).

"Pool Safety for Children." *The Injury Prevention Program (TIPP).* Fact Sheet. Elk Grove Village IL: American Academy of Pediatrics (1994).

"Pool Safety Survey." Survey Sheet. Fort Lauderdale FL: Broward County Public Health Unit, Drowning Prevention Coalition (no date).

"Safe Kids Are No Accident. How to Protect Your Child From Injury." Booklet. Washington DC: National SAFE KIDS Campaign (November 1996): 7.

"Safety Barrier Guidelines for Home Pools." Booklet (362). Washington DC: Consumer Product Safety Commission (no date).

"Sensible Way to Enjoy Your Inground Swimming Pool." Booklet. Alexandria VA: National Spa and Pool Institute (1995).

"Sensible Way to Enjoy Your Spa or Hot Tub, The." Booklet. Alexandria VA: National Spa and Pool Institute (1995).

"'Spas, Hot Tubs, and Whirlpools.' Safety Alert." Fact Sheet. Washington DC: Consumer Product Safety Commission (1996).

"Warning! Avoid the Danger: Children Can Fall into Buckets and Drown." Pamphlet. Washington DC: Coalition for Container Safety (no date).

"Water Safety for Your School-Age Child." *The Injury Prevention Program (TIPP).* Fact Sheet. Elk Grove Village IL: American Academy of Pediatrics (1994).

17. Rules of the Road

"Air Bag Alert." Booklet (DOT HS 808 456). Washington DC: National Highway Traffic Safety Administration (September 1996).

"Air-Bag—Associated Fatal Injuries to Infants and Children Riding in Front Passenger Seats—United States." *The Morbidity and Mortality Weekly Report* 44 (1995): 845–847, reprinted www.cdc.gov (August 3, 1998).

"Babies & Air Bags Don't Mix." Fact Sheet. Washington DC: National Highway Traffic Safety Administration (no date).

"Child Passenger Safety." Fact Sheet. Washington DC: Traffic Safety Outlook. NHTSA Campaign Safe and Sober (no date).

"Child Passenger Safety Awareness Week—February 9–15, 1997." Sample Press Release. Washington DC: National Highway Traffic Safety Administration (1997).

"Child Transportation Safety Tips." Booklet (DOT HS 808 301). Washington DC: National Highway Traffic Safety Administration (December 1998).

Committee on Injury and Poison Prevention. "Selecting and Using the Most Appropriate Car Safety Seats for Growing Children: Guidelines for Counseling Parents." *Pediatrics* 97, no. 5 (May 1996): 761–762.

"Kids Aren't Cargo." Fact Sheet. Washington DC: NHTSA Campaign Safe and Sober (no date).

"Motor Vehicle Occupant Injury." Fact Sheet. Washington DC: National SAFE KIDS Campaign (December 1998).

"Questions and Answers Regarding Air Bags." Document. Washington DC: National Highway Traffic Safety Administration (January 17, 1997).

"Safe Kids Buckle Up." Pamphlet. National SAFE KIDS Campaign (October 1994).

"Safety Belt Use: Traffic Safety Tips." *NHTSA Facts* (Summer 1996).

"Statement by Ricardo Martinez, M.D., Administrator, National Highway Traffic Safety Administration, November 1, 1996." Fact Sheet. Washington DC: U.S. Department of Transportation (November 1996).

"Take Vince and Larry's Crash Course on Child Safety Seats." Pamphlet. Washington DC: Department of Transportation (1985).

"Traffic Injuries." *Safe Kids Are No Accident! How to Protect Your Child From Injury.* Booklet. Washington DC: National SAFE KIDS Campaign (1996).

18. Hazards in the Community

"Attention Walkers!" *Safe Kids Are No Accident: A Traffic Safety Magazine for Kids* (September 1996): 6–7.

"Bus Stopper Kit." *Pupil Transportation Safety Institute Resource* (Fall 1996): 7.

"Falls from Shopping Carts Cause Head Injuries to Children." *Safety Facts.* 2nd ed. Booklet. Washington DC: Consumer Product Safety Commission (no date).

"Get to School!" Learning Partners, www.ed.gov (January 6, 2000).

"How to Cross Safely." Fact Sheet. Syracuse NY: Pupil Transportation Safety Institute (1995).

"Kid's Guide to Safe Walking, A." Pamphlet (FHWA-SA-96-057). Washington DC: Department of Transportation (April 1996).

"Kids, the School Bus and You." Pamphlet (DOT HS 808423). Washington DC: National Highway Traffic Safety Administration (July 1996).

"Parents, Safeguard Your Child: Suggestions to Parents on Preventing Traffic Accidents Involving Their Children." Pamphlet (3217). Heathrow FL: American Automobile Association (no date).

"Parents and Teachers School Bus Safety Alert." Fact Sheet. Washington DC: National Highway Traffic Safety Administration (no date).

"Patterns for Life." Cardboard Grow Chart (DOT HS 808 457). Washington DC: National Highway Traffic Safety Administration (no date).

"Pedestrian Safety." Fact Sheet. Washington DC: NHTSA Campaign Safe and Sober. www.nhtsa.dot.gov (April 11, 1999).

"Pedestrian, Walk Safely." Pamphlet (DOT HS 808 166). Washington DC: National Highway Traffic Safety Administration (December 1994).

"Prevent Pedestrian Accidents: Elementary School Children." Fact Sheet (DOT HS 808 166). Washington DC: National Highway Traffic Safety Administration (August 1990).

"Prevent Pedestrian Accidents: Preschool Children." Fact Sheet (DOT HS 807 608). Washington DC: National Highway Traffic Safety Administration (August 1990).

"School Bus Safety." Fact Sheet. Washington DC: NHTSA Campaign Safe and Sober (no date).

"School Bus Safety Facts." Fact Sheet. Syracuse NY: Pupil Transportation Safety Institute (1995).

"Shopping Cart Injuries: Victims 5 Years Old and Younger." Consumer Product Safety Commission, www.cpsc.gov (April 1999).

"Shopping Cart Injury." Fact Sheet. National SAFE KIDS Campaign (December 1998).

"Traffic Safety Outlook: Pedestrian Safety." Fact Sheet. Washington DC: NHTSA Campaign Safe and Sober (September 1996).

"Traffic Safety Outlook: School Bus Safety." Fact Sheet. Washington DC: NHTSA Campaign Safe and Sober (September 1996).

"Walk Alert!" Pamphlet. Ft. Lauderdale FL: National Safety Council, South Florida Chapter (no date).

"Walking With Your Eyes." Teacher's Guide for the Video (US GPO:1994-301-717:00056). Washington DC: National Highway Traffic Safety Administration (1994).

19. The Street-Smart Kid

"Baby-Sitting Reminders." *The Injury Prevention Program (TIPP)*. Fact Sheet. Elk Grove Village IL: American Academy of Pediatrics (1994).

"Halloween Safety." Fact Sheet. Washington DC: Consumer Product Safety Commission (no date).

"Helping Kids Protect Themselves: A Booklet for Children and Adults." Booklet. Washington DC: National Crime Prevention Counsel (1996).

"Just in Case . . . Parental Guidelines in Case You Need a Babysitter." Pamphlet. Arlington VA: National Center for Missing and Exploited Children (1988).

"Just in Case . . . Parental Guidelines in Case Your Child Might Someday be Missing." Pamphlet. Arlington VA: National Center for Missing and Exploited Children (1985).

"My 8 Rules for Safety." Fact Sheet. Arlington VA: National Center for Missing and Exploited Children (November 1996).

"Parents Guide to the Internet." Booklet (MIS 97-6609a). Washington DC: Department of Education, Office of Educational Research and Improvement (no date).

"Safety Tips for Halloween." Fact Sheet. Lake Park FL: Florida Branch of National Center for Missing and Exploited Children (no date).

"Your Inside Look at Crime Prevention." Booklet. Washington DC: Bureau of Justice Assistance (no date).

Appendix D. Baby Food

"Preventing Foodborne Illness: When Grandparents Take Care of Grandchildren: What You Need to Know About Food Safety and Young Children." Food and Drug Administration, www.cfsan.fda.gov (August 1999).

Tamplin, Mark L., Brenda Somes, and Carrie West. "Keep Infant's Food Safe." National Food Safety Database, www.foodsafety.org (December 18, 1999).

Appendix G. Room-by-Room Checklist

"Back-To-School Safety Checklist." Consumer Product Safety Commission, www.cpsc.gov (June 1999).

"Child Care Safety Checklist for Parents & Child Care Providers." Pamphlet. Washington DC: Consumer Product Safety Commission (no date).

"Childproofing Your Home: 12 Safety Devices to Protect Your Children." Pamphlet. Washington DC: Consumer Product Safety Commission (no date).

"Government Says Riding Lawnmowers Are Not Children's Toys." News from CPSC, Release 94-071 (May 5, 1994).

"Healthy Homes: In All Living Areas." Housing and Urban Development, www.hud.gov (July 1999).

"What Can I Do to Protect My Children from Dangerous Nursery Equipment?" Kids in Danger, www.kidsindanger.org (July 1999).

Index